HARD CHOICES, EASY ANSWERS

HARD CHOICES, EASY ANSWERS

VALUES, INFORMATION, AND AMERICAN PUBLIC OPINION

R. Michael Alvarez and John Brehm

PRINCETON UNIVERSITY PRESS PRINCETON, NEW JERSEY

Copyright © 2002 by Princeton University Press
Published by Princeton University Press, 41 William Street,
Princeton, New Jersey 08540
In the United Kingdom: Princeton University Press,
3 Market Place, Woodstock, Oxfordshire OX20 1SY
All Rights Reserved

Library of Congress Cataloging-in-Publication Data
Alvarez, R. Michael, 1964–
Hard choices, easy answers : values, information,
and American public opinion / R. Michael Alvarez and John Brehm
p.cm.
Includes bibliographical references and index.
ISBN 0-691-08918-3 (alk. paper)—ISBN 0-691-09635-X (pbk.: alk. paper)
1. Public opinion—United States. 2. Political culture—United States.
3. Values—United States. 4. Political psychology. I. Brehm, John, 1960– II. Title.
HM1236 .A46 2002
303.3′8′0973—dc21   2001050023

British Library Cataloging-in-Publication Data is available.

This book has been composed in Berkeley Book

Printed on acid-free paper. ∞

www.pupress.princeton.edu

Printed in the United States of America

1 3 5 7 9 10 8 6 4 2

Contents

List of Figures

List of Tables

Acknowledgments

JUST A FEW MONTHS after one of us (Alvarez) defended his dissertation, a long conversation began one afternoon in which we both realized that the literature on public opinion lacked a clear and straightforward analysis of uncertainty in public opinion. Our first stab at the problem, on a piece of scrap paper, turned out to be a very useful approach. If we conceptualized survey responses about issues to be represented by draws from an underlying statistical distribution, then we could use inferential statistical techniques new to political science to better understand public opinion. These new techniques would permit us to test hypotheses about what drives people to provide a response to a survey question *and* to test hypotheses about the underlying variability or variance in their opinions.

This idea led to three publications in the *American Journal of Political Science*, where we applied our inferential statistical technique to study opinions about abortion (1995), affirmative action (1997), and the Internal Revenue Service (1998). Each of these articles contains a discussion of our inferential statistical technique, the substantive application, and our speculations about why we found very different determinants of both policy choice and policy variability across these different domains of public opinion.

The fact that we found so much complexity—and so much regularity—underpinning American public opinion was what drove us to write this book. By expanding, elaborating, and deepening our studies of public opinion across a wide range of social and political issues, and across masses and elites, we have developed what we believe to be a new understanding of public opinion in the United States. We expand upon our theoretical and methodological contributions in the early chapters that follow, and then we present a wealth of empirical results about both policy choices and policy variability. We conclude with a discussion that links our results and findings with the past research on public opinion.

Throughout our research on this project, many colleagues and scholars provided us with very detailed and useful comments. Our first paper on abortion attitudes was presented at the 1993 annual meeting of the American Political Science Association, and we received very useful advice from John Aldrich, Bob Luskin, and Arthur Sanders. The second paper in this project, on attitudes about affirmative action, was presented at the 1995 annual meeting of the Midwest Political Science Association; subsequently this paper won the 1996 John Sprague Award for the best application of a quantitative method to a substantive problem in political science. Morgan Kousser, Lynn Sanders, Paul Sniderman, Laura Stoker, the Duke-UNC Political Psychology Group, and the seminar group at the University of California, Santa Barbara all gave helpful commentary on this research. Our paper on attitudes about the Internal Revenue Service was presented at the 1996 annual meeting of the American Political Science Association, where we received helpful advice from Chris Achen, Neal Beck, Charles Franklin, John Scholz, Renee Smith, and the political psychology workshop at the University of Minnesota.

More general, but no less important, discussions and debates with our students and colleagues have helped to sharpen our arguments and analyses. We thank Jim Adams, John Aldrich, Larry Bartels, Neal Beck, Adam Berinsky, Tara Butterfield, Fred Boehmke, John Cacioppo, Charles Franklin, Paul Freedman, Garrett Glasgow, Paul Gronke, Melissa Harris-Lacewell, Jonathan Katz, Donald Kinder, Jonathan Nagler, Wendy Rahn, Paul Sniderman, John Sullivan, John Transue, Fang Wang, Catherine Wilson, Matthew Wilson, and John Zaller. We particularly wish to thank Adam Berinsky and Monique Lyle for their extensive comments on the entire, if early, manuscript.

As the initial draft was being circulated, we received advice from many wonderful anonymous reviewers, and from Lew Bateman, Chuck Myers, and Jeremy Shine. Also, Dennis Chong and Jim Kuklinski provided detailed comments and discussions that have greatly strengthened this book.

Research we present in chapter 8 was first unveiled at the 1996 meeting of the American Political Science Association, where we received the advice of James Kuklinski and Milton Lodge. The material in chapter 9 was presented at the 1999 annual meeting of the International Society for Political Psychology; this research was coauthored with Hein Goemans. The underlying inferential statistical methodology was presented at the 1999 Southern California Political Methodology Program conference at Lake Arrowhead.

Along the way many others provided more practical assistance. Several of our students—Jim Battista, John Rattliff, Brad Gomez, and Dan Lipinski (all of Duke) and Fang Wang (Caltech)—provided assistance with our empirical analyses. Karen Kerbs provided vital clerical assistance. William Greene gave useful econometric advice and LIMDEP assistance. The data used in our studies were originally collected by many different researchers and organizations. We use data from the General Social Surveys (chapter 5); the 1991 Race and Politics Survey collected by Paul Sniderman, Philip E. Tetlock, and Thomas Piazza (chapter 6); Harris Associates (chapter 7); the National Election Studies (chapter 8); and the Survey on the Military in the Post–Cold War Era collected by Peter Feaver, Richard Kohn, and the Triangle Institute for Security Studies (chapter 9).

In order to better explicate our empirical findings, we have chosen to focus on estimates of the effects of the causal variables rather than on the coefficients. The coefficients, however, can be found at our website, www.pupress. princeton.edu/alvarez.

We dedicate this work to our families: Sarah and Sophia; and Kate, Laurel, Robin, Joe, and Jeff.

HARD CHOICES, EASY ANSWERS

CHAPTER 1

A Fickle Public?

IN MANY WAYS, politics is about conflict. People have conflicting goals, or they have conflicts over the means to achieve shared goals, and one of the most important purposes of a political system is to channel this conflict into political compromise. But other times, compromise is impossible to achieve, and conflict over political means or ends can result in events from polite arguments among family over the dinner table to riots, revolutions, and wars.

Many of the conflicts we read about in the newspapers, or watch on television, are struggles between politicians fighting for political power or to get some legislation enacted. The conflict may be between organizations, such as the fight between the National Right to Life Council and the National Abortion Rights Action League over abortion policy. Often, the conflict is between branches of government, as in struggles within a legislature to pass a bill, which then is vetoed by a president or state governor. And sometimes the conflict is between nations, in the form of low-level trade conflicts or even as all-out warfare.

Just as politicians, interest groups, and even nations engage in political conflict, so do everyday citizens. In the course of life's events, Americans discuss, debate, and argue about issues that concern their lives. These debates cover the political and social spectrum, ranging from local issues such as whether a stop sign should be installed at a street intersection in their neighborhood or how their local school district should teach children about responsible sexuality, to state-level issues such as whether public universities in their state should practice affirmative action, and to national-level issues such as what (if anything) the federal government should do to allocate the billions in budget surpluses. Americans have opinions about these issues, and many others, and are usually more than willing to discuss them when they come up in their lives.

But even though Americans have opinions about all sorts of political issues and like to argue about politics, it is not true that these opinions are easily developed or fixed in stone. Instead, just as there is conflict in the political world, there is also conflict in the minds of Americans about many of these same issues. Should abortion remain legal, and if so, under what conditions? Is affirmative action necessary to alleviate decades of racism in America? Should the full rights of marriage be extended to gay men and lesbians? These are all issues that are difficult to answer, as each involves conflicting values and principles.

In this book, we propose that it is possible to understand systematically the origins and nature of intrapersonal conflict over politics. Along the way, we will also demonstrate that mass public opinion has foundations in widely shared core values and beliefs, but that the public often finds it difficult to identify which values are most relevant.

When Americans answer questions in public opinion surveys about these conflictual issues, their responses seem remarkably fickle, ill-informed, and inconsistent. Sometimes scorning, sometimes ridiculing, commentators as varied as Walter Lippman in the 1920s, Philip Converse in the 1960s, and John Zaller in the 1990s, have each derided the American public as being uninformed about politics and ill-prepared to participate in a representative democracy.

One important example of the apparent conflict in American opinion is seen in the attitudes of white Americans about affirmative action in recent years. Affirmative action is an issue of real politics in American society, and the various dimensions of the affirmative action debate are ones on which Americans do have opinions. Affirmative action and other racial issues expose the raw fault lines of political struggle, as groups fight over economic resources and political power.

But in path-breaking research published in 1993, Paul Sniderman and Thomas Piazza found that there was conflict in the minds of white Americans about affirmative action. Their research found that 17 percent of white Americans who said they supported affirmative action and quotas in university admissions for black students changed their responses when asked "Would you still feel that way, even if it means fewer opportunities for qualified whites, or would you change your mind?"

On the other hand, 23 percent who were opposed to university affirmative action programs also switched to support when asked "Would you still feel that way, even if it means that hardly any blacks would be able to go to the best colleges and universities, or would you change your mind?" To be fair, Sniderman and Piazza note that the percentages of survey participants who change their answers on affirmative action are much lower than percentages who change their answers on other social policy issues, indicating that on affirmative action, the minds of Americans are more made up about this issue than on social policy issues.

This research about the internal conflict in the minds of white Americans did not go unnoticed by politicians and political activists. In fact, the Sniderman and Piazza research was directly applied to a real world political purpose. The coauthors of the California Civil Rights Initiative (Proposition 209 in the 1996 California general election), Glynn Custred and Thomas Wood, read the Sniderman and Piazza research and other public opinion polling data and knew that while most Americans supported affirmative action programs in principle, they might oppose race- or gender-based preference or quota systems.[1] Custred and Wood wrote Proposition 209 in terms of ending preference systems, not affirmative action programs, a move that most observers see as critical for understanding the dynamics of the Proposition 209 campaign.

Polling data gathered right in the heat of the 1996 general election campaign demonstrates the effectiveness of Custred and Wood's efforts to draft Proposition 209. The *Los Angeles Times* poll conducted October 17–21, 1996, in California, interviewed 1,290 registered voters.[2] First, the poll posed a simple question to respondents, essentially only reading to these registered voters the title of this ballot initiative. Of the 838 registered voters who had heard of Proposition 209, 40 percent favored it, 29 percent opposed it, and 31 percent didn't know.

But then the poll asked about opinions on Proposition 209, providing more information: "If passed, Proposition 209 would prohibit the state or localities from using race, sex, color, ethnicity, or national origin as a criterion for either discriminating against or granting preferential treatment to any individual or group in public employment, public education, or public contracting. If the November 5th election were being held today, would you vote for or against Proposition 209?" Of the 1,290 registered voters in the sample, 52 percent said they would support Proposition 209, 30 percent said they would oppose it, and 18 percent said they did not know how they would vote.

On the surface, the differences in just these two questions in one telephone poll on the Proposition 209 measure seem to support the basic point of the critiques of an informed American public opinion: the difference between reading the ballot measure title versus the short description of the measure for those saying they would support Proposition 209 was 12 percent. So perhaps the clever authors of Proposition 209 were just manipulating public opinion in their attempt to ensure passage of this initiative.

But a few weeks later, 51.3 percent of the just over ten million voters in the 1996 general election cast votes for Proposition 209, with 42.8 percent voting against it and 5.9 percent not voting on this particular ballot measure. The close correspondence between the yes vote in November, and results from the second October *Los Angeles Times* poll question on Proposition 209, is very important. As the information in the second question is virtually identical to the short description of the issue in the ballot book received by all voters, there was stable and slight majority support for Proposition 209 as the measure was worded. The only change between the second poll question and the final vote really was the drop in the no-opinion percentage from 18 to almost 6 percent, and a corresponding rise in the percentage of opponents from 30 to almost 43 percent.

By understanding public opinion on the affirmative action issue, Custred and Wood were able to write Proposition 209 in a way that facilitated passage of this initiative. What seemed like conflicting or muddled thinking by Americans on this issue instead became the basis for a critical watershed in California politics, because affirmative action programs at many levels of government in

California ended after 1996—especially in the University of California education system.

But is there internal conflict in the minds of Californians or Americans about affirmative action? Or instead of being conflicted, are Americans just unclear and uncertain about what affirmative action policies are and how they work? This is a central question about public opinion regarding affirmative action, since understanding what drives opinion will shed light on how and why public policies change as they did in the case of California's Proposition 209.

Abortion provides another important example of the potential conflicts in American public opinion. Americans seem deeply divided about the issue of abortion, and this conflict often leads to apparent fickleness in survey responses about abortion policy. Recently the Gallup Organization conducted extensive polling about abortion.[3] At a superficial level, American adults seem convinced of abortion's legality: 28 percent believe that abortion should be legal under any circumstances, while 51 percent say it should be legal only under certain circumstances. Thus, 81 percent of American adults believe that abortion should be legal, at least under certain circumstances.

But digging deeper into the issue, the Gallup Organization posed many specific circumstances where abortion might be considered. And it is in the specifics that the opinions of Americans begin to look muddled. When should abortion be legal?

- When the woman's life is endangered: 84 percent
- When the woman's physical health is endangered: 81 percent
- When the pregnancy was caused by rape or incest: 78 percent
- When the woman's mental health is endangered: 64 percent
- When there is evidence that the baby may be physically impaired: 53 percent
- When there is evidence that the baby may be mentally impaired: 53 percent
- When the woman or family cannot afford to raise the child: 34 percent

Despite what looks like strong support for the legality of abortion, there clearly are cases where Americans agree that abortion should be legal (in cases where the woman's health is in danger or the pregnancy was caused by rape or incest), cases where Americans are in disagreement (when the baby is thought to be physically or mentally disabled), and cases where Americans believe that abortion should be illegal (economic reasons for abortions).

While American opinion in these specific cases does range from strong support for abortion to strong opposition, these differences are really not so inconsistent. When the circumstances for an abortion are cast in terms of the mother's life, invoking notions of women's rights, Americans support the woman's right to choose an abortion. When the circumstances for an abortion are cast in terms of a baby's life, invoking notions of the sanctity of a human life, Americans are deeply divided about abortion. When the circumstances for an abortion become purely economic, invoking notions of economic individualism, support for abortion plummets. These patterns suggest that instead of muddled and fickle beliefs, there might be some principles behind these survey opinions.

Yet what seems to be muddled thinking by Americans is also apparent in many of the muddled recent actions of the U.S. Supreme Court. Beginning over a decade ago, the Court has taken a number of cases and made a number of decisions which reflect the underlying American ambivalence about abortion. The 1986 case of *Thornburgh v. American College of Obstetricians and Gynecologists* saw the Court strike down (5 to 4) provisions of Pennsylvania law that required physicians to give their patients pro-life information, among other strict rules for physicians to follow, before, during, and after abortion procedures. Three years later, in *Webster v. Reproductive Health Services*, the Court in another 5 to 4 vote upheld Missouri laws prohibiting the use of public facilities or personnel to perform abortions. In 1990, the Court in one case (*Hodgson v. Minnesota*) threw out Minnesota's parental notification rules as too strict, but then upheld Ohio's parental notification procedure (*Ohio v. Akron Center for Reproductive Health*). By 1992, the Court upheld rules imposed on physicians, including rules that required that physicians provide pro-life information to patients and other requirements like those in *Thornburgh* in the *Planned Parenthood of Southeastern Pennsylvania v. Casey*. In the mid-1990s, the Court upheld some restrictions on antiabortion protesters in Florida (*Madsen v. Women's Health Center*), but threw out slightly more restrictive provisions in New York (*Schenck v. Pro-Choice Network*). Most recently, the Court struck down Nebraska's late-term ("partial-birth") abortion law in *Stenberg v. Carhart*. In the context of the conflicting evolution of abortion policy in these recent Supreme Court decisions, the ambivalence in the minds of Americans looks quite reasonable.

These examples cut right to the heart of a long-lasting debate in the public opinion literature about whether or not citizens have well-thought-out opinions about political affairs. The public opinion debate, perhaps beginning with the writings of Walter Lippman in the 1920s and now raging in the academic journals of political science and psychology, has seen three different accounts for the apparent muddle-headedness of American opinion.

Phillip Converse (1964) argued that weakly held and ill-formed opinions are evidence of "non-attitudes," opinions cooked up by respondents on their doorsteps in order to supply some answer to the interviewer. What was especially damning evidence for the political intelligence of the public was that such non-attitudes were not confined to arcane questions about poorly known types of public policy but could be found on just about every issue.

Working with survey data collected through the University of Michigan's National Election Studies during the 1950s, Converse amassed a wide range of survey responses about many issues that formed the political context of those times. He found that responses change in apparently random ways from interview to interview. Responses within interviews on apparently related questions are only weakly correlated with one another and are sensitive to question-ordering and question-wording. All of these empirical results pointed to a sweeping indictment of the notion that Americans were ideologically aware and informed about issues.

This minimalist view of the extent to which the public lacked ideological structure to their political thinking encountered three significant challenges, beginning shortly after publication of Converse's work: an argument that the questions used by Converse were poorly designed; a claim that the politics of the 1950s were an unusually unstimulating period of politics; and the argument that the public attitudes toward politics stem from core beliefs and values, which are more enduring and stable than opinions on specific policy questions.

Christopher Achen, in a 1975 article, argued that the reason for muddled survey responses was muddled survey questions. Achen's key insight was that respondents' genuine opinion about policy should be thought of not as a single fixed point but as a distribution of opinions. When the respondent is interviewed on multiple occasions, the respondent is likely to offer different selections of opinions from the distribution. The more vague the question, the more likely that the variation in opinions would be wider. The result of applying such measurement error corrections to Converse's original panel data yields a portrait of survey respondents whose opinions are much more strongly intercorrelated, and more stable. Further, "[t]he well-informed and interested have nearly as much difficulty with the questions as does the ordinary man. *Measurement error is primarily a fault of the instruments, not of the respondent*" (Achen's emphasis, 1229).

A second source of criticism of Converse's original findings came from Norman Nie, Sidney Verba, and John Petrocik in their 1979 book *The Changing American Voter*. By extending the series of open-ended questions on candidates and parties from Converse's years through 1976, Nie, Verba, and Petrocik found that a much greater fraction of the public was able to think in ideological terms than had been reported by Converse. Further, when they turned to specific policy questions, the authors detected much stronger correlations among apparently related items, such as opinions on school integration and attitudes toward the scope of government, beginning after 1964.

But not everything was comparable across questions in the pre- and post-1964 studies. It turns out that there were some "innovations" in the design of the pre- and post-1964 survey instruments, as the important response choices were switched from a conventional Likert question format to a new format where respondents were asked to choose between a set of competing alternative choices. Also, the survey researchers slightly changed the way in which respondents were prodded to admit not having any opinion at all, which Sullivan, Piereson, and Marcus demonstrated in a 1978 article could account for the greater intercorrelations. Thus, it now appears that despite the large changes in American politics in the 1960s, there was not a corresponding increase in ideological thinking or ideological consistency.

The third challenge to the minimalist approach to public opinion is so fundamental that we consider it to be the second major school of thought about the nature of public opinion. While individuals may not have an over-arching ideology, they do hold enduring and strong core values and beliefs. The idea that American attitudes revolve around deeply held and widely shared core values is an old one. Tocqueville's discussion of American attitudes in the nineteenth century pointed to the tension between radical individualism, support for the community, and egalitarianism. In early public opinion re-search, Gunnar Myrdal (1944) saw the great struggle of American political ideology as the conflict between racism (a noxious core belief) and American democratic values. Core values permeate our political rhetoric and historical accountings, and the arguments for an important role for core values providing structure to public opinion evolved into a second major debate about American public opinion.

The prominence of core values as a replacement system for mass beliefs can be traced to a series of academic works. Milton Rokeach in 1973 evaluated both "terminal" values (desirable end states) and "instrumental" values (the means by which we accomplish them). An instrumental value might be some-thing like "ambitious" or "obedient," while a terminal value might be something like "a comfortable life" or "freedom." Individuals vary in the degree to which they hold different terminal and instrumental values, but while they may have different ideas about whether obedience is a value, the values of equality and freedom appear to be quite widespread in American opinion.

Rokeach found that the important American value of egalitarianism was strongly associated with the opinions of whites toward Martin Luther King's assassination in particular, and to racial desegregation efforts more generally. Egalitarianism also was closely associated with opinions about poverty, welfare, and the war in Vietnam for whites and nonwhites alike in Rokeach's data. Other research has examined the impact of another important American value, individualism, and shown that it, too, seems to be interrelated with opinions on social welfare and racial policies.[4]

This preponderance of evidence in favor of some significant role for core beliefs implies that the minds of most Americans are hardly politically void; rather, they are sensitive to ideas that have a broader currency than the pur-chase of immediate political choices. But the core values approach must con-front two serious criticisms, both raised by John Zaller in his celebrated 1992 book *The Nature and Origins of Mass Opinion* and in his article with Stanley Feldman in the same year. One is that the profusion of core beliefs and values renders the possibility of constructing a system of mass beliefs unlikely, and that even the construction of something resembling the liberal-conservative continuum is out of reach of such a plethora of monopoles of opinion. The second is that the core values approach is incapable of addressing the vast differences in levels of political awareness among citizens. In the pointed example in Zaller's book, respondents *might* have well-formed core values about U.S. foreign involvement in Nicaragua, but the values are unusable for those respondents who do not know where Nicaragua can be found or for whose side the contras were fighting.

In place of a core values approach, Zaller and Feldman offer what we consider to be a third fundamental approach to public opinion, the "belief sampling" approach: a multistep model of the relationship between mass opinion and survey response, dubbed the RAS model (receive-accept sample) and summarized in Zaller's book as follows:

> 1. Reception: The greater a person's level of cognitive engagement with an issue, the more likely he or she is to be exposed to and comprehend—in a word, to receive—political messages concerning that issue. (42)
>
> 2. Resistance: People tend to resist arguments that are inconsistent with their political predispositions, but they do so only to the extent that they possess the contextual information necessary to perceive a relationship between the message and their predispositions. (44)
>
> 3. Accessibility: The more recently a consideration has been called to mind or thought about, the less time it takes to retrieve that consideration or related considerations from memory and bring them to the top of the head for use. (48)
>
> 4. Response: Individuals answer survey questions by averaging across the considerations that are immediately salient or accessible to them. (49)

The key idea is that respondents maintain sets of *considerations* (potential public opinion expressions), not fixed, canned answers to questions. When asked to provide an answer to a specific question by an interviewer, the respondent samples from the set of considerations. Response instability becomes something to expect from respondents and, indeed, an object of intellectual study.

The Zaller-Feldman model is one that yields a picture of exceptional sensitivity to context. According to Feldman and Zaller, the model is capable of explaining a total of seventeen different effects ranging from interviewer and question-ordering effects, to priming effects of media and the effects of political information. This model is also one where predispositions serve one principal purpose: to resist or accept incoming political information. Predispositions do not account for the sampling of opinions in this perspective; this feature is handled by accessibility, a function of recency and salience. Instead, predispositions filter the messages from which the respondent will produce his or her sample of considerations.

In our view, the Zaller-Feldman perspective excessively minimizes the role of predispositions, which, in their view, affect only a respondent's ability to encode incoming information; they do not affect sampling from considerations. This is not just a matter of quibbling, since the predispositions approach predicts much greater consistency in answers, and a stronger role for predispositions in coloring response.

In the end, the public opinion literature is left with two currently separate and ultimately incomplete descriptions of American public opinion. The core values approach articulates a set of monopoles around which opinions might be based. The appeal of the approach is that such a diversity of core values could potentially describe a wider range of domains of opinion than could be captured in a simple left-right ideological spectrum. But this appeal is also a detraction in that prospects for a system of mass belief are unlikely. Such an approach provides neither an explanation for opinions that are unstable, nor can it capture differences between masses and elites in the stability of opinion. The Zaller-Feldman approach constructs what is in some ways a more satisfactory explanation of the relationship between masses and elites over public matters, and explicitly permits a model of response variability. Yet the approach leads toward a model of citizens as exceptionally minimal in their core beliefs, citizens who "make it up as they go along" when asked to respond to public opinion surveys.

Our argument stakes out an important middle ground between these approaches. In this book, we integrate core values and beliefs with the Zaller-Feldman approach and thereby produce a nuanced statement about American public opinion. There is no doubt that Americans are generally unknowledgeable and uncertain about political issues, and on that we agree with Lippmann, Converse, and Zaller. But there is no doubt that a profusion of core values and predispositions exist in the minds of Americans and that these values and predispositions provide important foundations for their opinions and survey responses. Here we agree with Tocqueville and Rokeach. We need to find areas of agreement with both sides of the public opinion debate.

Instead of making it up as they go along, we argue that respondents figure it out on the spot. When asked about an issue like affirmative action or race, Americans draw upon their core beliefs and predispositions to produce their answer. We show this simple fact repeatedly in later chapters, where time and again beliefs like egalitarianism, authoritarianism, and even racism provide foundations for survey responses. At the same time, even though there are foundations for public opinion in beliefs and values, identifying *which* value is relevant may not be obvious for the respondent. As a result, there is also a great deal of malleability or fickleness in public opinion. The malleability or fickleness may come from a simple lack of information about the issues or about how their values should matter for the issues (which we call uncertainty). Or it may come from conflict among values and beliefs (which we call either ambivalence or equivocation, depending on the way in which conflict produces or reduces fickleness).

Yes, this complex brew of values, predispositions, and their conflict makes the study of public opinion difficult for scholars. Yes, this same complexity also makes life difficult for political representatives, as they have to also filter through public opinion to try to understand the desires and values of citizens. But the complexity of public opinion, and the conflict it produces within the minds of Americans and in their debates about issues, produces the struggles over resources, which we call politics. So by better understanding the complexity of public opinion we will go a long way toward better understanding politics.

ROADMAP OF THE BOOK

Our aim in this book is to reconcile the core values with the Zaller and Feldman approaches. Part 1 outlines a new theory of the survey response. We begin with an argument drawn from the core values literature: specifically, that mass opinion orbits around predispositions or inclinations to interpret public opinion questions in particular ways. We argue that there is a profusion of predispositions at play in mass opinion. Chapter 2 discusses the range of these predispositions, including not only core values and beliefs, but also attitudes toward groups, affective evaluations of policy, and expectations about the performance of political actors. At one level, the diversity of these predispositions renders the possibility of simple systems of mass belief unlikely. But at another level we argue that the failure to unify mass beliefs into a single system is itself normatively appealing.

The problem with the core values literature, as raised by Zaller (1992), is that the connection between any particular predisposition and a particular policy choice may be opaque. In chapter 3 we borrow from the RAS model and argue that political "informedness" matters in survey responses in important ways. Answering a survey question is really partly a problem of interpretation: What does the question mean? Which predispositions are pertinent to the policy? The extent to which citizens are able to interpret policy questions in terms of their predispositions depends on their store of political information, as we argue in chapter 3.

Given that a survey respondent is able to summon one or more predispositions that pertain to a policy question, the problem for the respondent is to reconcile these potentially conflicting, potentially irrelevant, or potentially reinforcing value sets. In chapter 4 we specify a theory of response variability, arguing that the combination of political informedness and multiple predispositions can lead to one of three situations, or states. In the condition where a single predisposition presents itself in the policy choice, response variability decreases with the respondent's political knowledge; we refer to this as *uncertainty*. In the situation where multiple predispositions are mutually reinforcing, response variability decreases not only with the respondent's political informedness, but also with the extent to which the respondent adheres to the predispositions; we call this condition *equivocation*. In the final state, multiple predispositions lead to an internalized state of conflict about the choice; we refer to this last condition as *ambivalence*. Chapter 4 explains why a particular policy domain leads to one or another of these three states and outlines our inferential statistical model, which we use to adjudicate between the states.

In part 2 we examine these three different states of public opinion. We begin in chapter 5 with the problem of ambivalence. The idea that individuals may be internally conflicted about political matters is widespread in the literature (e.g., Hochschild 1981). As we have defined it, ambivalence is a state of intra-personal conflict, and as we argue in chapters 5 through 7, it is relatively rare across policy domains. We will demonstrate, however, that in one of the most heated debates in contemporary politics—attitudes toward abortion—ambivalence is a potent explanation for observed response variability. But although rare, ambivalence is not confined to abortion; we also show that attitudes regarding euthanasia in the United States are subject to ambivalence as well.

In chapter 6 we consider the problem of uncertainty, specifically turning to attitudes about racial policies and affirmative action. From Myrdal (1944) forward, the dominant characterization of mass attitudes toward racial politics has been that the public is internally conflicted or ambivalent about racial issues. We demonstrate that this is not so, that the public is uncertain, not ambivalent, about racial politics. There is little evidence that respondents are in a state of conflict over race; instead, their relative degree of knowledge about politics and race matters most. The difference is profound since it implies a much more optimistic prognosis for consensus about race in America than one that hinges on the resolution of internal value conflicts.

Multiple predispositions need not be conflictual, though, since they can also be mutually reinforcing. Chapter 7 discusses the state of equivocation, where respondents "speak in two voices" about politics. Citizens may have multiple expectations about what the government is able to do, and even if these expectations are logically contradictory, these contradictions need not be seen as such by survey respondents. In chapter 7 we examine attitudes about the federal bureaucracy, specifically the Internal Revenue Service, and demonstrate that survey respondents expect government to be responsive, honest, and equitable, all at the same time.

Part 3 (chapters 8 and 9) considers the relationship between masses and elites. One approach is to think about how elites understand the opinions of their constituents. Chapter 8 refocuses our attention on the issue of racial policies and affirmative action, using a different data source than we used in chapter 6. We use this different data source to consider how elites interpret mass opinion in the act of political representation. Here we consider the ecology of race, or the difference between individual and aggregate understandings about the reasons for opposition to affirmative action and other racial policies.

In chapter 9, keeping the same analytic focus, we switch our substantive and methodological perspectives to the issue of foreign policy. Here we use a survey that simultaneously measures the attitudes of civilian masses and military elites toward the scope of acceptable casualties for hypothetical conflicts and the extent of military autonomy from civilian control. The central question in this chapter is the extent to which masses and elites experience conflict in different ways, and we find that elite opinion is better crystallized than mass opinion, but that masses are equivocal about military policy while the military elites are ambivalent.

A fairly large amount of methodological work forms the basis for our analyses in chapters 5 through 9, but in general, our goal has been to keep the purely methodological discussions out of the text and to relegate them to appendixes available on the Internet for interested readers (at www.pupress.princeton. edu/alvarez). There, they can find details about the data sets we use, a discussion of methods employed, and a full presentation of the estimation results. In each chapter, however, we present graphical and tabular summaries of the estimation results so that readers who are not interested in the methodological details will not be distracted from our primary results.

Chapter 10 concludes our analysis. There we recount briefly our arguments and our empirical findings. We also discuss how our research provides an integration of the two main approaches used to understand American public opinion: predispositions and the RAS model. Our conclusion provides a detailed discussion of this integration and explains why it vastly improves our understanding of public opinion in the United States.

Part 1

THEORY AND METHODS

Predispositions

THE VERY CORE of the idea of democracy is that people believe in *something*. Maybe the something is self-interest, assessing any candidate or policy in terms of What's in it for me? Maybe the something is more collective, asking the candidate, What will you do for us? Maybe the something is more rarefied: Is this fair? or Is this right? The list of democratic theorists who assume a core of belief is prodigious: Rousseau, Locke, Mill, Dewey, Rawls, and many others. We are not aware of a single influential theorist who describes democracy and does not begin from some idea that people have meaningful beliefs and preferences about public life.

How do social scientists describe these somethings? There are a variety of terms, each implying a different level of conceptualization (is it abstract or concrete?), specificity (is this general or only with reference to a specific target?), durability (ephemeral or lasting?), and centrality (important to self-image or peripheral?).

In our work, the distinction between the durable and the ephemeral sources of answers to survey questions is crucial. We will refer to the durable class as *predisposition*, inclinations to judge an object in a particular way. We include under this label well-used foundations of beliefs: core values (e.g., Rokeach 1973), such as a preference for limited government; group attachments, such as a self-identification as being "black" or "fundamentalist"; affective judgments, such as being pro-labor or antiblack; impressions, such as a summary judgment of presidential candidates; and expectations, beliefs about what others are likely to do.

What evidence is there of anything durable in the minds of citizens as it pertains, even remotely, to politics? In a recent synthesis of the psychological literature on how people respond to surveys, Tourangeau, Rips, and Rasinski (2000) identify three different sources for answers: "impressions or stereotypes; general attitudes or values; [and] specific beliefs or feelings about the target." (172)

At one extreme of specificity, there is a portion of the public that has well-defined, specific, and firm beliefs and feelings about political targets. Some respondents actually have answers to survey questions in their heads, in part perhaps because the questions are so well known. An example might be "Do you approve or disapprove of the president's performance?" Some respondents have such a high degree of familiarity with politics that they have well-defined beliefs over a wide range of topics, yet these are probably rare. As a general source of explanation for response variability, one would probably not look to this category.

At the other extreme of specificity in content about the political targets are impressions, which refer to vague summaries that reflect one's overall judgment about an object, the general balance of positive or negative assessments, independent of specific information. Impressions are not based on memory (in that specific details can be recalled), but are "on-line" (Hastie and Park 1986; Lodge, McGraw, and Stroh 1989), easily summoned.

There is powerful evidence that voters keep these on-line tallies for purposes of evaluating candidates. Lodge and colleagues demonstrate through experiments that although subjects cannot recall the specifics of information that would cast candidates in a good or bad light, they do update their general impressions, or their on-line tally of the candidate.

But how relevant are impressions toward understanding response variability? There are two sources of ambiguity about their general utility for understanding survey response. One source is how a respondent would keep or use an on-line tally with reference to candidates considered in isolation, or to more complex objects of evaluation, such as matters of policy. Suppose one reads about the FDA decision to permit administration of RU486 for early termination of pregnancies. How does this new information affect your on-line impression about abortion? Or does this information affect a new tally about the FDA?

A second source of ambiguity arises from new research in social psychology and physiology. Cacioppo and colleagues (e.g., Cacioppo and Gardner 1999; Holbrook et al. 2001) argue that positive and negative streams of information do not automatically reconcile along a single dimension. Subjects can simultaneously maintain both positive and negative evaluations of an object. This simultaneous positive-negative evaluation could be a manifestation of internalized conflict, or it could be a disconnected yet simultaneous feeling of being "bittersweet" (the archetypal example would be the graduating senior's sense of triumph and elation upon graduating, and his/her feelings of sadness and anxiety upon leaving college). As Holbrook and colleagues show, this disconnectedness of positive and negative streams of information challenges the "simple theory of voting" (Kelley and Mirer 1974) in that respondents who have equal levels of likes about candidates are behaviorally more stimulated than those holding equal levels of dislikes about candidates.

In a middle area of specificity are those respondents who make their choices upon the basis of predispositions, durable cognitive structures that allow a respondent to render a judgment in a survey response. Predispositions have object-relevant contents, like identities (Who am I? Who does this person represent?), classifications (What category does this belong to?), expectations (What happens next? What follows?), and standards (Is this outcome good? What is fair?). Our definition is by necessity broad, and it invokes a wide range of potential modes for choice. In this chapter, we review four different forms of predispositions—values, group attachments, affective judgments, and expectations—and demonstrate their diversity in the American public.

However, in this mid-range of specificity it is clear that survey respondents have different puzzles to solve when answering a survey question than in situations where either firm beliefs or vague impressions are drawn upon to formulate an answer. Unlike the notion that survey respondents rely on strong beliefs to produce an answer, here respondents do not know an answer but instead construct one from their predispositions to make a choice on the basis of more than mere feelings.

Specifically, we postulate that typical survey respondents maintain multiple predispositions over many political and policy domains. It is even possible for more than one predisposition to be pertinent to any specific policy question. The problem for the respondent, addressed in the next chapter, is to identify *which* predispositions matter, and *how*.

This first stage in our model of survey response puts us in sharp contrast with the minimalist model offered by Converse in the 1960s. Instead of survey respondents who have few systematic and consistent preferences over politics, we argue that most respondents have many preferences, but that these preferences vary over policy areas. When multiple, contradictory preferences pertain to a policy choice, the problem becomes more complicated for the respondent. We take up the question of resolving multiple predispositions in chapter 4.

Our model of the survey response also puts us in contrast with the Zaller-Feldman RAS model. Predispositions organize respondents' answers to survey questions and do not serve solely as filters for incoming information. Thus survey response can be less variable, and less context-dependent, than argued by the RAS model.

Our use of the concept of *predispositions* also stands in contrast to an older distinction between *opinions* and *attitudes* (e.g., Smith, Bruner, and White 1956). Older uses of the idea of *attitudes* emphasized their stability and predictability: "to experience a class of objects in certain ways, with characteristic affect," or "to experience, and to be motivated by, and to act toward, a class of objects in a predictable manner" (Smith, Bruner, and White 1956, 33). The word denotes a chronic and enduring relationship between a person and another object or person. By this conception, Converse's demonstration of severe response instability would be strong evidence of the absence of political attitudes in the mass public. Our intention is to describe predispositions in a more primal, and not explicitly relational, sense, as in this older use of the idea.

In this chapter, we first review the four different predispositional forms, beginning with core values. We conclude by discussing the substantive and methodological impact of our argument and by developing the normative implications of pluralistic predispositions in the mass public.

VALUES

Core values comprise the most prominent of the categories of predispositions that structure American public opinion. Core values are deeply held, widely shared, enduring beliefs that establish "desirable modes of conduct or desirable end-states of existence" (Rokeach 1973, 7). Rokeach dubs those values, which describe modes of conduct, as "instrumental values"; examples of these include "ambitious," "obedient," and "forgiving." He refers to values describing desirable end states as "terminal values"; examples of these would include "a comfortable life," "national security," and "freedom."

The list of potential core values is enormous. Rokeach's study considered some sixty-four values, and even that list is an abbreviation. Some of the obvious values include equality, order, liberty, efficiency, health, security, wealth, and growth, but there are, no doubt, other highly internalized beliefs that could be considered core values.

How is it that such beliefs comprise a more general system for expression of public opinion? Both instrumental and terminal values play a key role as standards, permitting cognition of what is desirable and guiding behavior when activated.

> Values are multifaceted standards that guide conduct in a variety of ways. They (1) lead us to take particular positions on social issues, and (2) predispose us to favor one particular political or religious ideology over another. They are standards employed (3) to guide presentation of self to others (Goffman 1959), and (4) to evaluate and judge, to heap praise and fix blame on ourselves and others. (5) Values are central to the study of comparison processes (Festinger 1954; Latane 1966); we employ them as standards to ascertain whether we are as moral and as competent as others. (6) They are, moreover, standards employed to persuade and influence others, to tell us which beliefs, attitudes, values, and actions of others are worth challenging, protesting, and arguing about, or worth trying to influence or to change.
>
> Finally, (7) values are standards that tell us how to rationalize in the psychoanalytic sense, beliefs, attitudes, and actions that would otherwise be personally and socially unacceptable so that we will end up with personal feelings of morality and competence, both indispensable ingredients for the maintenance and enhancement of self-esteem. (Rokeach 1973, 13)

The utility of values for the survey respondent arises from the economy of a generalized standard that can be used in a wide-ranging set of political domains. Instead of maintaining separate political attitudes over diverse questions, respondents need only assess the relevance of the questions to a relatively limited set of core values.

Although not necessarily intrinsically "political," both instrumental and terminal values are directly relevant to political attitudes. A respondent who has a value that is pertinent to judgment of a political object is able to employ that value as a standard. According to Rokeach, two terminal values (freedom and equality) lead to a system of political ideology. These two values are clearly recurring in the study of American public opinion, dating back at least to Tocqueville's observations on nineteenth-century America. In academic work, "freedom" may more often be referred to as "individualism," and "equality" as "egalitarianism" (see Kinder 1983 for a detailed list of academic works). Indeed, the terms appear to be so popular in scholarly analysis that there is some evidence that "individualism" connotes standards for individual freedom, the scope of government, natural rights, and more (Lukes 1973).

We argue that some values are much more specific in their domain than others. Some of the core values that are pertinent to choices about abortion policy should surely include protecting human life (combined with a belief that life begins before birth) and prizing women's bodily autonomy. Values that are pertinent to choices about euthanasia include secular humanism, manifest in the (ultimate) control over one's own life, and depth of religious faith. (Both issues are examined in chapter 5.) If values are more specific than the spanning values of Rokeach's study, then the complexity of value systems is greater still.

Even though core values comprise a significant part of the predispositions that structure opinion, they are far from comprehensive. In the sections to follow, we consider alternative forms of predispositions.

GROUP ATTACHMENTS

Another of the important forms of predispositions that matter are group attachments. Indeed, in Converse's (1964) original work on the nature of belief systems, he found that a larger fraction of respondents (42 percent in the original study) would employ group identifications as a means to make sense of the differences between parties than they would any of the other levels of conceptualization. Being part of a group can be a powerful means to sort through certain classes of political problems.

Group attachments can be seen as a predisposition—a durable cognitive structure that allows a respondent to render political judgments—in a variety of forms. It encourages some respondents to understand politics in terms of the mutual interdependence among members. Group evaluations allow some respondents to judge policy by judging whom the policy advantages or disadvantages. Identifying with a group lets respondents sort the political world into those groups they like or dislike. Group can be a powerful cognitive shortcut, a means of describing oneself or others, and a persistent feature of political rhetoric and reasoning.

Race, in particular, is a very powerful and persistent group category that accounts for profound differences in attitudes. Since the first uses of surveys to gauge public reactions to policy problems, white and black respondents differ widely in support for racial policy, including school and neighborhood integration, affirmative action, housing laws, and other policy areas (Schuman, Steeh, and Bobo 1988). For example, in the National Election Studies series of questions on federal intervention in school, from 1964 through 1978, black respondents supported the idea by at least 30 percentage points more than white respondents. Even larger gaps could be found between white and black respondents on whether the federal government should intervene to ensure fair treatment in jobs (Schuman et al. 1988, 149–50). But racial differences persist in other matters of policy and politics that do not strictly pertain to race: in partisan identification, demands for domestic spending, and confidence in national institutions (Brehm and Rahn 1997).

One means by which group attachments help respondents make sense of politics is by providing a sense of "linked fate" (Dawson 1994). To the extent that group members see their fortunes as mutually interdependent, it may be quite reasonable for them to draw inferences from their assessments of how their group would fare as a means to decide how they should choose over policy for themselves. For example, to the extent that African Americans see their economic and political circumstances as linked to one another, then it would be rational for African American respondents to support policies that they believe aid them as a group, or to oppose policies that they believe hurt them as a group. Harris-Lacewell (1999) demonstrates that four distinct political ideologies—liberal integrationism, black nationalism, black conservatism, and black feminism—wax and wane in their strength depending upon exposure to different information networks. All of these ideologies ask why black Americans remain socially, politically, and economically unequal, and whether the role of white Americans is as obstacle, ally, or enemy. Race is a potent and clear social construction of group identity that matters a great deal to American public opinion.

One concern with the linked-fate conception of group attachments is that the concept does not completely solve the problem of structuring opinions. Respondents may not have to decide explicitly how a policy would affect them, but they do need to decide how the policy affects their group. One potential vehicle around the problem of drawing inferences about group conditions is to take cues from prominent members of one's group. Wilson (1999) demonstrates that those with strong group identifications (specifically among blacks, women, and evangelicals) have more systematically coherent beliefs, are more likely to mobilize, and (for women and blacks) more trusting of other people than those with weaker group identifications.

A second means by which group attachments help respondents make sense of politics is to classify which groups are associated with which political parties or political figures. Conover and Feldman (1981) posit one way in which respondents might use groups in order to construct evaluations of political actors. They construct a model of separate evaluations of liberals and conservatives on the basis of evaluations (feeling thermometer scores) of different groups, and a set of issue positions. Evaluations of liberals were influenced by feelings toward groups belonging to the "radical left" (e.g., radical students, black militants), "reformist left" (e.g., blacks, Chicanos, civil rights leaders), and "capitalism" (e.g., big business, Republicans, businessmen), and by positions on economic issues. Evaluations of conservatives were influenced by feelings toward capitalism, "status quo" (e.g., Protestants, working men, whites), and "social control" (e.g., police, military), and by positions on racial issues. In their model, how we think about the groups determines how we think about liberals and conservatives.

A third way in which group evaluations may help citizens sort political information was proposed by Brady and Sniderman (1985), in the form of the "likability heuristic." The idea is that respondents maintain feelings about politically relevant groups, such as liberals, conservatives, whites, Democrats, and Republicans, and beliefs about issues. As they put it, "What allows citizens to simplify political calculations efficiently is this two-sided, 'us vs. them' character of politics; the more attached they are to their side—and the more opposed they are to the other—the more they appreciate the differences between the issue positions of the two sides" (1075). It is this combination of affect toward groups that makes it possible for many in the mass public to accurately ascribe political attitudes about the groups.

Finally, partisanship itself might be regarded as a form of group evaluation. In the original "sociological" models of partisanship (Berelson, Lazarsfeld, and McPhee 1954), partisanship followed from socioeconomic position. But what was often overlooked was the hereditary role of partisanship. First-time voters, in particular, inherited party identification from their fathers (75 percent of the Elmira sample). Part of the inheritance, to be sure, followed from an inheritance of similar socioeconomic status. But part of the inheritance of party had to do with the relative political inexperience of new voters, who would rely upon standing cues about which party to support, and the group dynamic within the family that would encourage similar identifications. Partisanship as a group identification emerges in the Michigan school (Campbell et al. 1960) as well. Party forms a "psychological group," where membership is not delimited in a formal way, but in a subjective self-classification (297–98).

With each of these forms of group attachments and the potential roles such identifications might serve in making sense of politics, the singular question of which group identifications matter emerges. There are obviously a plethora of potential group attachments that an individual might call upon. What makes any one group politically salient? Even in those circumstances where ascriptive group memberships nominally provide considerable information about likely status of the individual (e.g., for blacks), the puzzle remains how that group identification becomes relevant to political choices. Is it because members of the group follow the cues of group leaders, because the policy consequences are obvious for members of the group, or because members share access to common information networks?

AFFECTIVE JUDGMENTS

Some predispositions are so affect laden that some scholars have difficulty considering them to be values. The idea that affect and values combined represent something different from affect or values separately is a controversial one, and no more prominent than in the debates over "symbolic," or "modern," racism.

To even the most cursory student of the scholarship on racial attitudes, it is obvious that researchers disagree over the basic forces that drive racial attitudes. One group (Kinder and Sears 1981; Kinder 1986; McConahay 1986) contends that symbolic racism, a combination of antiblack affect with traditional American values, drives white resistance to racial policy. By this argument, whites who oppose such policies as affirmative action or busing on the grounds that blacks are getting more than they deserve are motivated by a form of racism that has replaced overt expressions of racial superiority.

In contrast, Sniderman and his colleagues (Sniderman and Hagen 1985; Sniderman and Piazza 1993, Sniderman and Tetlock 1986) argue that symbolic racism fails because it confounds the policy choice with the attitude, while at the same time ignoring the continuing presence of simple antiblack affect as a source of white opposition to racial policy. Furthermore, Sniderman and colleagues argue that although symbolic racism is supposed to be the conjunction of antiblack affect and individualism, it is only weakly correlated with individualism itself.

Kinder and Sanders (1996, 292) strongly emphasize this combination of group evaluation *and* traditional values: "Symbolic (or modern or subtle) racism is neither prejudice, pure and simple, nor traditional values, pure and simple, but rather the combination of the two. . . . The point is worth emphasizing, because it is often misunderstood." One of the chief objections to the modern racism concept is that the scales used to measure this concept often treat policy choices as independent variables in the same models that purport to explain policy choices as dependent variables.

[I]t is gratuitous to equate opposition to affirmative action with racial prejudice—gratuitous because it would otherwise be possible to examine the actual relation between the two, and thus establish as a matter of fact, and not of definition, how and to what degree the two are connected. Quite simply, defining opposition to affirmative action as racism precludes falsification of the prediction that the two are indeed related, at the cost of making the relation between them a tautology. (Sniderman and Tetlock 1986, 135)

We will take up the question of the explanatory power of symbolic racism in chapter 6, on uncertainty. Symbolic racism is not the only form of an affective judgment that combines attitudes toward groups with expressions of core values. Brewer (1999) contends that attitudes about homosexuals may be understood in terms of a "symbolic homophobia," an expression of antigay affect in terms of violations of egalitarian principles.

EXPECTATIONS

Expectations comprise a fourth form of predispositions. Respondents are sometimes asked to make judgments about how likely certain things are to happen. We ask respondents to assess whether people can be trusted, what they expect when they interact with government agencies, and to make predictions about the likely success of different candidates or the future of the economy. Although core values may be relevant for some of these judgments, it is probably more reasonable to think of this form as an expectation.

Expectations can be as chronic and stable as other predispositional forms. Just as some people seem to be chronically risk-averse, others can be chronically trusting. Both the National Election Studies and the General Social Survey have, for years, asked a series of questions about the trustworthiness of others:

- Do you think most people would try to take advantage of you if they got a chance, or would they try to be fair?
- Would you say that most of the time people try to be helpful, or that they are mostly just looking out for themselves?
- Generally speaking, would you say that most people can be trusted or that you can't be too careful in dealing with people?

Although these questions clearly have the potential of invoking core values, it would be more accurate to think of these as expectations about what a generalized encounter with people is likely to be. Furthermore, generalized abstract social trust appears to be a highly durable and stable psychological construct, on par with the stability of partisan identification (Berger and Brehm 1997; Rahn, Brehm, and Carlson 1999).

Another form of expectations is covered in chapter 7, when we examine attitudes toward the Internal Revenue Service. The IRS is an archetypal form of the federal bureaucracy, and one that virtually every citizen interacts with every year (if only when filing tax forms). Scholars of public administration

(Goodsell 1985; Perrow 1987; Wilson 1967, 1989) contend that Americans have mutually contradictory expectations about the performance of bureaucracy, wanting on the one hand to have equitable treatment (treat all citizens the same), while allowing for responsiveness to unique conditions (treat certain citizens differently).

Although we outline four different predispositional forms, we do not intend to hold that these are the only durable cognitive structures that have the potential for guiding survey response. Indeed, one of the themes of this chapter is that predispositions can be plentiful, and take many forms. Not only does this diversity of predispositions hold for the mass public taken as a whole, it is quite possible—even probable—that individual respondents themselves possess quite a number of predispositions. The next task to consider is how to identify how respondents determine *which* of these predispositions are relevant.

CONCLUSION

An important component of our argument in this book is that there is a profusion of predispositions, including (but not limited to) a wide range of core values, affective judgments, group evaluations, and expectations. In this chapter we have only briefly touched upon what is really an enormous and continually expanding academic literature that discusses and elaborates on this seemingly disparate set of predispositions. We do not begin with the assumption that there is (or should be) a single organizing principle for Americans when they think about politics. We argue that such an assumption is clearly incorrect, and that research searching for single organizing principles of public opinion will quickly and correctly find that they do not exist.

America is a complex society, and Americans differ greatly in the ways in which they learn about politics and society throughout their lives. Ignoring the complexity of American society and the heterogeneity of the American life experience is problematic when trying to understand how we all think about politics.

Because of this profusion of predispositions, it is highly unlikely that an overarching left-right ideology would appear in mass survey data. Also, the typical approaches that researchers use to study public opinion enhance this problem, since methodologies ranging from the simple correlation analyses used by Converse to the nonlinear least-squares approach of Zaller rarely can allow for the differences that might exist across a set of survey respondents in how they conceptualize their political world. Virtually every technique used to study public opinion survey data assumes that all survey respondents think identically about politics or that if there is any heterogeneity it is simple and known to the researcher.

Last, research that assumes that Americans have a single organizing principle when they think about politics also ignores important realities of the political world and democratic political representation. While we will return to this discussion in chapters 8 and 9, politicians and political elites can play key roles in defining the predispositions that Americans use for understanding politics. If political elites do not present issues to the people in ideological terms, is it any surprise that ideological thinking is not widespread in our society? On the other hand, if political elites talk about an issue like affirmative action in ways that lead citizens (or some set of citizens) to think about affirmative action not in group terms but in egalitarian terms, should we be surprised to find that egalitarian thinking helps Americans construct their opinions about affirmative action?

Of course, our argument in this book about the multitude of predispositions that operate in American public opinion challenges the conclusions of past research. For example, our argument stands in sharp contrast to John Zaller (1992, 26), who writes: "There is, in other words, a tendency for people to be fairly consistently "left" or "right" or "centrist" on such disparate value dimensions as economic individualism, opinions toward communists, tolerance of nonconformists, racial issues, sexual freedom, and religious authority." What we will demonstrate is that the degree of integration of these values varies by the extent to which policy domains render them internally consistent, irrelevant, or contradictory.

A second consequence of the profusion of predispositions is normative. As the number of important core values increase in the polity, the probability that any one ordering could satisfy all those values decreases. In other words, not only is the diminishing likelihood of an overarching ideological ordering a substantive and methodological problem for public opinion research, any political ordering has the potential to run afoul of core political values. This is an old idea, dating to the eighteenth-century writings of Condorcet (1955) in *Esquisse d'un tableau historique*. Written while in hiding from the Jacobin government, Condorcet argued that the progress of human history would lead to flexible and tolerant political systems that could accommodate multiple political principles. His work on the "jury problem"—the observation that no voting scheme for a jury of at least three members could be assured of ascertaining guilt or innocence with certainty—led Condorcet to oppose capital punishment and put him in conflict with the revolutionary government. His observations about voting cycles on juries ultimately led to observations about political systems in general. Condorcet was a value pluralist long before twentieth-century political psychologists would define the term.

Indeed, more philosophical portions of our discipline would credit the term *value pluralist* to Isaiah Berlin (1992), who writes:

> What is clear is that values can clash—that is why civilizations are incompatible.
> They can be incompatible between cultures, or groups in the same culture, or

between you and me. You believe in always telling the truth, no matter what; I do not, because I believe that it can sometimes be too painful and too destructive. We can discuss each other's point of view, we can try to reach common ground, but in the end what you pursue may not be reconcilable with the ends to which I find that I have dedicated my life. Values may easily clash within the breast of a single individual; and it does not follow that, if they do, some must be true and others false. Justice, rigorous justice is for some people an absolute value, but it is not compatible with what may be no less ultimate values for them—mercy, compassion—as arises in concrete cases. (12)

This conflict of values—within individuals, or across polities—makes the place of values paramount in the plurality of predispositions, and indeed, in the empirical chapters of this book.

The core normative idea of the plurality of principles and the impossibility of procedures to conclusively sort these principles has currency in contemporary debates. Instead of institutional procedures, important political philosophers argue that agreement on norms of contestation, debate, and fairness facilitate construction of consensus. Rawls (1993) writes:

[G]iven the fact of reasonable pluralism, citizens cannot agree on any moral authority, whether a sacred text, or institution. Nor do they agree about the order of moral values, or the dictates of what some regard as natural law. We adopt, then, a constructivist view to specify the fair terms of social cooperation as given by the principles of justice agreed to by the representatives of free and equal citizens when fairly situated. The bases of this view lie in fundamental ideas of the public political culture as well as in citizens' shared principles and conceptions of practical reason. (97)

The observation that mass predispositions are numerous and not readily ordered into single dimensions of ideology, is not simply a problem for analysts of public opinion, but a broad and deep problem for pluralist democracy.

Knowing that the level and diversity of predispositions varies across the public presents only a half of the conditions necessary to understand survey response. Merely having strong predispositions is of little help to the survey respondent, if the respondent cannot understand the terms or topic of the question. The second component of any sensible model of the survey response is information, or the degree to which respondents are familiar with the conditions of the policy debate. We turn to questions about the role and meaning of information in the next chapter.

Why Does Political Information Matter?

WHEN SYSTEMATIC research on American public opinion began in the 1940s and 1950s, scholars assumed that citizens should be well informed about politics. One of the primary early works in the field, Berelson, Lazarsfeld, and McPhee's study of political behavior in the late 1940s, concluded: "The democratic citizen is expected to be well-informed about political affairs. He is supposed to know what the issues are, what their history is, what the relevant facts are, what alternatives are proposed, what the party stands for, what the likely consequences are. By such standards, the voter falls short" (1954, 308).

To put this into modern terminology, the early researchers hoped to find that Americans were *fully informed* about political affairs. Being fully informed would entail that Americans knew about the important issues of the day, that they had preferences about the direction of public policy, that they knew the positions taken by their political representatives on these public policy questions, and that they knew what the various levels of government were doing about these issues.

This premise, that ideal citizens in democracies need to be fully informed, is still widespread in research on public opinion. In a recent study of American political knowledge, Delli Carpini and Keeter began their work by asserting that "democracy functions best when its citizens are politically informed" because "a broadly and equitably informed citizenry helps assure a democracy that is both responsive and responsible" (1996, 1). Again, this premise leads researchers to lament the lack of political knowledge by Americans, which leads them to criticize the viability of democracy in modern society.

In many ways, however, it was clear even to researchers during the early years of public opinion research that these normative conclusions, and the premises upon which they were based, were not legitimate. Walter Lippmann, after all, prefaced his discussion of *Public Opinion* (1927) with a chapter about the "pictures in their heads" that an ill-informed public would have about political matters, especially those pertaining to foreign policy. E. E. Schattschneider countered the conclusions of the early work on public opinion: "If we start with the common definition of democracy (as government by the people), it is hard to avoid some extremely pessimistic conclusions about the feasibility of democracy in the modern world, for it is impossible to reconcile traditional concepts of what ought to happen in a democracy with the fact that an amazingly large number of people do not seem to know very much about what is going on."

(1960, 131–32). By assuming that democratic society functions best with fully informed citizens, early scholarship on public opinion in America produced very pessimistic conclusions about the operation of democracy in America.

Of course, the obvious answer to this research is that most Americans simply have too many other competing concerns—ranging from their jobs to their families to hobbies and other activities—to become fully informed about politics. So it is no great surprise that many Americans are fairly uninformed about politics; in fact, many are quite ignorant about most issues. What is important about the operation of democracy is accounting for why it is that some people are poorly informed on some issues, how they become better informed, and documenting how knowledgeable citizens interact with less-informed individuals.

While these works lamenting the lack of political knowledge by Americans were the subject of considerable debate among political scientists over the past forty years, some of the most notable contributions regarding whether citizens should be better informed about politics are from outside the field of political science.[1] One of these important contributions has come from economics, in particular, from the seminal book by Anthony Downs (1957). Downs, and those who have followed in his footsteps, compellingly explain why citizens have good reasons to be less than fully informed; further, the Downsian line of research has produced some important new ways to think about the role of information in shaping political opinions and behavior.

The second major development in the literature has come from the intersection between political science and psychology, from the work we discussed in the previous chapter. There, we showed how predispositions or values can provide some content to opinions about political affairs; these arguments were earlier summarized by Kinder and Sears (1985). But predispositions are increasingly seen as an important component of our developing understanding of the factors that shape public opinion, since predispositions and values provide the linkages necessary for citizens to relate new information to policy choices (Zaller 1992). Since much of the information citizens receive about politics comes from elite behavior and discourse, it follows that values and other predispositions are part of the process by which elites are shaping mass opinion.

In this chapter, we consider the problem of why information matters for understanding public opinion about policy choices. In particular, we focus on two different ways in which information is relevant for public opinion. Building from the important work of Downs (1957), we discuss how information directly shapes what citizens know about politics. Here we examine two different ways in which information about public policy has a direct impact on the opinions of individuals. First, information about some aspect of public policy can make citizens more certain about their opinion; second, information about public policy can persuade individuals to change their opinions.

We call these direct effects of information *uncertainty reduction* and *persuasion*, respectively.

Then, we turn to a discussion of how information makes predispositions and values relevant for policy choices, and how elite debates and behavior enter into this process. This effect of information draws upon the early work of Lazarsfeld, Berelson, and Gaudet (1944), and the more recent contributions of Popkin (1991) and Zaller (1992), on the ways in which elite discussions activate predispositions. Here we link the predispositions possessed by individuals with the political information they receive, thereby uncovering why it is that some predispositions structure certain beliefs about public policy while others do not. After developing our arguments for why political knowledge influences public opinion, we conclude with a discussion of how we measure political knowledge in our studies of public opinion in subsequent chapters.

INFORMATION AND REDUCING UNCERTAINTY

For our purposes, there are two important contributions made by Downs (1957): the elaboration of the spatial model in an explicitly political context and the discussion of information costs for citizens. Both of these ideas are fundamental contributions to political science, and they structure our analyses in later chapters. Oddly enough, neither aspect of Downs's work has had much impact on the study of American public opinion, even though his work has had a fundamental impact on the academic study of campaigns and elections. We view one of the major contributions of our work in this book as bringing his insights to this subject.

Information and Uncertainty

In the spatial model as introduced by Downs (1957), voters and candidates are arrayed only on a unidimensional ideological dimension. Voters have positions on the ideological dimension, candidates take positions as well, and voters are assumed to prefer candidates close to them on this ideological dimension. Armed with knowledge of the distribution of voter positions, and where candidates locate in this space, we can predict which candidate will win in an election.[2]

However, there is one thing that is almost always true about candidates for political offices: they are often quite vague or ambiguous about their positions on issues (Shepsle 1972; Page 1978). Thus, since candidates are not always clear about their stands (indeed, they often have strong incentives to be deliberately ambiguous) it should come as no great surprise that voters are often unsure about the positions of candidates on issues. V. O. Key (1966, 2) stated this best: "The voice of the people is but an echo. The output of an echo chamber bears an inevitable and invariable relation to the input. As candidates and parties clamor for attention and vie for popular support, the people's verdict can be no more than a selective reflection from among the alternatives and outlooks presented to them." Thus, there are good reasons to believe that voters are not well informed about the positions of candidates on policy issues, especially when candidates are ambiguous about their positions.

That voters are unsure of candidate policy positions has been incorporated into a number of theoretical and empirical models. In general, researchers have assumed that voter perceptions of candidate policy positions can be represented by probability distributions, which have central tendencies and distributions of points around the central tendency (Achen 1975; Alvarez 1997; Alvarez and Franklin 1994, 1997; Bartels 1986; Enelow and Hinich 1984; Franklin 1991). In this framework, the central tendency of the voter's belief is usually taken as the voter's best guess regarding the position of the candidate; the distribution of points around the central tendency is usually taken to be representative of the uncertainty in the voter's belief about the candidate's position.

This conceptualization of uncertainty has a straightforward application to how individuals might see their own beliefs about public policy issues, not just their beliefs about candidate positions. So we assume that citizens can be uncertain about their own political opinions, not just their opinions about where candidates stand on issues. This means that people have opinions that also can be characterized as having some sort of central tendency and a variance, the latter being our representation of their uncertainty about their opinion.

A simple way to picture uncertainty is to think of the voter's belief about a policy issue as a normal distribution, with a mean and a variance. We provide in figure 3.1 a hypothetical example, where the x-axis gives the range of potential beliefs on this issue (or this can be thought of as the ideological space), and the y-axis gives the possible distributions of the individual's position. In this figure, the three curves give three different levels of uncertainty, with the dashed line being high levels of uncertainty, the dotted line indicating moderate uncertainty, and the solid line representing low levels of uncertainty. For the purposes of our discussion here, we assume that the issue is affirmative action; with the far left being continuation of affirmative action policies and the far right being elimination of affirmative action policies.

In this example, each of the three distributions of the voter's beliefs about what to do with affirmative action policies have the same central tendency, or mean, since each distribution is centered just to the right of no change in affirmative action policies. Thus, this individual would believe that affirmative action policies ought to be reduced, but not necessarily eliminated. The key aspect of this figure is to see how varying amounts of uncertainty can be represented. When there is low uncertainty, the amount of variance in the voter's

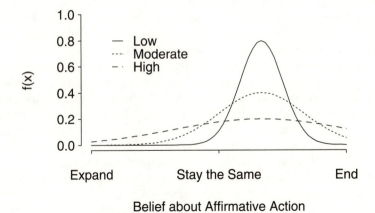

FIGURE 3.1. Voter uncertainty about their opinion on affirmative action

perception is very small; notice how the distribution clusters tightly around the mean. This means that the voter is quite sure about her opinion on changing affirmative action; the distribution of her opinion is somewhere very close to the mean. But, when she is very uncertain about affirmative action, notice that the distribution becomes very flat—in fact, in this example, it actually spans the entire issue, or ideological space. Although the voter's best guess at where her opinion on affirmative action might be is still the mean, she is now much less confident about her opinion regarding these policies.[3] When voters are highly uncertain, they are unsure about how close their opinion is relative to the central tendency of their belief.[4]

Keep in mind that although we have used the normal distribution in our example, in reality, there is no compelling reason for the beliefs of citizens to be distributed normally. In fact, nonsymmetric distributions might actually be more accurate, since it is possible that a person's perception might be highly skewed in one direction or another; this is likely in cases where individuals have extremist positions on issues, for example (Alvarez and Franklin 1997). When someone has an extremist position on an issue, and there are really no logically possible positions on that issue farther to the left or right (depending on which extreme the individual is at), then it simply has to be the case that their opinion has a skewed distribution, with some of the probability mass tending toward the center of the issue space. In any case, our point here is to use the normal distribution as an example, not to claim that the distributions of citizen beliefs are necessarily so smoothly and symmetrically distributed.

So far we have talked about uncertainty only in the context of the perceptions of voters about the policy positions of candidates running for office. That has been the focus of most of the research on the role of uncertainty in political science (Alvarez 1997; Alvarez and Franklin 1994; Bartels 1986; Enelow and Hinich 1984; Franklin 1991). Our intention here is to make this argument more general and to focus on the beliefs of citizens—their own positions on important issues of public policy—not on the positions of candidates.

Thus, we portray someone who is poorly informed about a particular public policy as being uncertain (as described above) and we substitute the voter's own belief about a dimension of public policy for his belief about a candidate's position, giving us the representation in figure 3.1. Again, a citizen with an uncertain belief is one whose belief has a relatively flat and diffuse distribution across the issue space; a citizen with a certain belief is one whose belief has a very tight distribution around the central tendency of their belief.

Next, conceptualizing uncertainty in this fashion also sheds considerable light on how new information might affect the beliefs of voters about some public policy, as well as how their attitude might be influenced by new information. An intuitive way to formalize this process is to use a simple Bayesian model of political learning (Achen 1992; Alvarez 1997; Bartels 1993; Calvert and MacKuen 1985; Zechman 1978). In this Bayesian framework we think of beliefs as weighted functions of past beliefs (or predispositions) and new information, where the weights express the citizen's uncertainty.

By making some simplifying assumptions about the statistical distributions of citizen's predispositions or beliefs, the new information they receive, and their new beliefs, we can obtain a useful formulation of the central tendency and uncertainty of their new beliefs (Alvarez 1997).[5] That is, the citizen's new belief, after receiving some new information is simply the weighted combination of their predispositions and the new information, where the weights are the certainty of their predisposition and the new information, respectively. Using this formalized model of citizen learning, we can easily see how it is that new information can influence a person's beliefs about public policies.

New information can have two different effects. The first is probably the easiest to understand and to document empirically. That is, if a citizen has an uncertain predisposition to begin with, and the new information is very certain, then the person will have a much more certain belief after obtaining this new information.[6] If, however, that predisposition is quite certain, even a very certain piece of new information will have little influence on the certainty of the new, updated belief about the policy issue. Therefore, new information—especially certain new information—will produce more certain beliefs, especially when the predispositions were uncertain (what we referred to earlier as *uncertainty reduction*).

New information can also have a second kind of effect on beliefs about issues of public policy. When an individual has uncertain predispositions but then encounters relatively certain new information, where the new information indicates that their belief about the issue should be different from their predisposition, then new information can also change the person's underlying belief. In the context of the formalization above, the new information (provided it is certain and has a central tendency divergent from the prior belief) can lead to a significant change in their new belief. In the terminology of figure 3.1, the new information can change the central tendency of the citizen's beliefs; which is why, we call this effect of new information *persuasion*.

Differences in Information between Citizens

Downs (1957) developed logical reasons for citizens to be poorly informed in a democratic society. In general, citizens will not be perfectly informed about political issues because it is costly for them to be well informed. And some citizens will be better able to reduce these information costs than others, which implies that there will be significant differences between citizens in how well they are informed about politics.

Downs argued that there were two major classes of information costs in a democratic society: *transferable costs* and *non-transferable costs* (1957, 210). Transferable information costs are ones that can be borne by other individuals—costs of gathering, analyzing, and evaluating information. For example, these are the sorts of costs that citizens can transfer to elites and the mass media. Nontransferable costs are those that must be borne by the citizens themselves: the costs incurred by citizens in selecting among data sources, in actually learning the new information, and in using the new information to make a decision.

These two different types of information costs will be distributed unequally in a democratic society. This is particularly true in the case of nontransferable information costs. Some citizens are in occupations where they are exposed to more information and more accurate sources of information than individuals in other occupations; also some citizens are better educated and possibly better able to discern important new information and to incorporate that into their knowledge base. And because of differences in education, occupation, and social situation, some citizens are better at using new information to inform their decision-making process.

Information influences the policy choices made by citizens, but it does so differentially, depending on the ability of the citizen to bear information costs. Individuals who can bear more of the nontransferable costs of information, then, will potentially have more information and more accurate information to use in the development of their beliefs about public policies. These individuals may be more attuned to new information, or to changes in the information environment, which implies that their updated beliefs might respond to new information in different ways than individuals who cannot bear significant information costs. In the end, this means that we must be sensitive to the fact that information can have different impacts on the beliefs of citizens about public policy, depending on the ability of each individual to cope with the costs of information.

INFORMATION, PREDISPOSITIONS, AND ELITE DEBATE

One of the earliest works in the field of public opinion and behavior, *The People's Choice* by Lazarsfeld, Berelson, and Gaudet (1944), discussed how information and elite debate made political predispositions relevant to political behavior. In their early studies of behavior in the context of presidential election campaigns, they found that presidential campaigns (certainly a case of elite debate and information) made political predispositions much more relevant for voters.[7]

In particular, Lazarsfeld and colleagues found that the 1940 presidential campaign had three main effects on voter predispositions. The first of these they called *activation of predispositions*. In this process, the interest of voters increases as campaign information begins to flow in earnest; as interest increases so does voter exposure to additional sources of information. These voters are exposed to a great deal of information, which they selectively sample by tuning into information that is in line with their existing predispositions, and by tuning out information that does not reinforce their predispositions. Last, this large quantity of selectively perceived information is used to make active the standing predisposition of each voter; their partisan predisposition has been activated. That is, the new information brought predispositions into the mind of the voter.

The second primary effect of campaign information on voter predispositions was the *reinforcement effect*. Here, new information from the campaign essentially only serves to preserve, or to strengthen, existing decisions made by the voters. So information does not awaken the existing predispositions, or change how the predispositions influence opinions and behavior; instead, information only maintains or enhances the role of predispositions in shaping the particular decision.

Last, Lazarsfeld found that some small percentage of voters were actually *converted* by new information in the campaign. That is, the information generated by elite competition for office actually led some voters to behave contrary to their political predispositions. So in these cases campaign information actually overwhelmed the voters' predispositions and led them to make a decision they would not have made were their predispositions their only guide to decision making.

Thus, they found that information from elite discourse played a critical role in determining how and whether political predispositions influenced voter decision making in presidential elections. While this important set of findings did not receive a great deal of attention in the public opinion literature for many decades, the role of information in making predispositions relevant for political decision making has been dramatically highlighted in recent research on public opinion, most especially in the work of Zaller (1992).

This role of information in making predispositions relevant for political decision making is at the heart of Zaller's contribution to the study of public opinion: "Thus, the impact of people's value predispositions always depends on whether citizens possess the contextual information needed to translate their values into support for particular policies or candidates, and the possession of such information can, as shown earlier, never be taken for granted" (25). But he recognizes the fundamental point we raised in our discussion of Downs's work: that information is not equally distributed throughout the citizenry of a democratic society; thus, how information from elite debate affects the beliefs of any particular citizen depends on the amount of information that citizen has about the issue or candidate.

Zaller demonstrates this through his examination of a number of different issues of public policy. In each issue he examines, Zaller consistently shows strong support for the activation of political values or predispositions; the activation is strongest for individuals who are the most politically informed. When elite debate about a public issue is consensual, activation of political predispositions will occur, especially among the most politically informed, and citizens will come, over time, to agree with the elite consensus. But when elite debate about a political issue is conflictual, activation of predispositions still occurs disproportionally among the politically informed, but in the end the citizenry will be divided along the same lines as the elites (Zaller 1992, chap. 6).

Information, therefore, matters for the study of public opinion, since it helps make political predispositions relevant for political policy and candidate choices citizens make in democratic society. When there is a consistent flow of information from elites, predispositions can be activated or reinforced, especially among the politically informed. The common activation or reinforcement of predispositions will lead citizens to a common belief about the particular issue. If information from elites and the mass media is not consistent or is conflictual, however, then predispositions can be activated differentially, leading politically informed citizens to have more polarized beliefs about policy issues. So which predispositions matter for structuring citizen beliefs about public policy issues, and how they matter, will be dependent on information and elite debate.

Chronic and Domain-Specific Information

In our analyses below we will, where possible, examine two different dimensions of political information. We call the first *chronic information*, which simply covers how informed the individual is about politics in general. We all know some people who are self-described political junkies, who participate in on-line debates about politics, who stay up late at night watching congressional debates on C-Span, or who get up early on Sunday mornings to see the political pundits argue on television. These are people who are high in chronic political information.

The second dimension of political information we term *domain-specific information*; this concerns how well informed the individual is about the particular issue at hand. For no matter how great a citizen's overall knowledge of politics, there will always be some issues that political junkies know well and others that they know nothing about. Also, citizens who rarely follow politics are often well informed about a local school board decision or a state or federal employment policy that affects their lives; no one would be surprised to find that people with newborns or infirm elderly parents living at home might be very well informed about the passage of the Family Leave Act by Congress in 1993.

The importance of the distinction between chronic and domain-specific information has long been known and debated by researchers of American public opinion. The logic that because of individual or group differences in information access or cost, or differences in interests and experiences, some people will be very well informed about only certain issues is compelling. So compelling, in fact, that researchers began to search for "issue publics" (Almond 1950; Converse 1964).

The search for issue specialists, or issue publics, has floundered, however; while some researchers have been able to find evidence of groups that are better informed about some issues relative to other groups, most researchers have had difficulty finding issue specialists in American public opinion.[8] How much stake we should put into the "non-results" is not clear, because much of the research has focused on different ways to study domain-specific information in the context of omnibus electoral surveys. Of course, if the researchers who come up with the survey questions do not ask about the right issues, or ask about the issues in the wrong ways, then issue publics will be difficult to spot in these surveys.

The non-results regarding issue publics in America, however, have lead most recent researchers to focus on chronic political information, sometimes also called political awareness. Studying the general levels of political information held by Americans was the subject of Delli Carpini and Keeter's 1996 book, *What Americans Know about Politics and Why It Matters*, and plays a central role in Zaller's important study of public opinion (1992). There are vast differences in America in chronic political information, with some Americans very well informed but most, poorly informed (Delli Carpini and Keeter 1996). Furthermore, chronic information plays a critical role in determining the impact of information flows from elites to the mass citizenry (Zaller 1992).

In general, these two different dimensions of political information link with the three ways in which new information influences public opinion. Domain-specific information will generally have a direct effect on public opinion; given that it is about a specific issue, it will affect the individual's opinion about the particular issue. Thus, we expect domain-specific information to typically lead to either variance reduction or persuasion.

Chronic information, on the other hand, is less specific information about politics. A chronically informed citizen is simply someone who is exposed to a great deal of political information, either by nature of their profession, their friends and family, or their interest in politics. Being chronically exposed to political information, however, will generally lead to two of the information effects we have discussed. Chronically exposed individuals can be persuaded; this is an indirect effect of chronic information, since the individual will either be more likely to be exposed to domain-specific information or will receive related information, which in some way leads them to change their beliefs about the particular policy issue. More likely, though, is that chronic information will lead to the activation of predispositions. Chronically exposed citizens are more likely to be exposed to arguments about how to think about politics; they are more likely to be exposed to elite discussions about the "right way" to think about an issue; and they are more likely to be aware of general elite debates about issues.

THE MEASUREMENT OF INFORMATION EFFECTS

The first two sections of this chapter have argued that information has three different fundamental influences on public opinion about policy issues: it influences the uncertainty citizens have about policy issues; it can persuade citizens to change their beliefs; and it influences the way in which predispositions or values become important for structuring beliefs about policy issues. Since information is so inherently important for understanding public opinion, information will be an important aspect of our analysis of opinions about public policies in subsequent chapters.

Information and Affirmative Action

In chapter 6 we discuss the beliefs of Americans about affirmative action and other racial issues, building upon our previous work (Alvarez and Brehm 1997). The survey data we use in that chapter comes from a study conducted in 1991 by Sniderman, Tetlock and Piazza. In that data there are a number of questions we use to construct information measures. First, we are able to develop two different measures of chronic information. The first of these is a very simple and generic measure: the respondent's level of educational attainment. The second measure stems from two different factual information items included in this study asking respondents factual questions about two of the branches of the federal government. The exact wording of each survey question was as follows:

- Number of Supreme Court members: "Please tell me how many members of the U.S. Supreme Court there are?"
- Maximum number of presidential terms: "And how many (four-year) terms can the President of the United States serve?"

The correct answers to these two factual information items are nine members of the Supreme Court and two four-year presidential terms: 37 percent of the survey respondents provided the correct answer for the Supreme Court question and 86 percent were correct about the maximum number of presidential terms. We then used these responses to develop a summary measure of chronic information by giving one point for respondents who provided the correct answer for each question. Our summary measure of chronic information is the number of correct answers divided by two (the average number of correct answers for a respondent).

The 1991 Sniderman, Tetlock, and Piazza data also included three factual information questions that specifically targeted information about blacks in America. The first of these questions asked respondents to tell the interviewer the *percentage of poor who are black*: "Just give me your best guess on this one—what percent of all the poor people in this country would you say are black?" Then, respondents were asked about the *percentage of people arrested who are black*: "Of all of the people arrested for violent crimes in the United States last year, what percent do you think were black? Do you think it is closer to (ten, twenty, thirty, forty, fifty, sixty percent)?" Last, survey respondents were asked about the *percentage of black males who are unemployed*: "Of all the black males of working age in the United States, what percent do you think are unemployed? Do you think it's closer to (five, ten, fifteen, twenty, twenty-five percent)?"

In our coding of correct responses to these factual information questions about the status of blacks in America, we defined a correct response on each of these three items as being (1) that 20 to 30 percent of poor people in America are black (20.2 percent of survey respondents were correct); (2) that 40 percent of people arrested for violent crimes in 1990 were black (19 percent correct); and (3) that 10 to 15 percent of black males of working age are unemployed (29.6 percent correct). Each respondent was given a point for a correct answer on each domain-specific factual item; we then calculated the average number of correct answers for each respondent.

We plot the distribution of each of these information measures in figure 3.2. The top panel illustrates the distribution of the first measure of chronic information, educational attainment; the middle panel shows the distribution of the other chronic information measure; the bottom panel gives the distribution of the domain-specific information measure.

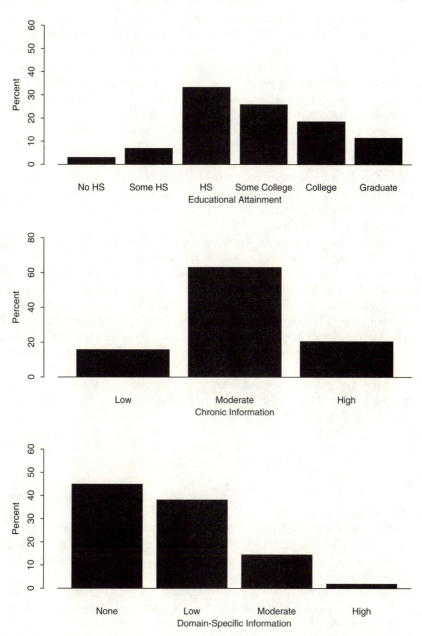

FIGURE 3.2. Education, chronic information, and domain-specific information

Both measures of chronic information have similar distributions; each is relatively symmetrically distributed about the middle of the possible range. Most of the respondents in this 1991 survey study had a high school education (33 percent) or had attended some college classes (26 percent). Thus, almost 60 percent of the survey sample had at least some college education. Turning to the chronic information measure, there we see that 63 percent of the respondents to this survey were able to answer one of the two factual political information items correctly. Sixteen percent of the sample missed both correct answers, while 21 percent were able to answer both questions correctly. These two measures of chronic information thus have similar distributions; also, they have a relatively modest and positive joint correlation (the Pearson correlation coefficient is .36) which demonstrates that individuals with a higher level of educational attainment also tend to score higher on the chronic information scale.

But the distribution of the domain-specific information scale clearly is distinct from the two chronic information measures in figure 3.2. First, the domain-specific information scale is essentially uncorrelated with a respondent's educational attainment (the Pearson correlation coefficient is −.008) and is only weakly correlated with the domain-specific information measure (the Pearson correlation coefficient is .08). Additionally, the distribution of the chronic information measure is skewed to the lower end of the measure, since 45 percent of the respondents were unable to answer any of the three domain-specific information questions correctly. Another 38 percent were able to answer only one of the three questions correctly, showing that the overwhelming proportion of respondents (83 percent) were at best able to answer one of these domain-specific information measures correctly.

Different Types of Domain-Specific Information

There are different ways in which we can measure domain-specific information; it can be broken down into "soft" and "hard" types of information. In our conceptualization, soft domain-specific information would be information held by an individual about some specific aspect of public policy that is general and nonspecific, for example, knowing that some particular aspect of public policy had changed.

On the other hand, hard information would be knowledge about a particular aspect of public policy that is very specific. Instead of just knowing that some domain of policy had changed, the individual would know exactly how that policy had changed. In our view, hard information about policy issues is likely to be less widely held by the public, since it is the sort of information that would be known by only those who are well informed about politics in general or who are knowledgeable about the policy in question.[9]

In this framework, our domain-specific measures about race would fall between the soft and hard information categories. That is, they ask individuals about general knowledge of the status of blacks in America, although they require specific information about proportions of people fitting specific categories. Hard information measures based on the same kinds of survey questions would likely be those that would ask survey respondents whether the percentages of black men who are unemployed had increased or decreased due to increases in the national minimum wage. Unfortunately, the survey data we use in our work on affirmative action and beliefs about race do not contain true, hard information questions.

But in other work, we have examined the differences between hard and soft information in structuring beliefs of Americans about the performance of the federal bureaucracy. In our previous work (Alvarez and Brehm 1998) we looked at respondent beliefs about the performance of the Internal Revenue Service using a survey conducted in 1987 called the Taxpayer Opinion Survey. One of the most intriguing features of the 1987 TOS is the extent to which the interviewer attempted to assess the respondents' knowledge about the changes in the 1986 Tax Reform Act. The TRA represented the culmination of years of activity from members of both parties (both Ronald Reagan and Bill Bradley were among the early proponents). Changes made during the markup sessions were complicated and many. In a battery of questions appearing very early within the instrument, respondents were asked to identify whether each of twenty-one aspects of the tax law had changed under the TRA, and if so, in what way. Table 3.1 displays the list of potentially changing aspects of the code, the correct answers associated with each, and the percentage of respondents getting each question correct.[10]

As the reader will note from table 3.1, nineteen out of the twenty-one items changed in one direction or another. A naive respondent who simply assumed that everything had changed would have been correct on 90 percent of these questions. Table 3.1 also notes the percentage of TOS respondents who correctly ascertained whether the aspect had changed. Nearly half knew that the dollar amount of the exemption had changed; the percentage of respondents who knew about the changes relative to other aspects of the code were substantially below this percentage. Even familiarity with whether an aspect changed (the soft information scale) proved to be a strong test of informedness about the code.

There is also a fair amount of variance in how often respondents gave the correct answer. The question with the most correct answers was the first one in the table, which asked whether the dollar amount of the exemption for individuals, spouses or dependents had changed; almost 45 percent of those surveyed answered that question correctly. Also, 40 percent of the respondents were correct in their assessment of what had changed about the deductibility of interest on consumer debt and credit cards. Both of these items had demon-

TABLE 3.1
Construction of Domain-Specific Information Scale

Aspect	Changed?	How?	% Correct
Dollar amount of the exemption for yourself, spouse, or dependents	Yes	Increased[1]	44.7
Personal exemption on a child's return	Yes	Eliminated[1]	14.1
Standard deduction on a child's return	Yes	Increased[1]	11.3
Deduction for being over age 65 or blind	Yes	Restricted[2]	17.2
Credit for child care expenses	No	(na)[2]	17.4
Exclusion of dividends of $100 / $200	Yes	Eliminated[1]	28.9
Tax on capital gains	Yes	Increased[1]	12.9
Tax on fellowships or scholarships' room and board	Yes	Reduced[2]	18.5
Taxable aspect of unemployment compensation	Yes	Increased[1]	19.2
Unreimbursed employee business expenses	Yes	Reduced[2]	25.2
Unreimbursed meals and entertainment expenses	Yes	Reduced[2]	39.0
IRA deductions	Yes	Reduced[2]	30.5
Deduction for married couples when both work	Yes	Eliminated[1]	33.8
Deduction for contributions to charity for those who do not itemize their deductions	Yes	Reduced[2]	34.2
Deduction for medical and dental expenses	Yes	Reduced[2]	18.6
Deduction for state and local income taxes	No	(na)[2]	34.3
Deduction for interest on consumer debt and credit cards	Yes	Reduced[2]	40.1
Deductions for other miscellaneous itemized items	Yes	Reduced[2]	25.3
Penalty for failure to pay	Yes	Increased[1]	17.8
Investment tax credit	Yes	Eliminated[1]	16.9
Need to report tax-exempt income	Yes	Increased[1]	12.5

Note: Columns "Changed?" and "How?" denote correct responses to the question: "As you may know, Congress revised many aspects of the Federal income tax law last year. Most of the changes they made are effective for the 1987 tax year. Here is a list of different aspects that are built into our income tax system. Some have been changed and some have remained the same. For each, tell me whether—from what you've read or heard—it has changed or remained the same. If you don't know about some of these, just say so. (Has it been increased, been reduced or restricted, or been eliminated?)" Column "% Correct" reports the percentage of respondents who correctly identified whether the aspect had changed (but not necessarily how). *Sources:* [1] *Summary for Individuals;* [2] *Highlights of the 1987 Tax Reform Act*, two IRS documents.

strable, and perhaps important, changes in the tax liabilities of these survey respondents.

But some of the changes in the 1986 TRA were poorly known by most respondents. In particular, only 11 percent correctly knew the change in the standard deduction on a child's tax return; and approximately 13 percent correctly knew about changes in the need to report tax-exempt income, or in the taxation of capital gains. These, of course, are aspects of tax law that are less likely to impact on large numbers of taxpayers; hence we would expect that fewer respondents in this survey would be correctly informed about these changes in the tax code.

We used these twenty-one questions to create two domain-specific information scales, which correspond to soft and hard information measures. The soft information scale simply records whether the respondent was aware that the particular aspect had changed, in some way; in other words, was the respondent correct about the changes listed in table 3.1? Thus, the soft information measure really is designed to assess the degree to which a respondent crossed the lowest threshold of informedness about the TRA (whether the twenty-one aspects of the tax code changed or not). On the other hand, the hard information scale examines whether individuals knew exactly how each of these different components of the 1987 Tax Reform Act changed. So this domain-specific information measure is designed to determine whether an individual passed a much more rigorous threshold of information concerning the 1987 TRA.

Figure 3.3 presents information on the distribution of the soft and hard information scales. Here we show two different sets of graphs, presenting the distribution of the two information scales. The top graphs give the probability density of the soft and hard information scales, which provide detail about the shape of the distribution of the two scales. The bottom graphs give the quantiles of the standard normal distribution, which help us discern how each distribution differs from the normal distribution.

One truly striking feature is that the vast majority of respondents scored extremely low on both scales, even when a guess that everything changed would have yielded extremely high scores. In fact, only 2 percent of the respondents exceeded this score. We also wish to note that the respondents scored at both extremes, ranging from those who answered none of the questions correctly to those who answered only one of the questions incorrectly.

Yet it is also quite clear in figure 3.3 that many more respondents were much better informed in a soft information sense than they were in terms of hard information, as can be seen in the figure, where the distribution of respondents for the hard information scale is skewed to the left, while the distribution of respondents for the soft information scale has a pronounced rightward skew. This is apparent in both the top and bottom rows of the figure, especially when the distribution of each information scale is compared to the normal distribution in the lower panels. So we see from this data that the respondents

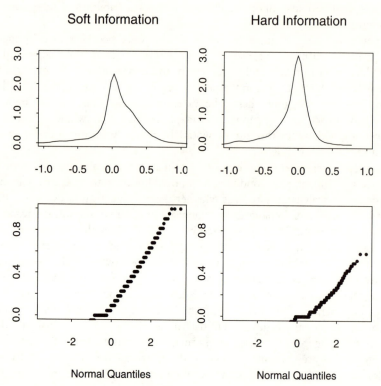

FIGURE 3.3. Distribution of information scales, 1987 Taxpayer Opinion Survey

in this survey were much more likely to cross the soft information threshold than they were to cross the hard information threshold.

These measures of domain-specific informedness are, in our view, truly unusual for attitudes toward public policy concerns. Consider Zaller's (1992) book, which explores the respondents' levels of political sophistication, in this case, constructed as a measure of "general, chronic awareness." Zaller writes:

> In using this sort of measure, I will be assuming that persons who are knowledgeable about politics in general are habitually attentive to communications on most particular issues as well.
>
> This measurement strategy is less than ideal. More narrowly focused measures of awareness—devoted exclusively, say, to intellectual engagement with foreign policy issues or race policy issues, and used exclusively in connection with reception of information concerning foreign or race policy issues—would be preferable to general awareness measures. However, such domain-specific awareness mea-

sures are rarely carried on opinion surveys and none are available for the cases I examine in this study. (43)

Likewise, Luskin (1987) constructs a measure of general political knowledge by tallying respondents' correct relative placement of the parties on a battery of eleven issues. Although the measure is composed of domain-specific information, Luskin explicitly aims for a more comprehensive notion of "information holding," presumably because (as argued earlier in the essay) "ideology as high sophistication is comprehensive" (863).

Despite the dependence of many scholars on chronic informedness as the means to assess how respondents incorporate messages about politics, it is perhaps possible that highly domain-specific information could be even more significant. If the models maintain that respondents' ability to counterargue against counter-partisan information (to "resist" in Zaller's model) hinges on the store of information the respondent possesses, it makes more sense for the respondents' arguments to be grounded in the specific domain of the communication and not simply their chronic connection to elite discourse. But this is a testable question, and we do want to allow for the possibility that chronic information matters, so we use the respondents' education level as a measure of political sophistication in many of our models. This will allow us to examine whether domain-specific information indeed outweighs chronic informedness in our models, or whether neither matters.

WHO IS INFORMED?

It now remains for us to consider which respondents are informed about affirmative action and about the IRS. Given the importance of understanding the impact of being politically informed on public opinion, it is also important for us to determine what factors lead some survey respondents to be better informed than others. This will allow us to then understand which respondents might be more likely to achieve any of the three different impacts of information on public opinion: variance reduction, persuasion, or the activation of predispositions.

Our theoretical expectations for which survey respondents are more likely to be politically informed is quite simple, and these expectations all revolve around the idea that individuals who have lower information costs are more likely to be informed than individuals with high information costs. This notion begins in the work of Downs (1957) and is continued in the recent literature (Alvarez 1997; Alvarez and Franklin 1994; Bartels 1986; Luskin 1987; Popkin 1991; Zaller 1992). We break down information costs into two different types: the costs of general political information and the costs associated with information about the specific public policy.

The approach we take toward understanding the determinants of political informedness in these two different domains of public opinion is to use statistical models that allow us to examine the effect of one variable upon another, while controlling for a number of other variables. In the case of modeling information levels for the affirmative action domain, we make use of ordinal probit models. These models are useful when the variable we wish to explain is ordinal and not continuous; we use the ordinal probit model extensively in subsequent chapters. However, the information variables for the domain of beliefs about the IRS are essentially continuous variables; this allows us to use a simpler statistical model in this case, multiple regression. (See our website, www.pupress.princeton.edu/alvarez, for discussion of statistical models.)

Who Is Informed about Affirmative Action and Race?

Regarding the chronic and domain-specific information measures we use in the case of affirmative action, we include two sets of variables in our ordinal probit model so that we can test for a series of different possible effects. First, to examine whether general information costs are important, we include as measures the respondent's age, the age squared (to control for the possibility of nonlinear effects of age), educational attainment, gender, and martial status. These are direct measures of general information costs. We also consider whether the survey interviewer thought the respondent to be intelligent. Second, to examine the importance of information costs associated directly with the issues of affirmative action and race, we use a series of questions: respondent employment, income level (low, moderate, or high), and family financial status, all of which are intended to control for the effects of economic competition on awareness about affirmative action and race; residence in a border or southern state, which controls for residence in locations where race has often been a serious issue; and whether the survey interviewer thought that the respondent was tolerant and sympathetic.

The results of our ordinal probit models for both chronic and domain-specific information are presented in table 3.2. In the first column we list the names of each of the independent variables in our ordinal probit model, while in the second through fifth columns we provide the coefficient estimates followed by the standard errors for chronic and domain-specific information, respectively. The asterisks indicate whether a particular coefficient estimate is statistically significant.

When we look at the determinants of chronic information about affirmative action and race we see that many of the general measures of information costs are statistically significant determinants of chronic information about this aspect of policy. The more educated a respondent is, and the more intelligent

TABLE 3.2
Determinants of Respondent Information: Affirmative Action and Race

Determinants	Chronic	S.E.	Domain-specific	S.E.
Age	0.019	0.01	−0.02**	0.01
Age squared	−0.00002	0.0001	0.0002**	0.0001
Education	0.32**	0.03	0.003	0.02
Employment	0.04	0.07	0.06	0.06
Females	−0.44**	0.06	0.06	0.05
Low income	−0.02	0.07	−0.14**	0.07
High income	0.19**	0.08	−0.09	0.08
Married	−0.07	0.06	−0.12**	0.05
Southern resident	0.04	0.06	−0.05	0.06
Border state resident	−0.10	0.11	−0.20**	0.10
Family finances	0.002	0.03	−0.05*	0.03
Tolerant	0.16**	0.08	0.10*	0.08
Intelligent	0.22**	0.06	−0.07	0.06
Sympathetic	−0.05	0.08	0.01	0.08
μ_1	0.38	0.24	−0.72	0.22
μ_2	2.5	0.24	0.39	0.22
μ_3			1.5	0.22
Sample size	1964		1964	
χ^2	374.4†		30.2†	

Note: Entries are ordinal probit estimates accompanied by standard errors. * represents a coefficient estimate statistically significant at the $p < .10$ level, one-tailed test; ** represents a coefficient estimate statistically significant at the $p < .05$ level, one-tailed test; † stands for a χ^2 estimate statistically significant at the $p < .05$ level.

the interviewer thought the respondent was, are both related to higher levels of chronic information. We also see that women are less informed about affirmative action and race than men. Additionally, though, two of the more specific measures of information costs are also statistically significant: high income respondents are better chronically informed than moderate income respondents, and the more tolerant the interviewer judged the respondents, the higher their chronic information.

The fourth column of table 3.2 shows the results for the domain-specific information measure. We see that one set of the general information costs measures are statistically significant: age and age squared. Additionally, marital status has a significant and negative impact on domain-specific information. But there are also a number of specific information costs measures that seem to be statistically related to domain-specific informedness. These are income (low-income individuals are less informed about domain-specific aspects of affirmative action and race), residence in a border state (these residents are less informed than residents in the remainder of the country), family finances (those whose family finances are worse are less better informed), and tolerance (those who are rated tolerant by the interviewer are higher in their levels of domain-specific information).

Who Is Informed about the IRS?

We take the same general approach to attempting to explain why some respondents are more informed than others on both aspects of information about the IRS—soft and hard information. That is, we begin with a set of general measures of information costs: gender, race, education, age and age squared, and attention to the news media. We also have a set of specific measures of information costs about the IRS, including whether the respondents are employed, their income, whether they had been audited, and whether they file a long form when they pay their federal taxes.[11]

We provide the multiple regression estimates in table 3.3, which is organized in a manner similar to the one in the last section. Again, the variable labels are given in the first column, and the multiple regression estimates and their associated standard errors appear in the second through fifth colulmns (for soft and hard information, respectively). Asterisks are again added to estimates that are statistically significant.

Beginning with the multiple regression results for the soft information scale, we see that many of the general information costs measures are statistically significant. Men are more informed in the soft sense than women, as are whites, those with higher educational attainment, and those who pay attention to the news media. We also see that two of the specific measures of information costs are statistically significant predictors of soft information: income and the filing of the long federal form, with higher income and filing the long form both leading to higher levels of soft information.

The fourth and fifth columns show the same multiple regression results for the hard information scale. Here, we see that fewer of the general measures of information costs are significant, with only whites and those of higher educational attainment being better informed on the hard scale. But we still see two of the specific information cost measures being statistically significant in this regression model: income and the filing of the long federal tax form.

TABLE 3.3
Determinants of Respondent Information: The IRS

Determinants	Soft	S.E.	Hard	S.E.
Constant	−0.19**	0.07	−0.27**	0.07
Men	0.02*	0.02	−0.003	0.02
Whites	0.04**	0.02	0.05	0.02
Employed	0.02	0.02	−0.02	0.02
Education	0.14**	0.04	0.12**	0.04
Income	2.4**	0.7	1.1**	0.6
Age	0.003	0.003	0.002	0.003
Age squared	−0.00004	0.00003	−0.00002	0.00003
News attention	0.11**	0.03	−0.002	0.02
Audited	0.02	0.03	0.01	0.02
Files long form	0.07**	0.02	0.03*	0.02
Sample size	999		999	
Adjusted R^2	0.14		0.04	

Note: Entries are multiple regression estimates accompanied by standard errors. * represents a coefficient estimate statistically significant at the $p < .10$ level, one-tailed test; ** represents a coefficient estimate statistically significant at the $p < .05$ level, one-tailed test; † stands for a χ^2 estimate statistically significant at the $p < .05$ level.

The Determinants of Informedness

We have demonstrated that there are predictable patterns across survey respondents in their levels of political information about both affirmative action and the IRS. In each of the statistical models presented in the last two sections, we have argued that a number of different attributes of individuals are important tools in our quest to find why some individuals are better informed about these aspects of public policy than others. No matter whether we are trying to understand why some individuals are more informed about affirmative action or the IRS, it is clear that a number of demographic attributes of individuals (age, education, race, and gender) all play an important role in providing people with the ability to become better informed about politics.

But we also saw that a number of measures of specific costs of information were important in our statistical models, in particular, when we looked at the more demanding kinds of political information (domain-specific information in the case of affirmative action, hard information in the case of the IRS). The processes by which people become informed in less or more demanding ways about politics depends significantly on their experiences with the specific public policy. In other words, citizens are becoming informed about affirmative action or the IRS, especially in domain-specific and demanding ways, through their real-life exposure to and experience with these different aspects of public policy.

WHY INFORMATION MATTERS

In this chapter we have advanced two arguments for why it is important to understand the role that information plays if we wish to understand what shapes American public opinion. First, *information reduces uncertainty and can persuade*. That is, with additional information about some issue of public concern, we should see individuals becoming increasingly certain in their opinions about that issue—and more confident of their answers on public opinion polls about the issue.

Second, *information makes predispositions and values relevant* for beliefs about public policy issues. When elites discuss policy issues in particular and consensual ways, it provokes some predispositions to be relevant in the beliefs of citizens about the issue. But if elite debate is conflictual, and this conflict produces different elite-level framing of an issue, then the predispositions invoked at the mass level will reflect this elite conflict; as a result, mass opinion about the issue can be similarly conflictual.

Thus, through these two different paths, political information has both direct and indirect effects on the beliefs of citizens regarding public policy. Information has a direct impact, since it affects the mechanics of attitude formation, that is, the beliefs of Americans as well as their uncertainty of their beliefs. In this way, information can lead directly to either persuasion and the changing of beliefs or the reduction of uncertainty about the belief. But information also has indirect effects on public opinions. Political information influences the ways in which citizens link predispositions to policy outcomes. We called this indirect effect of information the activation of predispositions or values.

These direct and indirect ways in which information "matters" for the study of American public opinion are critical components of our work in the next few chapters. The empirical examples in the rest of the book will illustrate how information is indeed reducing uncertainty about public opinion, as well as how information is provoking the relevance of certain predispositions over others. In the end, we will have a much fuller understanding of the role of information in democratic society.

There is a third important aspect of our discussion in this chapter that will also loom large in our later analyses: information costs and information levels differ significantly in the American public. As Downs (1957) argued, there are clear reasons to expect to see great informational differences among Americans. In fact, in both the examples we presented in this chapter, we saw substantial *heterogeneity* in the informational levels of Americans concerning general knowledge of politics and specific knowledge about racial issues and tax policies.

The fact that there is so much informational heterogeneity in the American public has important implications for our study. These informational differences will have to be taken seriously in our empirical work, a fact that Zaller (1992) also noted in his study of public opinion. We will use particular types of statistical models we developed in earlier work that allow us to control for different forms of heterogeneity, including informational, directly in our analyses (Alvarez and Brehm 1995, 1997, 1998). We discuss these statistical issues fully in the appendixes, available on the Internet at www.pupress. princeton.edu/alvarez.

The last subject covered in this chapter focused on different approaches to the measurement of information. We discussed the major conceptual distinction between chronic and domain-specific information; we gave examples of how measures for each type of information can be developed; and we described two different kinds of domain-specific information, hard and soft (sometimes it is possible in the available survey data to distinguish between these qualitatively different thresholds of information about specific public policies). We will use these different information measures extensively in the chapters that follow.

Ambivalence, Uncertainty, and Equivocation

IN CONVERSE'S SEMINAL 1964 STUDY of the stability of mass attitudes, those respondents who provided answers to survey questions, even though they did not have fixed and well-defined opinions, were said to be offering "doorstep opinions." They would invent survey answers at the moment of the interview, and in Converse's terminology, they had "non-attitudes." Only a minority of respondents possessed well-defined, organized, and stable opinions.

As we argued in the previous chapters, citizens may not always have opinions about arcane (or even common) aspects of politics, but they do possess core values, group evaluations, affective judgments, or expectations that permit them to sensibly answer questions. People who do not have well-constructed attitudes can still provide reasoned survey responses, based on their core beliefs and predispositions. But as Zaller (1992) rightly notes, possessing a predisposition begs the question of whether the respondent employs that predisposition in any specific matter of policy. Hence, in chapter 3, we identify how political information helps respondents to draw connections between values and political choices.

Our model of the survey response, however, contends that virtually *every* survey respondent constructs a response at the doorstep. Only the most survey-aware respondent would literally maintain survey answers in his or her head. Instead, respondents must decide what a question means in terms of standing predispositions—which values, if any, apply? How do these values instruct my choice, separately and in combination? Thus, we argue that it is the combination of multiple predispositions and the capacity of political information to make these predispositions relevant that determines the process by which respondents construct survey answers.

In this chapter we address four steps in the integration of multiple predispositions with political information. The first step is to ascertain what happens when multiple predispositions pertain to policy. The second step is to explicate how the distribution of survey responses will vary, depending on the resolution of multiple predispositions (i.e., are these predispositions contradictory, irrelevant, or mutually reinforcing?). This second step leads us to describe three states of mind in the mass public that characterize different forms of response variability, states that we refer to as *ambivalence* (internalized conflict over policy choice), *equivocation* (mutually reinforcing predispositions over choice), and *uncertainty* (when information alone affects the variability of choice). The third

Balanced triads

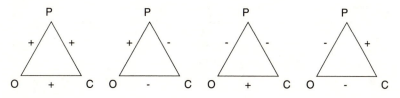

Unbalanced triads

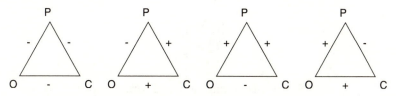

FIGURE 4.1. Heider's balanced and imbalanced triads

step develops our hypotheses about the conditions of policy choice and elite advocacy that lead to each of the three forms. The last section of this chapter describes our inferential method for identifying each of the three states.

WHAT HAPPENS WHEN MULTIPLE PREDISPOSITIONS PERTAIN?

We draw upon an old paradigm in social psychology to understand survey response when multiple predispositions are relevant. The problem of multiple core values has an analogue in research on balanced attitudes, especially when those values are in conflict. This older literature centers especially around the ideas of Fritz Heider (1946, 1948).

Heider enunciated theories of balance and imbalance between a person (P), an other (O), and some object (C), representing affective relations between the three as triangles with positively and negatively signed sides. The triad is balanced if the product of the three sides is positive, and imbalanced if it is negative.

The eight possible triads appear in figure 4.1. Suppose that C denotes President Clinton. The triad on the upper left represents a situation where one feels positively toward the other, and both feel positively toward Clinton. The triad immediately to the right is also balanced: one feels positively toward the other, but both feel negatively toward Clinton. The remaining two triads in the first row are also balanced.

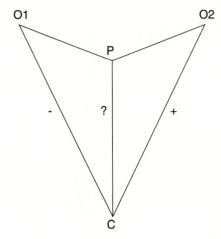

FIGURE 4.2. A difficult nested balance problem

Now consider the first triad of the second row. One feels positively toward the other, but the two hold differing feelings toward Clinton. This triad is imbalanced. Imbalance is a noxious psychological state that motivates behavior and attitudes to change (Heider 1946). In such a state of imbalance, one might expect that the individuals would do any of the following: repress consideration of the object (Clinton), modify attitudes toward either the other or the object, or divide consideration of the object into multiple components (by, say, agreeing with the other to dislike Clinton's health care proposal, and to like Clinton's support of free trade).

While the simple imbalanced triad may be uncomfortable for the individual, introduction of a second other may make it impossible for the individual to resolve the state of imbalance. Figure 4.2 depicts just such a situation. One feels positively toward two others (O1 and O2), for example, one's parents. One parent feels negatively toward Clinton, while the other feels positively. There is no signed relation that one could adopt with respect to Clinton that restores a state of balance to the entire system.

This hard balance problem has strong parallels with the problem of conflicting core beliefs. Instead of others in figure 4.2, replace O1 and O2 with core values, and replace the object (C) with a policy choice. The person holds both core values in esteem, but the two core values are at odds with respect to the policy choice. One context where it is highly likely that respondents find themselves torn between incommensurable beliefs is abortion attitudes, one of the key illustrations of chapter 5. In the context of understanding attitudes toward abortion, one core value might be respect for human life beginning sometime before birth, while the conflicting core value might be respect for a woman's autonomy in making such a decision. Under some policy considerations, only one of the core values might pertain. It is not too drastic a leap to imagine the survey respondent who values a woman's right to choose and who supports availability of contraceptives. It is also quite feasible to imagine the same respondent holding a belief that human life begins before birth, and supporting prenatal care for teenage mothers. Only when a policy consideration invokes both core values would the two values conflict.

Under conflicting core values, we expect that the dynamics of survey response would be quite different from circumstances where core values are pertinent, or when only one value is relevant. When there are two conflicting values, the respondent has two very different bases to formulate a policy choice. When there are two dimensions of evaluation, the variance of the subject's choice is increased or the probability that despite our best understanding of the subject's interests in opting for one side or another of the debate, our prediction will be incorrect.

While our usual focus of analysis in understanding policy questions is the respondent's choice or position on the policy, we suggest that there is an equally informative aspect of analysis in understanding the variance of a respondent's position. This idea of respondent variance is different from the sampling idea of variance. Instead of conceptualizing variance in terms of the range of attitudes possessed by the population, we argue that respondents themselves may possess a variance of attitudes. Respondent variance may look like measurement error, or respondent error (i.e., doorstep opinions), but it stems not from the inadequacies of either instrument or respondent, but from the difficult choices we ask respondents to make.

A UNIFIED MODEL OF RESPONSE VARIABILITY

Current understanding of the survey response has progressed significantly in recognizing that there are some consistent and important underpinnings to respondents' answers to survey questions and that the opinions individuals offer are drawn from a range of potential opinions and not some fixed archetypal attitude toward politics.

Recently, an excellent synthesis of theories of the survey response has been offered by Tourangeau, Rips, and Rasinski (2000) in their "belief sampling model." Their synthetic model assumes that when facing a question about some attitude, a respondent retrieves "considerations," which can be either factual information or values and predispositions. The respondent then evaluates the considerations in light of the particular question and integrates them into a survey response. The fact that respondents produce different answers over time, or that they have variable beliefs, is due not just to the considerations that are primed in the mind of the respondent but also to the evaluation, judgment, and integration of information and predispositions. Thus, the Tourangeau, Rips, and Rasinski model includes more cognitive processing than the Zaller model, and it imposes more structure on what constitutes the sampled considerations by including values, core beliefs, and other information.

Our model of the survey response is similar to that of Tourangeau and his colleagues in that we focus on the information and predispositions that respondents use in formulating their answers, and on how information and predispositions are integrated in the minds of respondents. Critically, we take their model but go one step further by specifying three distinct ways in which information and predispositions are accessed and integrated by respondents when they produce answers to survey questions, which determine the exact type of response variability we expect to find in survey responses.

Our approach to the survey response problem is to model the variability of responses as distributions. We begin by assuming that respondents maintain predispositions that are politically relevant, to varying degrees and in varying numbers. Some respondents may truly possess, with respect to a particular policy domain, absolutely no predispositions that could become relevant, no matter how politically aware the respondent is or how long he or she deliberates. We suspect, however, that in many policy domains, respondents will possess several predispositions, held to varying degrees. As Zaller (1992) points out, one of the difficulties will be for us to specify how it is that the respondent is able to resolve these (potentially) competing predispositions, and to explain how they are able to make these predispositions relevant.

We take Zaller's criticism of the core values approach as a research agenda, not as a fundamental indictment of the approach. So, why might an individual offer completely different answers at different times to the same policy question, even though the person holds the same underlying predispositions? Or, relatedly, why might two individuals who share identical predispositions offer two different answers?

It could be because the respondents have not deliberated over the political problem. Individuals may not have linked their predispositions to the policy domain, or may not have the information to make the connection. The respondents might not even know about the policy, or fail to see the relevance of the policy to the things they value. Last, some individuals might see the policy in terms of one set of values, while others see the policy in terms of other sets of values.

Or it could be because the policy problem requires a difficult choice. As teachers, we ask our students to recognize complicated policy questions as complicated; why should we expect that our survey respondents would see the same questions as easy choices? Many policy problems, including the two important examples of abortion and euthanasia that we discuss in the next chapter, involve choices that are incommensurable. Especially when we talk about fundamental individual rights, we talk in stark, black-and-white terms.

We either are willing to grant rights to others, or we are not willing to grant them rights. It is in situations like this that difficult choices must be made, and it should come as no surprise that difficult choices will involve competing and conflicting values and predispositions.

Our model argues that response variability results from two different questions:

- What happens to response variability when multiple predispositions apply?
- What happens to response variability as respondents elaborate on the problem, or acquire more extensive political information?

Most contemporary scholarship on multiple values and public opinion implies the potential for internalized conflict, whereby respondents feel torn between competing value positions (e.g., Katz and Hass 1988; Kinder 1983). A respondent who is personally conflicted would be likely to produce different answers to similar questions when asked at different times, or be sensitive to variations in context (such as changes in question-wording, question-ordering, or even to attributes of the interviewer).

But the relevance of multiple values need not lead to internalized conflict over policy choices. It is possible that the multiplicity of values is irrelevant to the structure of political attitudes. This may arise when respondents are able to reconcile potentially competing demands with relative ease. It may be that one of the values is more highly prized than the other. If a respondent favors liberty over equality (the classic "Goldwater" in Rokeach's 1973 study), equality over liberty (Rokeach's "Lenin"), wants neither ("Hitler"), or sees them as not in conflict (the "Social Democrat"), then the relevance of multiple values does not lead to more variable choice. A similar effect would emerge if the apparent strength of one value merely served to satisfy social pressures. A respondent who expresses strong support for racial equality, but only because he or she feels under social obligations to do so, may have little difficulty reconciling his or her attitudes along lines of racial resentment.

Another possibility arises when the multiplicity of values are mutually reinforcing. Such a scenario would be when two attributes of a policy choice are complementary, in fact or merely seen as such; respondents may value a policy both for its low cost and for its accomplishments. Citizens who found the supply-side economic reasoning of the early 1980s plausible may have believed general tax cuts were good because they reduced burdens upon them (a value of limited government), and because they believed that such cuts would lead to greater revenues by stimulating growth (a value of support for capitalism and growth). Obviously, others were skeptical of the capacity of tax cuts to accomplish both purposes. It is entirely possible that people can be wrong in their understanding of the effect of policies along multiple dimensions.

The role of information, the second question, likewise leads to different forms of response variability. Under most conditions, one would expect that the better informed the respondent is, the more likely it is that the person has a well-formed opinion on most matters of politics. This is the usual notion of the role of information in reducing uncertainty, and squares neatly with the role of information in Bayesian theory (Alvarez 1997).

But what of the respondent who finds herself torn between two mutually incompatible values? The respondent who wants a woman to have the right to choose to terminate her pregnancy and who also believes that human life begins before birth may not find his or her opinion more easy to resolve in the light of new information about late-term abortions. In a state of conflict between predispositions, information may heighten, not reduce, the conflict.

These two questions point us to two separate phenomena that may affect response variability: the effect of simultaneously holding two (or more) predispositions, and the effect of acquiring information. The result of the two phenomena leads us to describe three different states of mind:

- Ambivalence: Coincident predispositions induce wider response variability; information widens response variability. Ambivalence results when respondents' expectations or values are irreconcilable, such as we have demonstrated in the area of abortion policy for those respondents who believe both in a woman's right to autonomy over her body and that human life begins before birth (Alvarez and Brehm 1995).

- Uncertainty: Coincident predispositions do not affect response variability; information narrows response variability. Uncertainty results when respondents' expectations are not irreconcilable and when additional information reduces response variability. We have demonstrated that attitudes about racial policy are a question of uncertainty (rather than ambivalence), since respondents are not in a state of conflict between egalitarian and individualist values, but their opinions become more focused with additional (chronic) political information (Alvarez and Brehm 1997).

- Equivocation: Coincident predispositions induce narrower response variability; information narrows response variability. Equivocation means literally to speak with two voices. Equivocation results when those respondents who have high expectations in two or more areas are even more fixed in their opinions than those who hold high expectations in only one. Equivocal respondents want both expectations (e.g., bureaucracies should be both responsive and equitable), but see no contradiction or trade-off between them (Alvarez and Brehm 1998).

We expect that these three conditions will be the result of the information and predispositions that respondents tap into when posed a survey question, and that the information and predispositions, when integrated and evaluated in different ways, will produce predictable forms of response variability. How different policy attitudes become characterized by different states of opinion, and how we make operational and test for these states of opinion, are taken up in the next two sections.

INCOMMENSURABLES, ELITE VOICES, AND CHOICE

How is it that a policy domain becomes one of ambivalence, equivocation, or uncertainty? We argue that there are two general explanations, not mutually exclusive, but interdependent.

One explanation is that the nature of the choice itself leads to conditions of ambivalence, uncertainty, or equivocation. If citizens face choices between desirable incommensurables—literally, that to accomplish one value requires annihiliation of the other value—then that is a choice setting that is ripe for ambivalence. Note that this setting requires two separate features. First, the choice setting itself is one that is not subject to trade-offs or compromises, nor can it be reconciled as a single choice. This means that if one can accomplish both values, by implementing a policy that compromises or alternates between the values, one would not expect citizens to internalize a state of conflict about the choice. Further, the choice setting itself must involve two distinct choices, both of which are valued by the respondent. If the choice involves aspects of politics or social life that do not matter to the respondent, one would hardly expect them to be in a state of conflict. The result of these two features is that true conditions of ambivalence are probably rather rare in politics.

If the choice situation includes the possibility that both predispositions might be satisfied to some degree, then the setting is ripe for equivocation. Perhaps it is because the two predispositions are intrinsically compatible. For example, egalitarianism (a belief in the value of treating people equally) and humanitarianism (a belief in the value of treating people humanely) might be positively related, and it might be difficult to construct settings in which the two are conflicting. Perhaps it is because most citizens are unaware of the extent to which predispositions are exclusive. There were many people who believed that it is possible to reduce taxes, increase defense spending, and balance the budget (because the reduced taxes would spur economic growth, leading to greater revenues). Choice settings leading to equivocation might be quite common.

If a choice setting is one in which individuals would be inclined to rely overwhelmingly on a single predisposition, then the setting is prone toward uncertainty. The key question for the citizen would be, to what extent does this single predisposition provide guidance concerning the policy question. This may be due to settings in which a single predisposition is paramount, or that other predispositions are irrelevant.

But an alternative explanation for the three domains stems from elite behavior. To the extent that elite cues are important in telling us what policy means (in terms of standing predispositions), the nature of elite debate becomes a critical force leading to ambivalence, uncertainty, or equivocation.

Elites might advocate, consciously or not, for logically incompatible goals, even simultaneously. Depending on your understanding of Reaganomics, one might regard Reagan's appeals for decreased taxes, increased defense, and a balanced budget as a prime example. Perhaps elites advocate for logically incompatible goals, but not at the same time. At one moment, Clinton might call for the end of government as we know it, and at another, might laud the performance of specific bureaucrats. The net result of either of these would be the potential for equivocation, depending on the extent to which masses heed elite advocacy.

Elites might be persuasive in instructing masses about how to interpret the meaning of political questions. The interpretation itself might be an invocation of core values. Kinder and Sanders (1996) describe a significant change in the rhetoric of opposition to racial policies in the move from a frame of unearned advantages (an appeal to what they call "racial resentment," an affective judgment), to a frame of reverse discrimination (a claim of a violation of egalitarian principles). The result matters for the choices of egalitarians: when called to think in the unearned advantages frame, egalitarians support racial policy; when called to think in the reverse discrimination frame, egalitarians oppose the policy.

To the extent that elites are persuasive in helping the public resolve potentially conflicting predispositions, to choose along single, simplified dimensions, the policy domain is ripe for the condition of uncertainty. What would account for variability in response would be the extent to which masses are familiar with elite discourse, not how they reconcile potentially competing predispositions. Indeed, to the extent that elites are widely successful in promoting particular interpretations, the setting may become one of certainty (low response variability).

Can we reconcile these competing explanations for the origins of response variability? In some important ways, the two are intrinsically linked. For one, elite persuasion must be in terms of preexisting predispositions. The redundancy in the last sentence is essential: elites do not create predispositions; they activate them in the public. On some counts, this means that the malleability of the public is constrained by the values, beliefs, and expectations already in existence.

Another important point of linkage between the elite and mass-oriented explanations of response variability is that true ambivalence requires that the public care about the policy question, that the terms of the debate be real and understandable to much of the public. Real ambivalence is probably quite rare, and probably not strongly influenced by elite persuasion. Indeed, one interpretation of chronic political informedness is that respondents are aware of elite discourse. To the extent that greater information makes the choice harder, those who are more exposed to elite persuasion attempts are the more ambiva-

Low variance of opinion

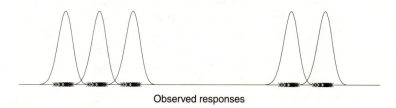

Observed responses

High variance of opinion

Observed responses

FIGURE 4.3. Distribution of potential opinions

lent. Conditions of uncertainty and equivocation, on the other hand, might be especially prone to persuasion, and the effects of the information measures consistent with the idea that those who are most exposed to elites are also the most fixed in their opinions.

MODELING AMBIVALENCE, EQUIVOCATION AND UNCERTAINTY

Our specific technical method is to use inferential statistics to model the heterogeneity of opinion. Three articles (Alvarez and Brehm 1995, 1997, 1998; and see also appendixes at www.pupress.princeton.edu/alvarez) explicate the specific statistical methods, all of which are variations on "heteroskedastic choice" methods. Our purpose in this section is to provide an intuitive understanding of the method. The core idea is that using evidence about predispositions and informedness lets one draw inferences about the most likely process generating the actual responses. (There are now several statistical packages capable of estimating these heteroskedastic choice models [e.g., Shazam, Stata, Gauss, LIMDEP], and at least one—LIMDEP—provides considerable assistance in interpreting the actual estimates.)

Figure 4.3 presents a graphical representation of our problem. Suppose that one could measure all the potential answers a respondent might offer to a particular survey question, and plot them along a continuum for five such respondents. The five sets of asterisks in the upper panel correspond to five such respondents. The possible answers offered by them are all fairly tightly packed, and we would consider them to exhibit low variance of opinion. By contrast, the five respondents in the lower panel have very dispersed sets of potential opinions, even to the point of overlapping with one another.

We have plotted a probability density function below each of the two distributions of potential answers about abortion policy. One feature of both of these distributions is its centrality, which corresponds to the most likely answer to the question at any given interview. The second feature of these distributions is the dispersion of those answers, which corresponds to how precise the centrality is as a predictor of the likely answer. Our method is to derive estimates for both the centrality (the most likely answer) and the variance of the distribution (the precision of that answer).

Generally, however, there are no multiple measurements of the same respondent. One usually has one or more cross-sectional interviews of different respondents in each cross-section. Even in panel studies where the same person might be asked at multiple times about the same policy domain, important aspects of the policy, the respondent, or the interview context might change. We then would need a means to gauge the centrality and dispersion of the potential distributions of opinions that does not rely upon multiple measurements.

We will draw inferences based on the observed responses of individuals sharing like characteristics to estimate the unobserved probabilities of response. The idea is that the actual distribution of responses provides the most likely estimates of the process generating the distribution of responses. Figure 4.4 contrasts two groups of respondents. The group in the upper section of the figure are those with low variance of opinion. We observe most of them answering in a consistent way, conditional on what we know about their core values; for example, those whose values are highly tilted toward valuing life before birth answer in a consistently pro-life manner, and those whose values tilt toward prizing women's bodily autonomy answer in a consistently pro-choice manner. This combination of information about values and the pattern of responses leads us to draw the inference that highly informed individuals are more consistent in their answers, or that the dispersion of potential answers is really rather constrained.

The group in the lower section of figure 4.4 are those with higher variance of opinion. For these respondents, the underlying distribution of opinions is quite wide. Since we only draw one response from each respondent, we do not directly observe the wide distributions of opinion. However, their opinions are more likely to be found away from the mode of the underlying distribution than those in the upper section of the figure. Our method relies on a battery

Low variance of opinion

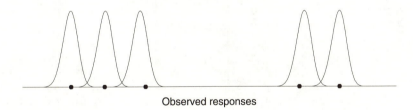

Observed responses

High variance of opinion

Observed responses

FIGURE 4.4. Distribution of potential opinions, one draw from distribution

of related statistical techniques to draw inferences about not just the mode of the distribution, but also the variance for each individual.

Remember that our distinction between ambivalence, uncertainty, and equivocation hinges upon the relationship between the estimated response variability and both information and the coincidence of values. Figure 4.5 presents the three prototypical forms of ambivalence, uncertainty, and equivocation as a function of information and values, with the effect of information in the top row, and the effect of coincident values in the bottom row.

Under ambivalence (the left-most column), as the respondent becomes better informed and as values increase in coincidence, response variability increases. In other words, under ambivalence, better-informed respondents have more variable opinions, as do those who elaborate upon both (potentially competing) predispositions. Under equivocation (the right-most column), the opposite attains: as the respondent becomes better informed and as values increase in coincidence, response variability decreases, that is, better-informed respondents have more crystalized (less variable) opinions, as do those who elaborate on more than one pertinent predisposition. The middle condition is uncertainty. Here, as with equivocation, increased information yields less variability; unlike either ambivalence or equivocation, the presence of multiple predispositions has no effect upon response variability.

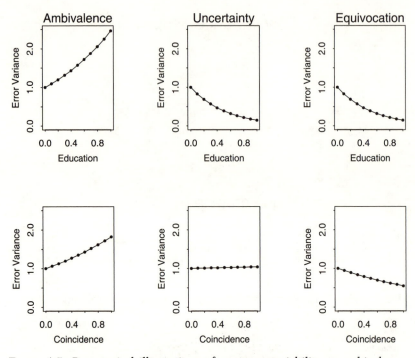

FIGURE 4.5. Prototypical illustrations of response variability as ambivalence, uncertainty, and equivocation

Our purpose in the next section is to explore these three domains of response variability. In chapter 5 we turn to the condition of ambivalence, when policy choices are made difficult by value conflict. Chapter 6 is an examination of the state of uncertainty, where information influences response variability. Then in chapter 7 we shift to a discussion of equivocation, where competing expectations, or core beliefs, lead respondents to have more fixed stated opinions.

Part 2

MASS PUBLIC OPINION

Ambivalent Attitudes: Abortion and Euthanasia

SINCE THE FOUNDING OF THE REPUBLIC, one of the central conflicts in American political life has been over the scope of individual rights. Most of the important political struggles in American history have centered on fundamental political rights, such as the long-lasting conflicts about the basic rights of African Americans, or the struggles of the woman's suffrage movement for the basic right to vote. Other political conflicts have centered on fundamental social rights, as best seen in the historic struggles over the division of church and state in American politics.

Conflicts over individual rights, both in the political world and in the minds of Americans, often seem impossible to resolve. Unlike a debate over how high to set marginal tax rates or how much money to spend on education, debates about individual rights simply offer little room for compromise, as there generally is no easy place for where common ground can be found in these debates over rights. For example, the struggles by African Americans over their right to vote really had no easy solution: either African Americans had the same political rights as white Americans, or they did not. While it might sound trite in this context, there really is no way to partly grant citizens the right to vote, and hence there really is no room for compromise in struggles over individual political or social rights.

What makes the polarity of debates about individual rights in America even more troubling is the fact that opinions about rights find their foundation in the basic values held by Americans. As we have earlier argued, when these basic values come into conflict in the minds of Americans, this value conflict will only make the resolution of debates about individual rights more difficult in the minds of citizens. Furthermore, as we will argue in subsequent chapters, when the minds of citizens are conflicted about an issue, political representatives will have great difficulty understanding the desires of their constituents and will have trouble formulating appropriate public policies.

In this chapter, we look at one form of this conflict—ambivalence—and how it affects American opinions about two of the most deeply conflictual social issues in our time, abortion and euthanasia. We start by defining exactly what we mean by ambivalence, and we contrast our definition to the prominent examples in recent research on American public opinion. While we show that ambivalence is prominent for attitudes about abortion and euthanasia, we also argue that ambivalence is a rare state of public opinion. In subsequent chapters we take up the more prevalent states of opinion, uncertainty (chapter 6) and equivocation (chapter 7).

WHAT WE MEAN BY AMBIVALENCE

We wish to be quite specific in our use of the term *ambivalence*, in frank contrast to its use elsewhere in the study of public opinion, especially in many popular discussions of American opinion where the term is often confused with uncertainty and a lack of information. *Webster's Unabridged Dictionary* defines it as the "simultaneous existence of conflicting emotions, as love and hate, in one person toward another person or thing." We want our use of the term to capture this same idea, that one reason opinions may be variable over time and context is that respondents experience strong, internalized conflict over the choices they are asked to make about policy or candidates for office. Ambivalence, in our usage, must be distinguished from alternative reasons for response variability (especially uncertainty) because of this internalized conflict. Internalized conflict is central to our definition of ambivalence.

In many ways, our definition of ambivalence (strong internalized conflict producing variable opinions) is consistent with how other public opinion researchers have recently used the concept (Feldman and Zaller 1992; Hochschild 1981; Zaller 1992). Hochschild's definition is by far the most thorough because she identifies five distinct types of internalized conflict in her in-depth interviews, which produce ambivalent attitudes. So while we want to be clear about how we define ambivalence, we also want to note that our use of the concept is consistent with previous scholarly uses of this term.

Moreover, in our use of the concept, ambivalence is distinct from indifference, even though when asked, many people may be indifferent between conflicting policy choices. That is, given a choice between, say, whether to restrict a woman's right to an abortion on demand or not, the respondents would be equally happy (or unhappy) with either. One would not really call a person who is indifferent about policy choices someone who is necessarily experiencing internalized conflict. An indifferent person has not internalized the choice, nor is that person conflicted between the two outcomes.

Sometimes, people may find multiple predispositions pertinent to a policy choice yet not consider the predispositions to be mutually contradictory. The respondent who is asked to think about the performance of a government agency may consider whether the agency is honest, or fair, or responsive. The respondent might even wish the agency to be all three of these things at once. But unless the respondent cares enough to internalize his or her thinking about the agency, or recognizes some way in which these three expectations are mutually exclusive, we do not consider that respondent to be in a state of internalized conflict over the evaluation of the agency.

Or, people might consider multiple predispositions as being relevant to a policy choice, but believe that one predisposition is really much more important than another. A respondent might think of welfare reform as restoring a degree of egalitarianism to policy, or that it is the humanitarian thing to do (Feldman and Steenbergen 2001), but conclude that it really has much more to do with humanitarianism than egalitarianism. Respondents who are able to reconcile potentially competing predispositions are not in the same state of internalized conflict that is experienced by those people who cannot reconcile predispositions.

This is to say not merely that scholars of public opinion need to be careful about their use of the word *ambivalence*, and not subsume into their use of that term states of mind that do not reflect internalization or conflict. Ambivalence is—and should be—conceptually distinct from other states of mind about public life. But our conceptualization is also implicitly an argument that real ambivalence is probably quite rare when thinking about matters of politics, because few aspects of political life lead to internalization. Those who participate in public opinion surveys can be questioned about an incredible array of topics. In a typical National Election Studies survey, for instance, respondents are asked to make choices about civil rights, abortion, defense policy, the federal budget, the environment, women's rights; to assess the traits of political candidates; and to provide their perceptions of where these candidates stand on the same set of issues. How many people would find these topics of sufficient immediacy that the topics would translate into considerations about what these topics mean for *them?*

Additionally, ambivalence is rare because these internalized predispositions have to be those that cannot be readily resolved. The policy choices that induce real ambivalence must be incommensurable ones, where the accomplishment of one choice necessitates the destruction of the other choice. Again, the best examples of political conflicts where we might expect to see ambivalent attitudes are ones involving questions like individual rights, where the choices involved are incommensurable and involve internalized value conflict. Because contemporary political debate has two such conflicts concerning individual rights on the agenda—the long-running debate over abortion rights and the much newer debate over euthanasia—we hypothesize that our findings about both issues should be characterized by ambivalence.

But it is here that we have another very important distinction to make between our definition of ambivalence and how the concept has been used by past scholars. Both Zaller (1992) and Hochschild (1981) argue that ambivalence is virtually ubiquitous, a roughly constant state of mind for most individuals. Hochschild states that "people do not make simple statements; they shade, modulate, deny, retract, or just grind to a halt in frustration" (238). In Zaller's subsequent empirical analysis, "respondents exhibited substantial amounts of internal conflict in all measures," a result that corroborates

Hochschild's contention (61). So these scholars contend that ambivalence is commonplace, where we contend that it is quite rare.

But both Zaller and Hochschild reach their conclusion about the ubiquity of ambivalence because their conceptualization of this state of mind is, in our opinion, too broad, and it conflates ambivalence (in our use of the term) with indifference and even uncertainty. Their evidence, then, would seem to be weak and ambiguous, since it is also consistent with uncertain or equivocal attitudes. Just because people have variable opinions, or have difficulty answering questions, or provide murky answers, or often say they have no opinion, does not necessarily mean that they have ambivalent opinions. As we will show in this chapter, and the two that follow, it is critical to include controls for all three states of public opinion. When we do so, moreover, we find that our suspicions about the rareness of ambivalence are confirmed.

In our systematic search for respondents' attitudes toward public policy, we have located only two domains where ambivalence appears possible for the mass public: abortion and euthanasia. (A different condition may exist for elites, as we show in chapter 9.) As we will show in the next two chapters, however, policy domains that scholarship routinely categorizes as prone to ambivalence prove to be either driven by uncertainty or equivocation. It is perhaps not too surprising that attitudes about abortion and euthanasia would fall into the category of ambivalence: these are choices that are meaningful and real for substantial numbers of respondents, and that represent clearly understandable and mutually contradictory outcomes regarding individual rights. We take up the discussion of each in turn.

ABORTION

For the last several decades, abortion has been one of the most conflictual issues in American politics. Candidates' positions on the legality of abortion, on restrictions on its availability, on parental consent, on state funding, and on numerous other dimensions of abortion policy, are among the first positions that both Democratic and Republican elites ascertain when a new candidate seeks office. Abortion positions also figure prominently in recent Supreme Court and federal court appointments, and are often a critical litmus test in many state and local political appointments as well. There is strong evidence that the two major political parties have realigned their electoral base because of abortion (Adams 1997). Many thousands of women every year contend with the difficult and personal choice about whether to have an abortion themselves. Thus, abortion is one of the most conflictual and prominent issues in contemporary American politics.

And yet, if one were to look at the positions of the American public on abortion in the decades since *Roe v. Wade*, one would probably conclude that the public appears to have come to some consensus about which forms of abortion should be legal, and which not. Luckily, we can look at these positions over the recent decades using survey data, since the General Social Survey has long included a complex battery of questions on abortion. The GSS battery asks respondents whether they believe abortion should be allowed under any of seven circumstances, for each scenario separately. The question reads, "Please tell me whether or not *you* think it should be possible for a pregnant woman to obtain a *legal* abortion . . ."

- If there is a strong chance of serious defect in the baby.
- If she is married and does not want any more children.
- If the woman's own health is seriously endangered by the pregnancy.
- If the family has a very low income and cannot afford any more children.
- If she became pregnant as a result of rape or incest.
- If she is not married and does not want to marry the man.
- If the woman wants it for any reason.

Figure 5.1 displays the percentage who answer that abortion should be legal for each of the seven scenarios, for all the years that the question has been asked.

The first obvious characteristic of the trends in abortion opinion is that there is remarkably little change in opinions about abortion in the last two decades. The "mother's health," "rape or incest," and "birth defect" series change by no more than 5 percentage points, barely larger than variation, which would simply be due to chance. The most variable of the series, whether abortion should be legal for any reason, only changes by about 10 percentage points from minimum to maximum. At the aggregate level, there is little here to indicate a high state of internalized conflict over abortion policy.

The second obvious characteristic of the trends in abortion opinion is that the policy choices cluster into three distinct groups. Abortion to protect a mother's health is supported by an overwhelming majority of the GSS respondents. This is not at all surprising, since exceptions for the health of the mother have always been part of abortion law in the United States (Ginsburg 1989). The second group are the exceptions due to rape or birth defect. These, too, are exceptions that are supported by huge majorities of the GSS respondents. Again, the survey results are consistent with the historical record of changes in abortion law: exceptions to abortion bans began to include both conditions from the late 1950s onward (Ginsburg 1989). The third group of exceptions are all of the four remaining cases: "too poor," "single," "does not want any more children," and "for any reason." Levels of support here range between 38 and 55 percent.

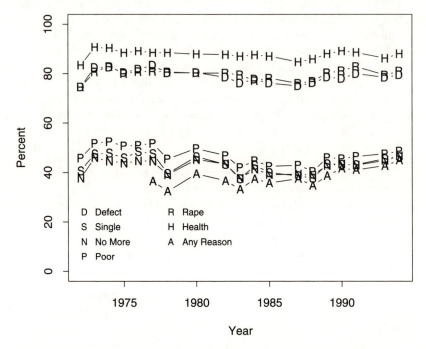

FIGURE 5.1. Attitudes toward abortion, 1972–94 General Social Survey

However, the nearly even split among GSS respondents between those who support and those who oppose abortion is surely evidence of the potential for aggregate, political conflict. But because these numbers remain so constant, these aggregate trends obviously cannot shed light on whether there is an internalized conflict over the question. In the end, we must turn to individual level evidence to determine if there is indeed internalized conflict regarding abortion policy in America.

Everything we know about the issues that become embedded within the debate on abortion suggests that it should meet the conditions that we set out in chapter 4 for ambivalence. The subject is something that invokes multiple, mutually incompatible predispositions. It is fundamentally impossible to both preserve the life of the fetus and to permit a woman full autonomy over a choice to abort the fetus. The issue is also one that is likely to be internalized, in the sense that many women (and men) have faced a choice, or are aware of others who have had to make the choice, of whether to have an abortion. The terms of the debate are far from the usual abstractions of politics, invoking as they do matters that are real, tangible, and accessible for many respondents. Thus, attitudes about abortion policy are prime candidates for the state of ambivalence.

Models of Abortion Policy Choice

There are two steps to development of a model of ambivalent attitudes toward abortion. The first part of our model, the choice model, estimates levels of support for abortion rights under each of the seven scenarios. For the development of this model, we draw from the previous research on abortion attitudes. In order to accumulate sufficient variables to test this model, we use both the 1982 and 1987 GSS.[1] The second step is the development of the variance model, which we discuss in the next section.

Two very strong predispositions dominate choices over abortion policy: feminism and religiosity. By feminism we mean that pro-feminist respondents value a woman's right to choose, not just in the matter of abortion, but also over career, marriage, education, and social roles, denoting a preference for a woman's autonomy to make every choice that affects her.

The 1982 and 1987 GSS surveys permit two very different approaches to the predispositions at work in policy choice. One method (for the 1982 GSS) uses proxy measures for predispositions. These proxies are conceptually closer to the true concepts than most such measures, in that one is an attitudinal manifestation of pro-feminist attitudes, and the other is a demographic measure, which is likely to be highly correlated with religiosity. The second method (for the 1987 GSS) employs confirmatory factor models to generate scales for feminism and religiosity. We take these two approaches in chronological order.

ABORTION CHOICES IN THE 1982 GSS: PROXY APPROACHES

Luker (1984) describes the conflict in attitudes concerning abortion as stemming from fundamental conceptions of the role of women. While direct questions about women's roles would be especially useful, we lack such direct measures for the particular years of the GSS question. We do, however, have a measure of support for the Equal Rights Amendment. By the later years of the campaign by pro-ERA activists, many of these activists explicitly linked support for the ERA with abortion rights (see Mansbridge 1986, 122–28). We include "supports ERA," the response to the question, "Do you strongly favor, somewhat favor, somewhat oppose, or strongly oppose this amendment?" It is scaled from 0 (strongly oppose) to 1 (strongly support).

Figure 5.2 displays the distribution of support for the ERA in the 1982 GSS. The graph on the left shows the proportion of respondents who claim to know what the ERA means. The vast majority said they did know what the amendment meant, which is of some interest, considering that both advocates and opponents exaggerated the potential content of the amendment (Mansbridge 1986). In the graph on the right, the majority of the GSS respondents supported passage of the ERA—the right two bars swamp the left two—although

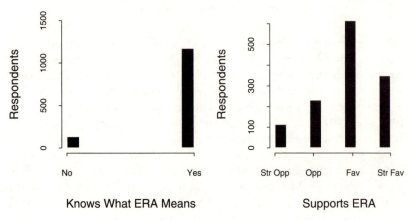

FIGURE 5.2. Distribution of ERA opinions, 1982 General Social Survey

the plurality only somewhat favored the amendment. By this proxy measure, one would describe the majority of GSS respondents as having at least weakly pro-feminist opinions.

Luker also found that religion remained a significant contributor to pro-life activism. We include several measures: "Catholic" is a dummy variable denoting whether the respondent is a Catholic; "attend church" records the frequency of the respondent's church attendance', scaled from 0 (never) to 8 (several times a week); "religious intensity" gauges whether the respondent expressed a strong religious intensity, scaled from 0 (not religious) to 1 (very strong religious preference).

Figure 5.3 displays the distribution of two religiosity measures in the 1982 GSS. The graph on the left demonstrates religious intensity. The vast majority of respondents claim to have strong to very strong religious preferences. The graph on the right documents how often the respondents claim to attend church. Here, the distribution is much more uniform, but, again, the majority of respondents attend church at least on a monthly basis.

Although these are proxy measures for the relevant predispositions, they indicate a very strong potential for conflict. The majority of respondents are both pro-feminist and pro-religious, setting up the incommensurability of choices about abortion policy.

We include two dummy variables for race and gender: "black" and "male." Black Americans have had persistently stronger opposition to abortion than whites, even after controlling for religion, education, social status, and region (Brehm 1993; Combs and Welch 1982; Hall and Ferree 1986). Gender has not had a convincingly consistent relationship with abortion attitudes, even though some activists see abortion policy as a question of women's rights.

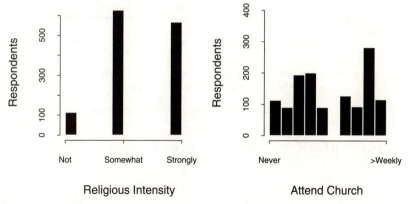

FIGURE 5.3. Distribution of religiosity, 1982 General Social Survey

ABORTION CHOICES IN THE 1985 GSS: CONFIRMATORY FACTOR APPROACHES

The 1985 GSS permits a different and more systematic approach to measuring the predispositions relevant to abortion. Here, we have eight attitudinal measures that allow construction of feminism and fear-of-God scales, as we have four measures for each predisposition. Table 5.1 presents the confirmatory factor loadings for both of these scales.

The upper portion of table 5.1 presents the loadings for the feminism scale. Here, we code the answers to the questions such that a strongly feminist respondent would agree with the first question, and disagree with the remainder. The freed factor loadings are all close to 1, implying that there is considerable shared variance among the indicators. The lower portion of the table documents the loadings for the fear-of-God scale. With this scale, we code the conceptions of God that are hierarchical (master, judge, creator, and redeemer) as 1, and those that are nonhierarchical as 0 (spouse, lover, healer, liberator). The loadings for this scale, unfortunately, are not as strong. Only the conceptions of God as master and judge share much common variance.

Next, to show the distributions of these two scales, figure 5.4 presents the histograms for our two derived scales for feminism and fear of God, and their interaction. The distribution on the feminism scale is quite dispersed, covering the full range on the scale, with a peak at approximately 0.6. The majority of the respondents to the 1985 General Social Survey are moderately pro-feminist. The fear-of-God scale is much more asymmetric: although there are observations at all points on the 0–1 scale, the mode is decidedly close to the maximum. This implies that the majority of GSS respondents believe in God in a hierarchical form. The interaction between the two demonstrates that being

TABLE 5.1

Confirmatory Factor Scales for Feminism and Religiosity, 1985 General Social Survey

Question	Loading
Feminism	
A working mother can establish just as warm and secure a relationship with her children as a mother who does not work (SA = 1).	1.00
It is more important for a wife to help her husband's career than to have one herself (SD = 1).	0.73 (0.02)
A preschool child is likely to suffer if his or her mother works (SD = 1).	0.82 (0.02)
It is much better for everyone involved if the man is the achiever (SD = 1).	0.92 (0.02)
Fear of God	
There are many different ways of picturing God. We'd like to know the kinds of images you are most likely to associate with God. . . . Master (1) or Spouse (0)	1.00
Judge (1) or Lover (0)	0.49 (0.03)
Creator (1) or Healer (0)	0.24 (0.02)
Redeemer (1) or Liberator (0)	−0.31 (0.02)

Note: Cell entries are unstandardized factor loadings; standard errors are in parentheses.

both pro-feminist and believing in a God as master is quite common. Although the scale is skewed toward the low end, the mode is just below the halfway point on the scale.

To further examine the bivariate relationship between the two predisposition measures, we present their scatterplot in figure 5.5. In fact, if one examines the scatterplot of the two scales, it is apparent that a significant portion of the GSS respondents exhibit high degrees of both feminism and religiosity. Also, there is little apparent correlation between the two predisposition measures.

We again employ a set of control variances for race, gender, Catholic Church background, and religious intensity, coded in a manner parallel to the 1982 GSS analysis. This ensures that our analysis for the 1985 GSS is as similar as possible to our 1982 GSS model, so that we can directly compare results between the two GSS samples.

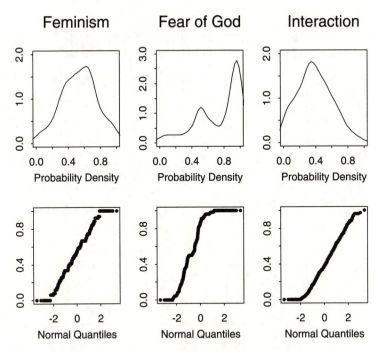

FIGURE 5.4. Distribution of feminism and religiosity, 1985
General Social Survey

Specification of the Variance Model

As with the choice model, we employ two distinct approaches to the specification of the variance model. Because we do not have direct indicators of the predispositions in the 1982 GSS, we use elaboration measures for the variance model for that year. In the 1985 analysis, we do have measures of predispositions and can directly model the interactions. In both analyses, we require measures of the respondents' informedness.

The elaboration measure we use from the 1982 GSS to measure predispositions is unique. Our basic assumption is that individuals who possess strong attachments to both of the underlying core principles should have a harder time making a decision about abortion; hence they should have a greater error variance. A respondent's ability to elaborate multiple arguments indicates stronger commitment to the principles underlying those arguments. To measure elaboration, we need to know respondents' motivation, their ability to

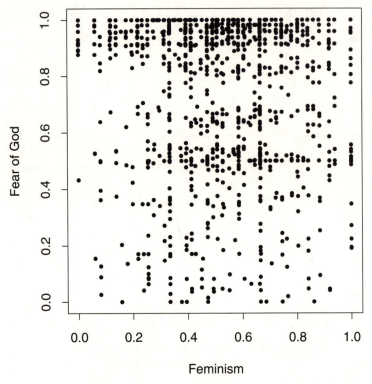

FIGURE 5.5. Scatterplot of feminism and religiosity, 1985 General Social Survey

process the communication, and the degree to which they evaluate the policy choice under both pro-life and pro-choice dimensions.[1]

There are two aspects of a respondent's motivation to process the information about abortion: commitment to a prior position and self-identification of the prominence of the issue. They may say that they are firm in their opinions about abortion; under ordinary circumstances, one would expect there to be less underlying variance to their positions. When both pro-choice and pro-life positions are salient, the more firm they profess to be and the more their answers will be sensitive to the context of the choice. "Firmness of opinion" is one of two measures of motivation, where respondents' answers are scaled from 0 (for those who are very likely to change opinions) through 1 (for those who are very unlikely to change). An alternative aspect of motivation is the respondent's self-assessment of the importance of the issue. Those who say that abortion is not important at all would be unmotivated to process any communications about abortion, whereas respondents who say that abortion is the most important issue would be highly motivated. Also included is "abortion importance" as a variable scaled from 0 (not important at all) through 1 (most important).

We measure the ability of respondents to process the communication by their self-reported level of information on the issue on abortion. But there are some glaring weaknesses in using these self-reports here: respondents will be inclined to exaggerate their level of informedness, and information does not directly represent ability to understand the information. Nonetheless, the respondent's assessment of whether he or she has enough information is a useful indicator. We code "abortion info" on a scale from 0 (very little information) through 1 (all the information).

Beyond the usefulness of information as a measure of ability, the self-report highlights a significant difference between ambivalence as a source for error variance and the alternative explanations: the role that information plays in resolving conflict. Under three of the alternatives (uncertainty, ambiguous questions, and the desire to appear informed), we expect the error variance to be less for those who are better informed about abortion policy than those who are relatively uninformed. Under ambivalence, we expect that additional information should not account for any change in the error for respondents' policy choices. The 1982 GSS also asked how much information they had on the abortion debate, how firm their opinions were about abortion, and how important the abortion issue is to them. We include measures for all three of these in the error variance part of the model. Note that one would probably not expect strength of opinions on abortion to affect the direction of support, but it would affect the difficulty respondents have in stating their position.

The third component of the variance model is the degree to which the respondent has cognitive information about the core principles of abortion. One way of ascertaining that is to ask the respondent to elaborate on the reasons for and against abortion, as the 1982 GSS asked, in an open-ended question. We include both "pro count" and "con count," which are simply counts of the number of reasons for and against. Since we are arguing that it is the simultaneous presence of both attitudes that should increase error variance, we look toward the product of the two.

It is possible that respondents would be able to rehearse both the reasons for and against abortion without being in a state of conflict about the policy (because of uncertainty, ambiguity of the questions, or a desire to appear informed). Those respondents who rehearse both sides of the question because they are well informed about the terms in the political debate (or have a desire to appear so) should have less error variance throughout. Our argument will be that ambivalent respondents should have greater error variance for the difficult policy questions and less error variance for the easy questions than respondents who do not elaborate both sides.

TABLE 5.2
Estimated Effects on Attitudes toward Abortion, 1982 General Social Survey

Variable	Mother's Health	Birth Defect	Rape	Too Poor	Single	No More Kids	Any Reason
Black	−.05	−.13	−.13	−.08	−.16	−.07	−.07
Male	.00	−.04	−.05	−.03	−.04	−.01	−.06
Catholic	−.05	−.07	−.04	.01	−.02	.01	.02
Religious intensity	−.11	−.10	−.04	−.15	−.13	−.09	−.10
Attend church	−.20	−.18	−.23	−.30	−.33	−.28	−.35
Know ERA	.00	.00	−.03	.08	.06	.06	.05
Support ERA	.08	.09	.03	.19	.22	.21	.22

Note: Cell entries are computed change in probability by moving from minimum to maximum on listed variable, holding all others at the mean. N = 1219.

Our measure for informedness in the 1985 GSS is decidedly weaker: using years of education as a proxy for exposure to chronic political information. As we noted in chapter 3, the respondent's educational attainment is the best predictor of chronic political information, although a relatively weak predictor of domain-specific information. In lieu of the elaboration measures available for 1982, education then constitutes the best available proxy for chronic informedness.

Results of the Choice and Variance Models

We estimate the heteroskedastic probit model for each of the seven indicators of attitudes toward abortion, and report the results of these estimates in tables 5.2 and 5.3. We order the estimates for the seven different indicators by the percentage of respondents in the 1982 GSS who answered yes to each question. The first three questions elicit overwhelming support from the GSS respondents: "mother's health" (90.4 percent), "rape" (83.9 percent), and "birth defect" (82.1 percent). None of the remaining four questions obtains a majority supporting abortion under the specific circumstance.

This initial observation is extremely useful for the present analysis. The pattern of support for the seven different alternative scenarios closely follows the historical record of legal abortion in the United States. Protection of the life of the mother has always been a component of abortion law. The first laws restricting the availability of abortion included explicit exemptions intended to protect the mother's health (Ginsburg 1989). If there is ever something approx-

TABLE 5.3
Estimated Effects on Attitudes toward Abortion, 1985 General Social Survey

Variable	Mother's Health	Birth Defect	Rape	Too Poor	Single	No More Kids	Any Reason
Black	−.02	−.08	−.04	−.07	−.07	−.04	−.01
Male	.04	.02	.02	.06	.04	.08	.03
Catholic	−.04	−.09	−.09	−.12	−.10	−.33	−.08
Religious intensity	−.09	−.22	−.18	−.32	−.27	−.04	−.25
Fear of God	−.07	−.05	−.06	−.13	−.10	−.08	−.06
Feminism	.24	.29	.28	.41	.42	.52	.31

Note: Cell entries are computed change in probability by moving from minimum to maximum on listed variable, holding all others at the mean. $N = 1219$.

imating an easy or valence question about abortion, it is to permit legal abortions when the life of the mother is in jeopardy. Likewise, the subsequent history of the expanding set of permitted circumstances for abortion moved rapidly to include probable birth defects. Ginsburg describes the emergence of abortion under circumstances other than for the health of the mother, with the terrible rubella epidemics of the late 1950s and early 1960s, and the horrific birth defects caused by thalidomide. These disasters led to more relaxed laws permitting so-called therapeutic abortions.

We will refer to the first three settings ("mother's health," "birth defect," and "rape") as the easy abortion questions, and the remaining four as difficult ones. Furthermore, we will demonstrate that it is only under the difficult abortion questions that two-sided elaboration leads to greater variance in the individual respondent's probability of support. As we argued above, the difference between easy and difficult questions is that under difficult questions, values are in conflict, whereas under easy questions, values are either nonconflictual or subordinated.

We begin with the choice component of these models. Note that the findings of the general literature on attitudes toward abortion policy remain entirely intact. Black respondents were more likely to oppose abortion under all seven of the scenarios, for both years: the coefficient on "black" is always negative, and in all but one case ("too poor"), the coefficient is statistically significant. The puzzle of strong black opposition to abortion remains confirmed in our estimates here.

Men are more inclined to oppose abortion under all seven alternatives for 1982, but the sign flips for 1985. The estimates are not statistically significant in four of the seven cases ("mother's health," "too poor," "no more kids," and "single") for 1982, but in 1985, men are *more* likely than women to favor legal abortion under all seven of the scenarios. While there might be some interest in the relationship of gender to attitudes about abortion, the evidence here is that gender is not an overwhelmingly strong or consistent predictor of such attitudes.

Religiosity clearly affects attitudes toward abortion, and in significant ways. Being Catholic is not the best reflection of religiosity as it pertains to abortion, however. The coefficient on Catholic is inconsistent across the seven models for 1982, and statistically distinguishable from zero in only two of those cases ("mother's health" and "birth defect"). Catholics are consistently likely to oppose abortion in the 1985 data. "Religious intensity" is consistently negative: those who have strong religious preferences are more likely to reject abortion under all seven scenarios, and to a statistically significant degree in all but two of those cases ("rape" and "no more kids"). Frequency of church attendance turns out to be the strongest measure in the model. The coefficient is always negative, always statistically significant. Note also that this is the only variable whose scale runs from 0 to 8 (instead of 0 to 1), so that at its maximum range, it has a powerful effect in undermining support for abortion. For 1985, religious intensity itself had the strongest effect.

With the 1985 data, we were able to employ a measure of religiosity conceived as a view of God as master, judge, creator, or redeemer. This measure of religiosity is consistently related to opposition to legal abortion, although never as much as the religious intensity measure. Further, the effect of the fear-of-God measure is inconsistent in strength; it is a much stronger predictor of opposition to abortion under the "too poor" and "single" settings than any of the others.

Mere knowledge of the ERA has no influence on support for abortion; in no case were the coefficients on knowledge of the ERA significant, and the variable does change sign. Support for the ERA, however, is a powerful predictor of support for abortion rights in all but one of the scenarios ("rape").

In the 1985 analysis, we were able to construct a measure for feminism. In every case, not only is it strongly related to support for legal abortion, but it is also the strongest predictor in the entire analysis. While gender is not related to support for legal abortion, feminism clearly is strongly related, whether measured as knowledge of or support for the ERA, or by the feminism scale.

The most relevant portion of the analysis for establishing the presence of ambivalence is the variance analysis. We think the foregoing findings are useful in and of themselves, since they demonstrate the many bases of attitudes toward abortion and point to possible sources of conflict. But the most intriguing aspect of the problem arises in the variance model.

Rather than simply examining the direction and statistical significance of the interaction between the expression of reasons for and against abortion, we can look at the magnitude of these effects. Because of the different specifica-

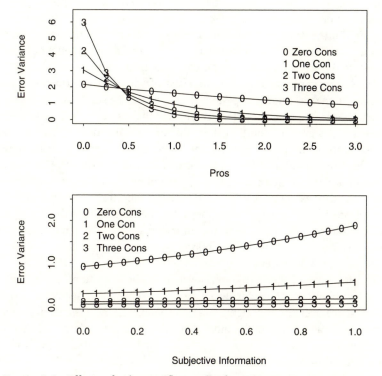

FIGURE 5.6. Effects of value conflict and information on error variance in "mother's health" scenario, 1982 General Social Survey

tions of the variance model, the method for displaying the variance differs for 1982 and 1985.

For 1982, we plot the estimated error variance of each policy choice across the possible combinations of reasons for and against abortion, holding the other variables in the variance models constant at their mean values. The horizontal axis in each graph counts the number of reasons in favor of legal abortion ("pros") from 0 to 3 mentions. There are four curves on each graph, each indicating increasing numbers of reasons in opposition to legal abortion. The degree to which respondents offer one-sided elaborations appears in the "zero cons" line (for positive elaborations), and across the four lines at the point of "zero pros" (for negative elaborations). The highest degree of two-sided elaboration appears in the "three cons" line for increasing "pros."

The first pair of graphs (figure 5.6) demonstrates the effects of value conflict and information on error variance in the "mother's health" scenario, the scenario that achieved the highest levels of support throughout the series. In the upper graph, the more reasons that the respondent can provide to support legal abortion, the lower the error variance: all of the curves are downward sloping. Furthermore, the more reasons that the respondent can provide to oppose abortion, the lower the variance: as we increase the number of "cons" from 0 to 3, each successive curve is closer to the horizontal axis.

The lower graph demonstrates the effect of additional information on the variance in the respondent's opinions. Here, we use the subjective-information measure, asking participants to ascertain for themselves how informed they are about the issue of abortion. But this measure has defects, namely, that respondents would probably exaggerate their informedness, and fail to report that they were ill-informed, even if that was the case. What we see is that the effect of additional information varies, depending on the number of reasons the respondent can provide in opposition to legal abortion. When a respondent cannot provide any reasons to oppose legal abortion, being subjectively well informed leads to an increase in the estimated variance. When a respondent can provide at least one reason to oppose legal abortion, the effect of subjective information is nonexistent.

The meaning of the two graphs relative to the conditions we set out to identify ambivalence is decidedly ambiguous. We would certainly not characterize choice over abortion rights when the woman's health is endangered as a condition of ambivalence: the more that the values are in conflict (when the number of pros and cons increases), the less the variance. It is probably closer to a state of uncertainty in that individuals who elaborate multiple reasons become less variant in their opinions compared to those who elaborate few reasons, or only on one side. But the effect of our measure of subjective information here runs counter to the criterion that information should reduce variance in the uncertainty condition.

The picture is entirely unambiguous in the pair of graphs in figure 5.7 documenting the effect of value conflict and information in the most pro-choice scenario ("any reason"). The upper graph displays the effects of one- and two-sided elaboration on reasons to oppose or support legal abortion. When respondents cannot provide a reason to oppose abortion, the effect of elaborating additional "pros" is to sharply decrease variance: the curve labeled "zero cons" is downward sloping. But when respondents can provide at least one reason to oppose legal abortion, the effect of additional "pros" increases variance, and the rate of increase increases with each additional reason in opposition. Furthermore, as the lower graph shows, the effect of increasing subjective information leads to greater variance. In other words, the more that respondents are able to think about reasons for and against abortion, and the more they consider themselves well-informed, the more variable their opinions are. This is the condition we refered to earlier as ambivalence: the simultaneous presence of coincident values, which leads to a state of intrapersonal conflict.

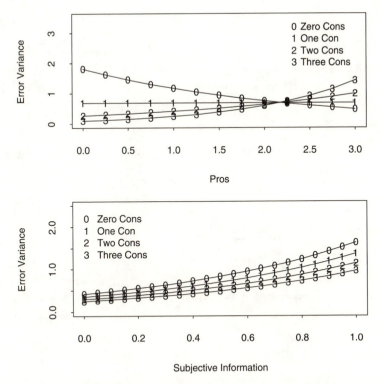

FIGURE 5.7. Effects of value conflict and information on error variance in "any reason" scenario, 1982 General Social Survey

Similar results obtain for the 1985 abortion questions. Here, we have no direct measure of informedness, and rely upon education as a proxy for chronic political awareness. We do, however, have two distinct measures of the values that could be in conflict: a retributive conception of God, and a sense of feminism. As figure 5.5 showed, there are quite a number of the GSS respondents who happen to score highly on both the fear-of-God and feminism measures. To ascertain the extent to which these values are simultaneously and equally strongly present in the respondent's mind, we employ a very simple transformation to generate a coincidence scale:

$$\text{Coincidence} = 1 - |\text{ Fear God} - \text{Feminism }|.$$

We refer to this as a coincidence scale because it captures the extent to which a respondent holds two predispositions simultaneously. It is not a conflict scale, since multiple predispositions can be reinforcing. We rely upon our statistical method to assess conflict among coincident predispositions. This

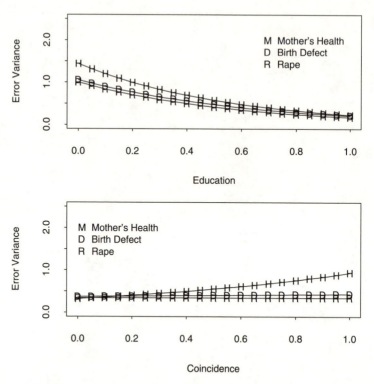

FIGURE 5.8. Effects of value conflict and information on error variance, most widely supported abortion scenarios

measure will range from 0 (scales are opposite in strength, e.g., high on feminism, low on fear-of-God) to 1 (scales are equal in strength).

The first pair of graphs (figure 5.8) displays the effects of education (top graph) and coincident values (bottom graph) on the variance for the three scenarios where legal abortion is widely supported ("mother's health," "birth defect," "rape"). The better educated the respondent, the less variable the respondent's opinions are about abortion. In the lower graph, we demonstrate that as values become coincident, the variance increases, but only for the "mother's health" condition. Under our criteria, we would clearly classify choice about abortion in the "birth defect" and "rape" conditions as ones of uncertainty, since the effect of multiple predispositions does not appreciably change the variance, and that the variance decreases with information. Our criteria are slightly less dispositive in the "mother's health" condition. Although the information measure functions as it should for the uncertainty category, there is a modest effect

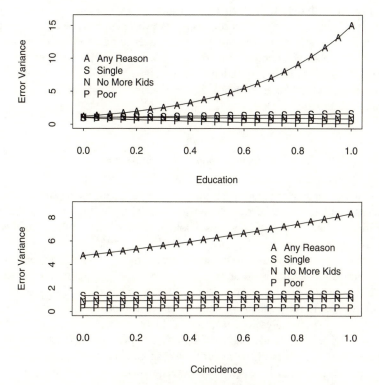

FIGURE 5.9. Effects of value conflict and information on error variance, less widely supported abortion scenarios

of coincident values, suggesting that there is some ambiguity for this scenario of abortion choice between ambivalence and uncertainty.

The next pair of graphs (figure 5.9) present the effects of education (top graph) and coincident values (bottom graph) on the remaining four scenarios. In general, neither education nor coincident values has much of an effect upon variance in abortion attitudes for the three middle conditions ("too poor," "single," "no more kids"); all of the curves are essentially flat. The effect of the two variables on variance in the most pro-choice condition ("any reason") is quite clear, and quite strong. As respondents become better educated, and as they become more likely to equally value a retributive view of God and feminism, they are quite clearly more variant in their opinions.

In other words, even in this setting where, presumably, individuals are most likely to be ambivalent, ambivalence as a state of internalized conflict surfaces only in the more pro-choice scenarios. When there is an additional overriding concern—the woman's health is jeopardized, the fetus's life would be severely marred by birth defect, the woman is pregnant as a result of a felonious act of violence—the choice about abortion is not one that elicits conflict (in the form of increased variance of choice). When the overriding concern is removed, when the reasons for abortion are not life-threatening, the picture is somewhat ambiguous. Only when respondents are not offered justifications for abortion (i.e., abortion legal for any reason), do we see evidence that respondents internalize a conflictual choice.

Conclusions about Abortion Attitudes

We have demonstrated that the attitudes of American citizens toward abortion policy are rooted in conflicting core beliefs. This is especially true for the more "difficult" abortion policy questions—policy issues that have historically been areas of great political conflict. Clearly, to understand attitudes toward abortion policy in the United States, one must understand the core beliefs that constitute the foundations of these attitudes.

In the broader realm of American politics, our work here has at least two implications. In the particular context of the abortion debate, neither the pro-life (e.g., Operation Rescue and National Right to Life Committee) nor the pro-choice (e.g., National Abortion Rights Action League) activists represent the policy preferences of the majority of respondents to the present survey. The policy positions of the activists are unequivocal, one-sided in support for or opposition to abortion. What we have demonstrated is that ambivalence and internal conflict reign over the four most difficult policy scenarios explored in this particular survey. Ironically, the most recent Supreme Court decision, *Casey v. Planned Parenthood*, may have come closest to the preferences of the public by sustaining both *Roe v. Wade* (and the possibility of legal abortion under certain circumstances) as well as *Webster v. Reproductive Health Services* (which permitted significant restrictions on the availability of abortion to minors).

Second, our results unfortunately imply that abortion attitudes in the American public may be difficult to change. Because abortion opinions are not influenced by additional information, simply educating the public about abortion (either about the need for continuing abortion policies or about why abortion policies need to be restricted) will not fundamentally alter abortion beliefs. Abortion rights, like any other individual rights, involve incommensurable choices. But equally important, we have shown that abortion rights beliefs are also structured by conflicting and incommensurable predispositions that determine both the variability of abortion attitudes and the specific policy choices of the public. Thus, resolution of the abortion rights debate in American politics will not be a simple matter.

EUTHANASIA

We also expect to find ambivalence in another domain of public opinion: attitudes concerning suicide and euthanasia. The topic meets the conditions we elaborated for internalized conflict. The issue involves incommensurable choices about individual rights, of the same life-or-death variety as abortion. There is, of course, a strong impetus to discourage suicide and euthanasia. As we will show, a significant proportion of the public find euthanasia or suicide acceptable, but only in cases of incurable disease. Respondents would permit euthanasia only in the instances where the person contemplating suicide is in a condition where abject misery would be the best description of the quality of life. Thus, like attitudes about abortion rights, attitudes about giving people the right to take their life can be weighed against equally dire alternatives.

Euthanasia is fast becoming an important issue in U.S. politics. As the aging of America continues, and medical science continues to develop ways to prolong the life span of adults, euthanasia will grow as a hot-button issue. In 1994, Oregon's electorate passed into law a ballot measure called the Death with Dignity Act, which provided euthanasia for terminally ill adults under a set of restrictive conditions. Challenged by many religious groups—especially the Catholic Church—Oregon's voters nevertheless again supported euthanasia in their state in 1997.

Recently, laws about euthanasia in Washington State, New York, Florida, and Michigan have been challenged in courts. In 1997, the United States Supreme Court examined the New York and Washington cases, and issued a narrow ruling. The Court found that there is no general constitutional right to physician-assisted suicide, so the New York and Washington laws that banned euthanasia were constitutional. But on the other hand, the Court did imply that there could be a constitutional right for certain groups, like the terminally ill, to have access to physician-assisted suicide. But until a relevant case reaches the Supreme Court, the constitutionality of euthanasia in the United States is still unclear. With legislative activity on physician-assisted suicide in both the national capital and in many states, it is clear that this is a controversial issue that will be widely debated in coming years.

One difficulty, however, in proceeding with a study of attitudes about euthanasia is that, as best as we can tell, the area is unexplored by political scientists and other scholars of public opinion. What little social scientists do know about public opinion concerning suicide follows indirectly from related issues, such as scholarship on reasons for changes in suicide rates (e.g., Lester 1998; Saunderson, Haynes, and Langford 1998; Swanwick and Clare 1998) or in support of suicide among the elderly or terminally ill themselves (e.g., Sullivan et al. 1998).

There is also, of course, the great sociological tradition studying suicide, stemming from the work of Emile Durkheim (1951). Durkheim's book *Suicide* is a masterwork of early social science, first disputing the idea that suicide originates in personal madness or in imitation, and then arguing that suicide has social origins. Particularly relevant here is Durkheim's argument that "normlessness" (or in his terms, *anomie*) precipitates suicide, specifically, that the more society lacks regulation and order, the more people despair of their opportunities. Durkheim found anomie in economic crisis, family catastrophe, and social disorder.

We have an opportunity to consider different choices about suicide and euthanasia in drawing upon five questions from the same 1985 General Social Survey we used earlier in this chapter to study abortion rights beliefs. The percentages reflect responses in the affirmative

- When a person has a disease that cannot be cured, do you think doctors should be allowed by law to end the patient's life by some painless means if the patient and his family request it? (Euthanasia, 66.6 percent.)
- Do you think a person has the right to end his or her own life if this person has an incurable disease? (Incurable, 45.5 percent).
- Do you think a person has the right to end his or her own life if this person has gone bankrupt? (Bankrupt, 7.7 percent.)
- Do you think a person has the right to end his or her own life if this person has dishonored his or her family? (Dishonored, 7.8 percent.)
- Do you think a person has the right to end his or her own life if this person is tired of living and ready to die? (Tired of Life, 12.6 percent.)

The first point to note is that, just as we saw in the previous section on abortion attitudes, there is a broad range of levels of support for different forms of suicide or euthanasia. Only one of the questions (euthanasia) elicits a majority in favor of permitting the practice; the second closest (incurable) falls just short of majority support. It is interesting to note that what varies across these two conditions is not the root cause of suicide—in both cases it is an incurable disease—but in the action. In the latter case, it is the person with the disease who ends his or her own life, while in the former, it is the patient's physician who is the responsible actor. (Note also that the first question is phrased in the form of taking action, rather than the form of consciously failing to act, such as honoring a do-not-resuscitate order). For each of the last three conditions, the vast majority of respondents consider bankruptcy, shame, and being tired of living to be insufficient justifications.

There are two broad value sets that may affect attitudes about euthanasia and suicide. The first, stemming from the research on support for suicide among the ill, is the importance of religion and religious values. Those people who believe in an afterlife and believe that consciously taking their own life would preclude oneself from heaven (or its equivalent in non-Christian religions), are less likely to consider suicide to be acceptable—*even if terminally ill themselves.* Consequently, we expect that these attitudes should generalize to survey respondents who are not in such a dire situation.

We measure the respondent's religion and religiosity in a variety of ways. First, we include the measure developed in the previous section on abortion for the vision of a retributive God ("fear of God"). Second, because of the dominant perspective among fundamentalists, of not only the existence of heaven but also of a retributive God who would punish those who commit suicide, we include a dummy variable for Fundamentalists. And last, we measure the intensity of religiosity by two other measures: frequency of church attendance and professed religious intensity.

Alternatively, we will consider measuring religiosity in terms of an expressed value about the nature of the world, which we refer to in the subsequent discussion as a "good world" expectation. Table 5.4 includes a summary of the confirmatory factor results for those predispositions we consider relevant to attitudes toward suicide. The top set of questions and corresponding loadings correspond to those that measure the "good world" expectation. The scale intends to capture a belief that life on earth is fundamentally good. The strongest loadings are for those indicators that either describe the goodness of the world, or disagree with statements that humans are "perverse and corrupt" or "vain and foolish." We expect that the more that individuals maintain a "good world" expectation, the less likely they are to approve of suicide and euthanasia.

The second class of explanations for attitudes regarding suicide comes more directly from the work of Durkheim, in the form of normlessness, or anomie. The more that individuals believe that the world is unfair, that there is a lack of natural order to things, or that one has little control over one's destiny, the higher the level of overall normlessness. We measure these with four indicators, which appear in the second section of table 5.4. Note here that the three strongest loadings—for the lot of the average man (which fixes the scale), for the interest that public officials take in ordinary people, and for whether it is fair to bring a child into the world—share a high degree of common variance, even though they appear to be about very different aspects of normlessness. The last item, while statistically significant and of correct sign, is less clearly aligned with the other three.

How are these predispositions distributed among the public? The distribution of "good world" and normlessness appears in figure 5.10.[2] The left histogram demonstrates the distribution of "good world" beliefs. Note that the vast majority of the public comes very high on this scale, with relatively few pessimists. In sharp contrast, we see in the right histogram that the distribution of normlessness is much more widely dispersed. Some individuals are very low on the scale, while others are quite high, and many others fall somewhere between the extremes.

TABLE 5.4
Measurement Model of Predispositions Pertinent to Suicide,
1985 General Social Survey

Question	Loading
Good World	
There is much goodness in the world, which hints at God's greatness.	1.00
The good person must avoid contamination by the corruption of the world.	−0.41 (0.03)
God reveals Himself in and through the world.	0.27 (0.03)
Human nature is fundamentally perverse and corrupt.	−0.76 (0.03)
It is dangerous for a human to be too concerned about worldly things like art and music.	−0.61 (0.03)
Harmony and cooperation prevail in the world.	0.44 (0.03)
Most human activity is vain and foolish.	−0.71 (0.03)
Normlessness	
In spite of what some people say, the lot (situation/condition) of the average man is getting worse, not better.	1.00
It's hardly fair to bring a child into the world with the way things look for the future.	0.62 (0.03)
Most public officials (people in public office) are not really interested in the problems of the average man.	0.44 (0.03)
Some people say that people get ahead by their own hard work; others say that lucky breaks or help from other people are more important.	−0.14 (0.03)

Note: Cell entries are unstandardized factor loadings; standard errors are in parentheses.

Is there evidence in the joint distribution of these scales that people experience a high degree of coincidence of these values? Figure 5.11 shows the scatterplot matrix of the scores on the values. Not too surprisingly, "good world" and normlessness tend to be negatively correlated, with the general slope of the scatterplot running along the opposite diagonal (upper right and lower left graphs). There are, however, quite a few individuals who express both a high degree of normlessness and a belief in a "good world," in that there are significant numbers who fall along the 45-degree line. Not surprisingly, the two

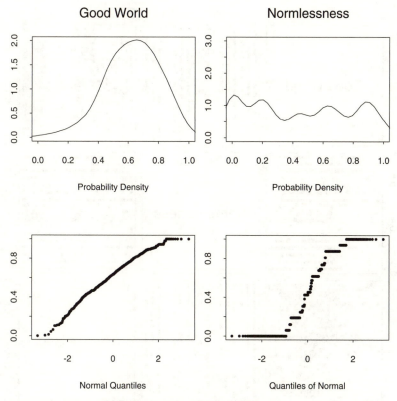

FIGURE 5.10. Distribution of "good world" and normlessness, 1985
General Social Survey

religious values are reasonably correlated. Respondents who tend to hold a retributive vision of God are also likely to believe that God created a fundamentally good world. The most widely dispersed set of predispositions are those for "fear of God" and normlessness, with respondents scattered throughout most of the full range of both scales. In other words, there are a considerable number of people who believe not only that God will act retributively for their sins, but also that the world has lost its fundamental order. This scenario should make it ripe for the possibility of internalized conflict.

Results of the Models of Euthanasia and Suicide

Our selection of measures for the choice model, then, include the items for religion and religiosity, and each of the three predisposition sets ("good world,"

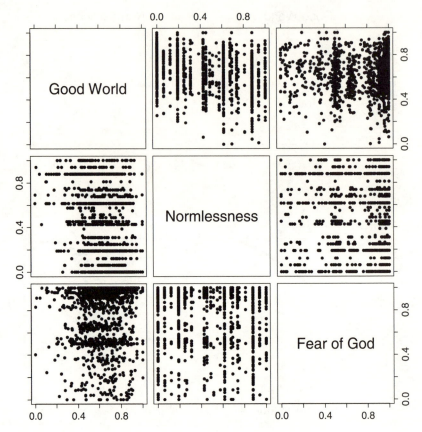

FIGURE 5.11. Scatterplot matrix of "good world," normlessness and fear of God, 1985 General Social Survey

normlessness, and fear of God). In the variance model, we include the coincidence measure (one minus the absolute value of the difference of each pair of predispositions), and education as our proxy for chronic informedness. The computation of the effects of these variables upon support for suicide appears in table 5.5.

The first point of note is that religiosity consistently undermines support for euthanasia or for personal justifications for suicide. The effects of religion (especially as measured by church attendance) are consistently negative, and the effect of church attendance is even more pronounced in the two settings where taking one's life is, on the margin, acceptable to significant numbers of respondents. Nearly two-thirds of the sample concurred that euthanasia was acceptable. From the marginal effects, we would conclude that a regular

TABLE 5.5
Effects of Religious Attitudes on Euthanasia and Suicide, 1985 General Social Survey

Coefficient	Euthanasia	Incurable	Bankrupt	Dishonored	Tired of Life
Fundamentalist	−.05	−.28**	−.07	−.03	−.01
Attend church	−.23**	−.76**	−.02**	−.01**	−.04**
Religious intensity	−.05	−.29**	.03	−.02	.04
Good world	.01	.12	.01	.06**	−.04
Normlessness	−.02	.18**	.04	.04**	.04**
Fear of God	−.03	−.03	−.02**	−.06**	−.03**

Note: Cell entries are first derivative of probability link function evaluated at the mean. $N = 1161$, ** indicates estimates significant at $p < .05$.

churchgoer would be substantially less likely—by 23 percent—to permit euthanasia. This effect is even more pronounced when we look at the first of the suicide settings (suicide for an incurable disease). Churchgoing respondents are almost certain to oppose suicide under these circumstances. Similar results obtain for those who are fundamentalist and religiously intense.

The effects of church attendance, fundamentalism, and religious intensity decline considerably once we move to the remaining three suicide conditions. Of course, one reason for the much smaller effects is that the sample is so skewed in their opinions about the legitimacy of suicide under bankruptcy, dishonor, or being tired of life; with the mean shifted so far to one side of the scale, effects will be attenuated.

The effects of the religious values are of interest as well. In general, positive beliefs about the state of the world have only a weak correspondence to attitudes about the legitimacy of suicide or euthanasia. It is only in the dishonor condition that the effect of the "good world" view is statistically significant, and here in a positive direction. A retributive view of God consistently depresses support for the legitimacy of suicide, and the effects are statistically significant for the three extreme conditions. Further, relative to the other measures in these extremely skewed conditions, the effect of this view of God is on par with, or greater than, the effect of any other value set.

Durkheim would perhaps be satisfied with the importance of anomie as an explanation for the legitimacy of suicide. The effect is strongest when the condition is suicide because of an incurable disease. The effect is also consistently in a positive direction for all four of the suicide conditions, but in a negative direction for the sole euthanasia condition.

In brief, then, religious values and normlessness significantly affect attitudes about the legitimacy of euthanasia and suicide. We hope that these results may help to turn scholarship toward the study of what has, to our knowledge, been a thoroughly understudied aspect of public opinion on what is becoming an important matter of public policy in America.

What do we expect for the prospects for internalized conflict over these questions? Our requirements were that the choices be irreconcilable, that the terms of the debate be accessible and familiar to most respondents, and that the predispositions lead in contrary dimensions. Similar to the debate over abortion, one should expect internalized conflict to be most likely when respondents cannot rely upon external conditions to resolve the choice. Like the "mother's health" condition, one would probably not expect a high degree of internalized conflict under the euthanasia condition, or perhaps under the condition of an incurable disease: in both cases, death is inevitable, and the effect of life is to prolong a highly undesirable condition. One would be more likely to find internalized conflict—ambivalence—in the three suicide settings that do not attempt external justification.

These conjectures are exactly what we find. Figures 5.12 and 5.13 display the response variance as a function of coincident predispositions and education. The horizontal axes in the coincident predispositions graphs range from 0 (perpendicular predispositions) through 1 (parallel predispositions), whereas it ranges from 0 (least educated) through 1 (most educated) in the education graph. In each graph the vertical axes are the estimated response variance.

Two of the predispositional sets had virtually no effect on response variance (figure 5.12). Respondents who maintained that God created a good world *and* were anomic increased slightly in their response variance in the most extreme suicide condition, but were virtually flat for the other conditions. The interaction between the two conceptions of God ("good world" and fear of God) had no discernible or consistent effect upon response variance.

The pattern is quite distinct for the effects of the interaction of a fear of God and normlessness, and for education (our proxy for informedness). Here, the more that one simultaneously held a fear of God and believed in an anomic world, the more internalized conflict we see, but only under the suicide conditions. The effect of additional years of education also increases response variance under the three most extreme suicide conditions.

By the criteria we set out in the previous chapter, three of these settings demonstrate ambivalence: suicide due to bankruptcy, shame, and being tired of life. One condition is clearly not one of internalized conflict: euthanasia because of an incurable disease. But one condition is ambiguous, that for suicide because of an incurable disease: the values appear to conflict (in the upper part of figure 5.13), but education appears to reduce variance (in the lower part of the same figure).

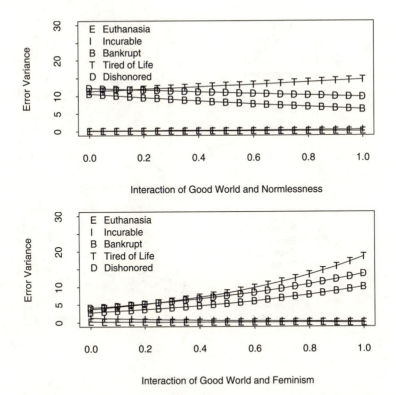

FIGURE 5.12. Response variance as a function of coincident predispositions

DISCUSSION

This chapter makes a number of important contributions to the general argument of the book. First, we demonstrate that in certain domains of public discourse, mass choices about the appropriateness of specific policies depend on strongly held principles and values. The strength of religious values among wide swathes of the American public has been noted time and again by researchers of public opinion. Americans are an unusually religious people, quite likely to identify themselves with organized religions, to report active attendance and participation in religious institutions, and to cherish specific aspects of religion. We demonstrate that these religious values play a very important role in attitudes toward two of the more controversial aspects of contemporary political life: abortion and assisted suicide.

But religious beliefs are not the only values that matter in these debates. At the same time that religion matters, aspects of secular life matter, too. In the debate over abortion, the importance of feminism can hardly be minimized,

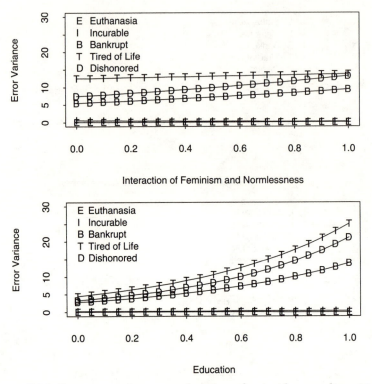

FIGURE 5.13. Response variance as a function of coincident predispositions and education

and in the specific aspects of choice about abortion under those very settings most strenuously argued by pro-choice interests, feminism matters most. In our analysis of attitudes about euthanasia and suicide, we find that Durkheim was right: normlessness—the sense that the society has lost its fundamental order—significantly increases a respondent's willingness to forgive suicide.

We also show that, under very specific conditions, the interplay between these religious and secular values can have a pronounced effect upon the variability of survey response. Those respondents who are most torn between the conflict of religious and secular values are those who are most likely to be internally conflicted, or in our nomenclature, *ambivalent*, about abortion.

Moreover, we show that not all choices about such fundamentally incommensurable alternatives as life and death lead to such internalized conflict. When there is a countervailing concern—the health of the mother, the viability of the fetus, the long-term prospects for the ill—internalized conflict is not the best description. Instead, the condition we call *uncertainty* is much more apt.

What this means is that contrary to the vast majority of scholarship contending an ambivalent public, the public is probably not ambivalent in the sense that we use the term. As long as we require "ambivalence" to represent the "simultaneous existence of conflicting emotions," then ambivalence is rare, even under these settings where all the preconditions for internalized conflict appear to be present.

That the ambivalent state of mind is rare, though, should not be interpreted as a positive statement about American public opinion, however. First, by our conceptualization, political debates about incommensurable choices, involving incommensurable values and predispositions, will be deeply divisive and difficult to resolve. To the extent that there are ambivalent issues in U.S. politics, there will be political conflict. Moreover, as we examine in chapter 8, ambivalence makes political representation difficult, if not impossible, as internalized conflict in the minds of Americans spills over into the rhetoric of political elites and the mass media. Third, the other two states of public opinion that we discuss in the next two chapters, uncertainty and equivocation, each involve other dilemmas for political life in the United States.

So in the next chapter, we continue this theme by turning to the question of American attitudes toward race and racial policy, an area that is, by many counts, the core of the "American dilemma." There we will show that uncertainty, not ambivalence, is critical to understanding public opinion about race and racial policy.

Uncertainty and Racial Attitudes

THE COMPLEX ISSUES surrounding racial and ethnic differences in American society have sparked many political controversies. During the debates about the framing of the U.S. Constitution, discussions about whether slavery should (or could) be addressed within the Constitution itself were long, involved, and difficult. Less than a century after the founding of the American republic, the nation was torn apart by a violent civil war, with slavery and the role of blacks in society central reasons for the bloody fighting. In the early twentieth century, with black Americans still lacking full political and civil rights, other racial and ethnic groups were also systematically discriminated against, especially Asian immigrants on the West Coast. By the 1950s and early 1960s, issues of racial and ethnic discrimination boiled over, resulting in large-scale changes in public policies designed to redress these centuries of inequality and discrimination in American society. With the passage of the Voting Rights Act, and with the initiation of many federal, state, and local affirmative action programs, many policies were established to address racial and ethnic discrimination.

But these many, diverse programs came under criticism and attack by the mid-1990s. The efforts to apply the Voting Rights Act in redistricting plans with the creation of majority-minority districts were criticized from the political right and left, and were attacked in legal cases, some of which ended up in the U.S. Supreme Court. In the important *Shaw v. Reno* decision, the Court held that race could not be used as a criteria in the drawing of district lines. Similarly, affirmative action programs were attacked in state capitals across the nation; and in the wake of the passage of California's Proposition 209 (which ended affirmative action programs in California), many other states weakened or eliminated their own affirmative action programs.

In the last four decades, there has naturally been an enormous amount of academic research trying to answer one central question: Why are white Americans opposed to the development and implementation of public policies designed to end centuries of racial inequality and discrimination? In many ways, the classic statement of this problem comes from Gunnar Myrdal's *An American Dilemma*. Myrdal (1944) laid out a central theme for research on the beliefs of white Americans about racial politics:

> The "American Dilemma" . . . is the ever-raging conflict between, on the one hand, the valuations preserved on the general plane which we shall call the "American Creed," where the American thinks, talks, and acts under the influence of high

national and Christian precepts, and, on the other hand, the valuations on specific planes of individual and group living, where personal and local interests; economic, social, and sexual jealousies; considerations of community prestige and conformity; group prejudice against particular persons or types of people; and all sorts of miscellaneous wants, impulses, and habits dominate his outlook. (lxxix).

Thus, the dilemma of race in American politics is argued to arise from a conflict in the minds of white Americans between traditional American values like equality and individualism, and principles of self-interest and simple prejudice.

That opinions on racial issues are so fundamentally conflictual for most Americans has led many to argue that racial opinions are gut-level issues: firmly held, consistent, and difficult to change (Carmines and Stimson 1980; Kinder and Rhodebeck 1982; Nie, Verba, and Petrocik 1979; Sniderman and Hagen 1985). Racial issues like affirmative action, desegregation, and enforced busing are seen by some scholars as being so deeply ingrained in the conflict between traditional American values and self-interest or prejudice, and in the rhetoric of politicians and political elites, they have become "easy issues" (Carmines and Stimson 1980). Thus, American opinion about racial issues has long been seen as one area of public policy about which Americans have real and coherent attitudes (Kinder and Sanders 1996).

It is clear, though, that this is too stark a portrait of racial issues in American society. Page and Shapiro (1992), in their study of the dynamics of opinions about racial issues since the late 1940s, found that

> [t]he expressed attitudes of white Americans toward black Americans have undergone a great transformation over the last forty or fifty years, a change greater than on any other issue. On a wide range of policies related to public accommodations, employment, schools, neighborhoods and housing, and intermarriage, whites moved from advocating total separation and an inferior status for blacks to favoring legal equality and substantial desegregation. (68)

In their sweeping study of the contemporary politics of race in American society, Sniderman and Piazza (1993) also found strong evidence demonstrating the malleability of opinions about racial issues: "It has long been assumed that whites can be dislodged from the positions they have taken on many issues of race by calling their attention to countervailing considerations" (178).

The implication of both the Page and Shapiro and the Sniderman and Piazza findings is that public opinion about racial issues is sensitive to the information that citizens have about this complex of social issues. Page and Shapiro present compelling evidence to explain the changes in public opinion about race in the last few decades: "the fundamental source of change was demographic, the northward migration which led to blacks' achievements in northern urban environments and whites' recognition of those achievements" (80). The innovative work by Sniderman and Piazza is perfectly consistent with this historical argument, since they find that many white Americans will change their stated opinion about many different types of racial policy once they are given new information.

However, finding that opinions about racial issues can be changed by new information does not mean that white Americans are well informed about the reality of racial relations in American society. David Shipler (1977), who conducted five years of extensive qualitative studies of the opinions of white and black Americans about themselves and each other, noted early in his recent book that

> most whites rarely have to give race much thought. They do not begin childhood with advice from parents about how to cope with racial bias or how to discern the racial overtones in a comment or a manner. They do not have to search for themselves in history books or literature courses. In most parts of America, their color does not make them feel alone in a crowd; they are not looked to as representatives of their people. And because they almost never have to wonder whether they are rejected—or accepted—because of their genuine level of ability or the color of their skin. As a result, few whites I interviewed had considered the questions I put to them. Many struggled to be introspective, but most found that I was taking them into uncharted territory, full of dangers that they quickly surrounded with layers of defensiveness. (10–11)

This lack of information about race relations by white Americans has been echoed in quantitative analyses as well (Nadeau, Niemi, and Levine 1993).

On the other hand, the malleability of opinion about racial issues might stem not from new information but from ambivalence produced by core value conflict. Rokeach (1973) identified a large number of respondents who were torn between two terminal values—freedom and equality—over diverse policy choices, including race. Katz and Hass (1988) attribute whites' conflict over racial policy to two competing value orientations, a Protestant ethic and a humanitarian-egalitarian one.

Can competing core beliefs produce internalized conflict about racial policies? Many scholars working on the issue of racial opinions believe the answer to be yes. McConahay (1986) argued that the difference between respondents' reactivity to "old-fashioned" racism scales (racial superiority) and those measuring "modern" racism denotes a zone of ambivalence about race. Katz and Hass (1988) and Katz, Wackenhut, and Hass (1986) argue that white subjects experience psychological tension and discomfort in response to the presence of cues activating conflicted racial attitudes. Gaertner and Dovidio (1986) demonstrate that a residual core of racism exists in their subjects, even among those professing a generalized support for racial policy.

The question of what determines variability in racial opinions is quite important in the context of our research in this book. The differences between uncertainty and ambivalence over policy choices point to two criteria we can use to differentiate the concepts in our empirical studies. Uncertainty reduces with additional information, while ambivalence does not; hence, if we can demonstrate that better-informed respondents have less variance in their responses, it indicates uncertainty. Ambivalence stems from a choice between incommensurables, and the literature points to the role of competing values; hence, if we can demonstrate that as competing values become increasingly important to an individual, that individual's response set becomes more variable, which indicates ambivalence. These criteria establish well-defined conditions to adjudicate between ambivalence and uncertainty.

The rest of this chapter takes up this very question: Are the beliefs of white Americans about racial issues better characterized as being ambivalent or uncertain? Additionally, we also delimit the exact role core beliefs play in the determination of an individual's beliefs about racial issues. In the end, we find strong evidence demonstrating that two core beliefs, modern racism and egalitarianism, do strongly structure opinions about affirmative action and policies designed to alleviate racial inequality. When we turn to opinions about the status of blacks in American society, however, we find they are strongly influenced by modern racism and antiblack affect. This shows the importance of modern racist beliefs across different racial issues, as well as the fact that as we change issue domains, some of the core beliefs that determine opinions on specific issues shift with the issues. But the opinions of Americans about these issues are not set in stone. The variability we do see in opinions about racial issues is shown to be a function of uncertainty, not ambivalence.

CORE BELIEFS AND RACIAL ISSUES

Even a quick read through the academic research on racial attitudes demonstrates that researchers collide over the basic forces that drive racial attitudes. One group (Kinder 1986; Kinder and Sears 1981; McConahay 1986) contends that "symbolic" racism, a combination of antiblack affect with traditional American values, drives white resistance to racial policy. By this argument, whites who oppose such policies as affirmative action or busing on the grounds that blacks are getting more than they deserve are motivated by a form of racism that has replaced overt expressions of racial superiority. Sniderman and his colleagues (Sniderman and Hagen 1985; Sniderman and Piazza 1993; Sniderman and Tetlock 1986) argue that symbolic racism fails because it confuses the policy choice with the attitude, while at the same time ignoring the continuing presence of simple antiblack affect as a source of white opposition to racial policy. We take the level of conflict about the sources and meaning of white opposition to racial programs as one piece of evidence that individual attitudes may be in conflict.

Our point is not to settle, or even to breach, the argument over the existence of symbolic racism as a distinct source of racial attitudes. We want, specifically, to assess how levels of support for these values account for both the policy choices and the variability of those choices. In our research we develop six scales for pertinent values based on the 1991 Race and Politics Survey: symbolic racism, antiblack stereotyping, authoritarianism, anti-Semitism, egalitarianism, and individualism. The measurement of these core values of racial beliefs are discussed in this section.

The Race and Politics Survey is a data set collected by the Survey Research Center of the University of California, Berkeley.[1] The unique aspect of the survey was the profusion of split questionnaires, randomly assigned to respondents, made possible by a computer-aided telephone interview approach. Each of the four dependent variables we consider altered important components of the question. For purposes of scale construction, however, we were stymied by the split samples and employed only those questions that were asked of all respondents.

We use confirmatory factor analysis to develop six scales, each measuring one of the concepts that assume varying degrees of prominence in scholarly explanations for variation in racial attitudes. The overall fit for our confirmatory factor model is adequate with a goodness-of-fit index of .86. The first scale is a measure of modern racism. According to the various authors (e.g., Kinder 1986; Kinder and Sears 1990; Kinder and Sears 1981; McConahay 1986) symbolic, or modern, racism denotes a conjunction of antiblack affect with traditional American values, taking form in the belief that blacks are receiving more attention from government and advantages from the private sector than they deserve.[2]

We located three questions that tap into the idea of modern racism. One of these questions is a simple 3-point Likert scale asking respondents to rate (1) the amount of attention that government has been paying to minorities, (2) how angry they feel about giving "blacks and other minorities special advantages in jobs and schools," and (3) how they feel about "spokesmen for minorities who are always complaining that blacks are being discriminated against."[3]

This scale probably will not satisfy either group of partisans in the debate over the relevance of modern racism. As we noted already in chapter 2, one of Sniderman and Tetlock's chief objections to the modern racism concept is that the scales often treat policy choices as independent variables in the same models that purport to explain policy choices as dependent variables:

> [I]t is gratuitous to equate opposition to affirmative action with racial prejudice—gratuitous because it would otherwise be possible to examine the actual relation between the two, and thus establish as a matter of fact, and not of definition, how and to what degree the two are connected. Quite simply, defining opposition to affirmative action as racism precludes falsification of the prediction that the two

are indeed related, at the cost of making the relation between them a tautology. (1986, 135)

In order to be sensitive to these objections, in our earlier work we replicated all of our models excluding the modern racism scale, and a further replication where we only include the last item ("complaining") and found that our measure worked the best in our analyses (Alvarez and Brehm 1997). But in defense of the measure, we note that the specific policy referents in the measures are rather oblique. The "attention" variable asks the respondent to evaluate the amount of government attention to the problems of minorities, hardly on the same level of specificity as the dependent variables we discuss later in this chapter. The latter two questions ask about a diffuse anger provoked by a policy ("special advantages") or "complaining" spokesmen.

The weakness in these indicators as seen from the advocates of the symbolic racism concept is the absence of specific referents to traditional American values. If symbolic racism is the conjunction of antiblack affect and traditional American values, then these questions are decidedly weak as far as their emphasis on unearned advantages. The language here emphasizes "special advantages," which orbits somewhere near the meaning of unearned advantages.

In place of the modern racism scale, Sniderman and Piazza (1993) argue for separate consideration of alternative values: authoritarianism, anti-Semitism, individualism, and antiblack stereotyping. In a series of impressive bivariate analyses, Sniderman and Piazza demonstrate that authoritarianism is more strongly correlated with opposition to racial policy than measures of individualism (which they take to be the core of the modern racism argument).

The authoritarianism scale we use draws upon six indicators, which correspond to three aspects of the classic F scale of authoritarianism (Adorno et al. 1950, 228–41)—conventionalism, authoritarian submission, and authoritarian aggression—albeit to varying degrees of coherence. *Conventionalism* referred to "rigid adherence to conventional, middle-class values" and is measured here with "following God's will" and "improving standards of politeness in everyday behavior." *Authoritarian submission* meant a "submissive, uncritical attitude toward idealized moral authorities of the in-group" and is measured here with "preserving the traditional ideas of right and wrong." *Authoritarian aggression* referred to a "tendency to be on the lookout for, and to condemn, reject, and punish people who violate conventional values" and is measured by "respect for authority," "strengthening law and order," and "respect for American power."[4] All six of the loadings for the indicators are strong, but "preserving the traditional ideas of right and wrong" and "respect for authority" are the strongest pair.

Our scale for individualism is measured by three items: the importance of self-reliance, emphasizing individual achievement, and a Likert scale assessing anger at government interference.[5] This is admittedly a weak scale (with the lowest reliability), and any effect that it has in our subsequent analysis is likely to be attenuated due to the inferior level of measurement.

The next scale that we employ in our analysis measures anti-Semitism. Sniderman and Piazza (1993) find modest (approximately .3) correlations between assessments of negative attributes of blacks and agreement with elements of an anti-Semitic scale. In several analyses in their book, Sniderman and Piazza utilize anti-Semitism as a measure of prejudice because of "[their] belief that the heart of prejudice is captured by the notion of ethnocentrism" (107). We use five Likert scale questions (4-point scales that do not include the hedging response of "neither agree nor disagree"). At face value, one of the five questions does not seem to be anti-Semitic, as it asks respondents whether they believe that "most Jews are ambitious and work hard to succeed." We have reasons for including this question in our anti-Semitism measure. First, the reader should recall that the purpose of the scale is to measure a religious stereotype in order to denote prejudice and ethnocentrism. The significant part of the apparently anomalous question is "most Jews" in light of construction of a stereotype. Our second answer is data-driven: when we delete this question from the scale, the remaining loadings plunge by nearly 25 percent.[6]

Fourth, we construct a scale for egalitarianism. The nominal conflict between egalitarianism and individualism appears prominently in the literature on attitudes toward racial policy. Katz and Hass (1988) find in experimental work that priming subjects to consider one value or the other significantly increased scores on corresponding attitudes, but not on attitudes corresponding to the non-primed value. In other words, the two scales operate independently, and each has the potential to significantly affect preferences for racial policy. Lipset and Schneider (1978), in a review of a range of survey data, see the dynamic of attitudes toward racial policy as "between two values that are at the core of the American creed—individualism and egalitarianism" (43).

As with our scale for individualism, the scale for egalitarianism is somewhat weak. While the first variable is fixed at 1 (more money being spent to reduce unemployment), the next variable loads at only 0.33. The non–Likert scale question loads at half that (−.13). Again, we expect that the effects of the egalitarianism scale in the estimation will be attenuated.

Finally, we develop a measure of antiblack stereotyping. The scale performs adequately. All of the negative attributes (aggressive, lazy, boastful, irresponsible, complaining) have positive, large, and statistically significant coefficients.[7]

In figure 6.1, we present kernel density plots and quantile-quantile plots showing the distributions of beliefs of each measure of core values for white Americans in 1991. Figure 6.1 provides the distributions for anti-Semitism, authoritarianism, individualism, modern racism, antiblack affect, and egalitarianism. The top two rows show the distributions of our measures for anti-Semitism, authoritarianism, and individualism. Of these three predisposition measures, anti-Semitism has a distribution that appears very similar to a nor-

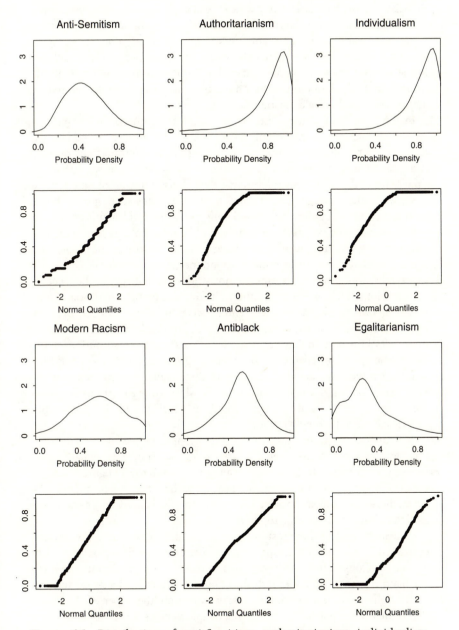

FIGURE 6.1. Distribution of anti-Semitism, authoritarianism, individualism, modern racism, antiblack affect, and egalitarianism

mal distribution, with a relatively wide spread across the range of the scale and a central tendency near the middle of the scale. This implies that while some white Americans have highly anti-Semitic beliefs, others do not, and most white Americans are somewhere in between. The other two core values shown in the top two rows of this figure have highly skewed distributions, with the overwhelming bulk of most white Americans being deeply committed to both authoritarian and individualistic values.

In the lower half of the figure we have the distributions for our modern racism, antiblack, and egalitarianism core values. Our measure of modern racism has a very diffuse distribution, with roughly equal proportions of white Americans being spread from the middle of the scale all the way up to the upper end of the scale. This implies that the beliefs of this set of Americans in 1991 was rather divergent, with many white Americans scoring quite highly on this measure of modern racism—showing that they hold significantly racist beliefs—while many others scored in the middle ranges of this scale. Likewise, our antiblack measure also has a relatively diffuse distribution, though it is somewhat more tightly concentrated around the center of the scale. This argues that while most white Americans are not stridently antiblack in their beliefs, they are not stridently problack either. The overwhelming proportion of individuals in our sample are somewhere in between these opposing sets of beliefs about blacks. Last, we show the distribution of the egalitarianism scale in the lower left of the bottom panel of figure 6.1. Like the other distributions in this figure, the spread of egalitarian beliefs among white Americans is relatively diffuse. But there is a decided skewness of these beliefs toward the lower end of this scale—toward non-egalitarian beliefs. Most white Americans fall below the midpoint of our scale for egalitarianism, which means that most white Americans are not strongly egalitarian.

In figure 6.2 we present a matrix of graphs that show the bivariate distributions for every pair of core belief measures we use. This figure is easily read: for example, the first (vertical) column and (horizontal) row of figure 6.2 depict the distribution of our anti-Semitism measure with authoritarianism, individualism, modern racism, antiblack affect, and egalitarianism, reading either down the left column or across the top row.

Visually, it is clear that most of these core belief measures are not strongly correlated. Evidence of a strong positive correlation in figure 6.2 would be clustering of observations in a particular element of this graph from the lower left-hand corner to the upper right-hand corner; evidence of a strong negative correlation would be clustering of observations from the upper left-hand corner to the lower right-hand corner. In a couple of cases we see some evidence of positive correlations between pairs of core value measures. For example, antiblack and anti-Semitic affect have a positive correlation (measured at .41); individualism and authoritarianism have a positive correlation (measured at .37); and modern racism and antiblack affect also have a modest positive corre-

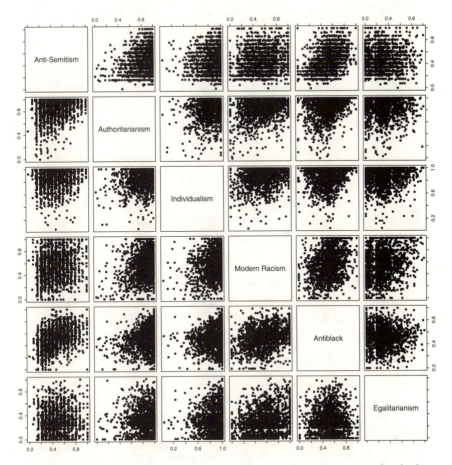

FIGURE 6.2. Scatterplot matrix of anti-Semitism, authoritarianism, individualism, modern racism, antiblack affect, and egalitarianism

lation (measured at .30). The remaining bivariate distributions all have correlations less than .30, as is evident in this figure. Thus, the evidence we have presented here makes us confident that we have developed six reliable measures for these important predispositions.

CORE BELIEFS AND RACIAL POLITICS

The six core belief scales allow us to evaluate the relative weight of the competing explanations for opposition to racial policy, in a mode that is similar to our analyses of policy choices in the other chapters of this book. But again we argue that understanding the choice is only one of the interesting aspects of the problem, and that understanding the *variability* in that choice, for each respondent, also matters. To this end, we employ our heteroskedastic probit technique to simultaneously model the probability that a respondent might choose a particular racial policy alternative and the amount of variance associated with that policy choice for the respondent.

Full details of our model specifications, the variable codings, and the heteroskedastic probit technique are in an appendix on our website at www.pupress. princeton.edu/alvarez. The important aspects of the analysis for our argument in this chapter are the different components of racial politics we examine as dependent variables; the core beliefs that are the important determinants of the individual's responses to each racial policy question; and whether ambivalence driven by conflict between core beliefs, or uncertainty driven by a lack of information, determines the underlying variability in each individual's policy responses. We discuss each briefly in turn.

First, we greatly expand on our earlier work on this general topic by examining a much broader array of racial policy choices (Alvarez and Brehm 1997): the same binary racial policy choices we analyzed in our previous work; ordinal racial policy choices; and ordinal opinion questions about blacks in American society. The dependent variables in our analysis are the following:

1. Racial policy choices (binary response):
   - Contracts: set-asides in federal contracts for black contractors
   - Taxes: tax increases for education of minorities
   - Housing: open housing laws
   - Universities: preferences for qualified blacks in university admissions
   - Job quotas: laws to require quotas for blacks in private-sector jobs
   - Jobs: federal government policies to help blacks get jobs
2. Racial policy choices (ordinal response):
   - Discrimination: laws protecting minorities from employment discrimination
   - Housing: blacks buying homes in white suburbs
   - White suburbs: programs to encourage blacks to buy homes in white suburbs
   - Interference: federal government interferes in attempts to fight racism
   - Overboard: federal government goes overboard to fight racism
3. Opinions about blacks (ordinal response):
   - Students: Do black children do as well in school as white children?
   - Knives: Are poor black children more likely to carry knives and weapons to school?
   - Advantage: Do blacks take advantage of opportunities to improve their economic position?
   - Employers: Are employers more likely to choose a black over an equally qualified white candidate?

- Fair trial: Does a white have a better chance at a fair trial than a black?
- Racist: Are whites more likely to be racist than blacks?

The one important complication to note as regards the use of these different dependent variables is that all the racial policy questions were part of randomized question experiments, which posed slightly different wording of questions to different respondents (Sniderman and Piazza 1993). We deal with this heterogeneity in a very simple way: we include in the choice function of each racial policy choice model a series of independent variables that control for the question wording each respondent received.[8] The second complication is that the questions concerning the opinions about blacks were asked of participants in a mail-back questionnaire; 53.9 percent of the respondents to the original telephone survey sent back their mail questionnaire, limiting our effective sample size for analyzing those questions to just under 1,200.[9] Finally, we restrict our analysis to only white respondents who answered these questions.

Second, the important explanatory variables for all of these different policy choices and opinions about racial politics are the six different core beliefs we discussed in the previous section: modern racism, individualism, antiblack stereotyping, authoritarianism, anti-Semitism, and egalitarianism. Each is a scale constructed on the basis of confirmatory factor analysis of various survey items, and each has been recoded to range from 0 to 1, where 1 indicates the maximum observed level of the scale. Our prior beliefs about the signs on each of the scales is that they should all be negative, with the exception of egalitarianism, higher levels of modern racism, individualism, antiblack stereotyping, authoritarianism, and anti-Semitism, and lower levels of egalitarianism, should all be associated with lesser support for racial policy. We additionally include the respondent's self-placement on a liberal-conservative scale and their own personal financial status as control variables in the choice model.[10]

Third, specification of the variance function reflects our desire to test two competing explanations for differences among Americans in the variation of their racial policy beliefs. As we argued above, these variations may reflect fundamental uncertainty about the policy choice under discussion. In other words, people may simply lack information about the policy choices and what they might imply, and that uncertainty will be reflected in the variance function of the heteroskedastic probit model (Alvarez 1997; Alvarez and Franklin 1994; Franklin 1991).

To control for the effect of uncertainty, we include in the specification of the variance function a variable measuring chronic information—a simple political information measure based on the earlier measures advocated by Zaller (1992)—using an additive scale that measures whether the respondent correctly knew the number of Supreme Court members and the maximum number of presidential terms. This variable is coded to range from 0 to 1, where 1 indicates correct answers to both factual political information questions. We expect the estimated coefficient to be negative, which implies that with increased political information the amount of variance in policy choices diminishes.

The 1991 survey data also includes three race-related factual items: the percentage of poor who are black, the percentage arrested who are black, and the percentage of black males who are unemployed. We used responses to these three questions to develop a domain-specific racial information measure. Although the mechanics of the difference are far from clear, chronic information measures regularly outperform domain-specific information measures (Zaller 1992).

The rival explanation for variability in attitudes toward racial policy is ambivalence induced by core beliefs underlying racial attitudes. We set two criteria in order to identify ambivalence. The first is that additional information should not reduce—and may in fact heighten—the response variability. The second criteria is that response variability should increase as core beliefs and values conflict. Prior research instructs us to attend to one particular source of conflict, between egalitarianism and individualism. To the extent that racial policies achieve egalitarianism by rejecting individualism, we should expect to see greater response variability among individuals who prize both egalitarianism and individualism.

To test for the core belief conflict, we include our coincidence measure, that is, 1 minus the absolute value of the differences of levels of egalitarianism and individualism. When we use this measure in the analyses reported below, we will refer to this as the interactive specification of the error variance.[11] To get a sense for what this measure means, recall that each of these core value scales is coded so that the minimum score is 0 and the maximum is 1. Thus, when we use the absolute value of the differences, when a respondent's level of egalitarianism and individualism are fully coincident (i.e., both are highly prized values), we get a measure of 1. When the respondent's level of egalitarianism differs from the level of individualism, the values are not fully coincident, and we get a value of 0. In this particular case, we expect that if the two values conflict, then this can only occur when the respondent is equally committed to the two values. Hence, if ambivalence is the appropriate characterization, we expect the coefficient on this measure to be positive and significant.

A second way in which these scales might influence variability in racial attitudes is through a form of measurement effect. Sniderman and colleagues (Sniderman and Hagan 1985; Sniderman and Piazza 1993; Sniderman and Tetlock 1986) have argued that researchers should not hold that opposition to racial policy is an indication of racism, since such opposition might be grounded in nonracial objections. This is tantamount to holding that racists are relatively fixed in their opposition to racial policy, but that nonracists might be quite variable in their attitudes. We estimate a second set of heteroskedastic probit models, including the two primary racial core values—modern racism and antiblack stereotyping—in the variance function. Our expectation is that people who are more racist on these scales will have lower variance, so the sign of the direct effects of modern racism and antiblack stereotyping should be negative. We call this the linear error variance specification.[12]

Core Beliefs and Policy Choices

This chapter discusses only the results from the interactive variance model (not the linear model), since it is the specification that allows us to examine whether variability in opinions and choices about racial politics are subject to ambivalence or to uncertainty. In addition, we find that there are few differences in the results across the two different specifications, paralleling and reinforcing the identical results we found in our earlier analysis (Alvarez and Brehm 1997).

We do not report the full heteroskedastic probit results in this chapter because the parameters and their standard errors are difficult to interpret on their own and focus, instead, on the estimated effects of each of the variables in the choice function of the model, shown for each of the variables in the model, controlling for all other effects as specified in each equation. The one thing to keep in mind is that we will be computing the effect of a change in the independent variable on the change in the probability of picking the binary choice (for the binary models) or on the change in the probability of picking the top two policy choices (for the ordinal models).

We begin with the results from the binary policy choices, which we present in table 6.1. The left column gives the independent variable under examination, while the remaining six columns give the particular binary policy choice we are interested in. Each entry gives the marginal effect of the particular independent variable, controlling for all the other effects in the statistical model. The asterisks denote coefficients which are statistically significant at two different standard levels.

The results in table 6.1 provide strong support for the hypothesis that modern racism plays a strong role as one of the primary core beliefs that undergird the responses of white Americans toward these particular policy choices about affirmative action. In each of the six policy choice models, we see that modern racism has a strong, statistically significant, and negative impact on policy response, demonstrating that the more an individual's core values lean toward racist beliefs, the less likely that person is to provide a positive response for any of these policy domains.

The only other measures that have such systematic effects are found in the last three rows of table 6.1: egalitarianism, ideology, and financial status. Clearly, the effects of egalitarianism are quite strong in these results and are statistically significant in each of the policy domains. That the effects are always

TABLE 6.1
Binary Probit Choice Function Effects
Interactive Variance Specification

Independent Variables	Contracts	Taxes	Housing	University sities	Job Quotas	Jobs
Modern racism	−.31**	−.21**	−.18**	−.50**	−.41**	−.70**
Individualism	−.16**	.07*	.03	−.12*	−.07	−.35**
Antiblack	.00	−.02	−.34	.02	−.11*	−.20**
Authoritarianism	.02	.08*	−.12**	.00	−.06	.16*
Anti-Semitism	.16**	−.10**	−.12**	.07	−.06	−.20**
Egalitarianism	−.11**	−.20**	−.08*	−.16**	−.30**	−.50**
Ideology	−.01*	−.01**	−.01*	−.01**	−.00	−.03**
Financial status	−.00	−.02**	−.01*	−.02*	−.02	−.07**

Note: * indicates a $p < .10$ level of statistical significance, one-tailed tests; ** indicates a $p < .05$ level of statistical significance, one-tailed tests.

estimated to be negative indicates that the more egalitarian people's beliefs, the more likely they are to provide a positive response to the particular policy question. The most general core value—ideology—does have a statistically significant, but negative effect, in each of these models, but it is a very small impact on policy choices. We see even weaker results for the financial status variable.

Next, we present the results for the ordinal racial policy choice models in table 6.2. This table is identical to the one just discussed for the binary choice models, except the columns have different policy choice variables. Note that even though we are now looking at different survey questions (questions with different wordings and with different possible responses), and using a different statistical model (ordinal heteroskedastic probit instead of binary heteroskedastic probit), the general pattern of results here is virtually identical to those shown in table 6.1.

That is, we find here that modern racism is again by far the dominant core belief, since it strongly predicts individual responses to these questions about racial policy. In each of the models, we see that modern racism has a negative, statistically significant, and substantial impact on the probability that a respondent would pick one of the top two response categories. Next, we again see that egalitarianism plays a strong role as a core principle structuring responses to questions about racial policy, since here we obtain negative, sizable, and significant effects (except for the housing question) for this core belief. One difference between these results and those presented for the binary choices,

TABLE 6.2
Ordinal Probit Choice Function Effects: Racial Policy
Interactive Variance Specification

Independent Variables	Discrim- ination	Housing	White Suburbs	Interference	Overboard
Modern racism	−.26**	−.10**	−.56**	−.31**	−.72**
Individualism	.10*	.03	.05	−.29**	−.15**
Antiblack	−.10**	−.11**	.08	.08*	−.31**
Authoritarianism	.08*	−.06**	.06	−.06	−.17**
Anti-Semitism	−.14**	−.18**	−.11*	−.13**	−.18**
Egalitarianism	−.22**	−.01	−.43**	−.13**	−.18**
Ideology	−.02**	−.01**	−.02**	−.02**	−.01**
Financial status	−.02**	−.01**	−.05**	−.02**	−.03**

Note: Entries are the predicted marginal effects for the probability that the individual picked the top two categories. * indicates a $p < .10$ level of statistical significance, one-tailed tests; ** indicates a $p < .05$ level of statistical significance, one-tailed tests.

though, is that in table 6.2 the role of anti-Semitism is generally about equal to that of egalitarianism. For each of these core values, the more strongly the individual holds the belief, the more likely the person is to give a positive response to the policy question.

We also see in table 6.2 that both ideology and financial status again play some marginal role in structuring responses to these ordinal questions about racial policy. Whereas in table 6.1 we found that ideological principles played a slightly stronger role than did financial status, here we see that financial status plays an equal if not greater role in determining the responses of white Americans to these different racial policy questions.

The last table presenting the effects of core beliefs in determining the responses of white Americans to questions about race relations and affirmative action are given in table 6.3. Again, this table is organized just like the two proceeding ones, except that we have six different dependent variables lined up in the columns of this table.

Notice that in table 6.3 we have turned from examining individual responses to questions about affirmative action and racial policies, to questions specifically about the behaviors and status of blacks in American society. With such a shift in our focus comes a not-too-surprising shift in the patterns of the results we obtain. We still see that white American responses are strongly structured by one core belief (modern racism), with the one exception being

TABLE 6.3
Ordinal Probit Choice Function Effects: Blacks
Interactive Variance Specification

Independent Variables	Students	Knives	Advantage	Employers	Fair Trial	Racist
Modern racism	−.01	−.21**	−.28**	−.42**	−.36**	−.29**
Individualism	.04	.15**	−.01	−.08	−.15	−.15*
Antiblack	−.19**	−.54**	−.48**	.06	.03	−.14**
Authoritarianism	.31**	.23**	.23**	−.07	−.29**	.11*
Anti-Semitism	.04	−.37**	−.16**	.07	.03	.23**
Egalitarianism	−.22**	.11	−.14	−.08	.01	−.02
Ideology	.02**	−.01*	−.01	−.01	−.02**	−.01
Financial status	.05**	−.02**	−.00	−.01	−.00	−.02

Note: Entries are the predicted marginal effects for the probability that the individual picked the top two categories. * indicates a $p < .10$ level of statistical significance, one-tailed tests; ** indicates a $p < .05$ level of statistical significance, one-tailed tests.

that we do not obtain a statistically significant effect for this belief in the students model. Otherwise, modern racism seems to have the same impact on survey responses as it did in the affirmative action results presented in the previous two tables.

But beyond modern racism we see very mixed evidence for the impact of the various core beliefs. Neither of the core principles that were important for affirmative action beliefs—egalitarianism and anti-Semitism—plays a strong or systematic role in predicting responses about blacks. Nor do we see ideology or financial status having strong and systematic impacts in these results. We do see that simple antiblack affect has a relatively strong, statistically significant, and negative impact in four of the six models, however (students, knives, advantage, and racist).

These results tell a very important and general story about the factors that drive white Americans to give the survey responses they do to questions about affirmative action, racial policy, and blacks. When it comes to questions about affirmative action and policies designed to address racial inequality, white American responses are driven primarily by two core principles, modern racism and egalitarianism. To a much lesser extent, their responses are also determined by ideological beliefs and personal financial status. Thus, on one hand, there is no question that racist beliefs still exist in the minds of white Americans, and that these ideas are important determinants of their responses on items about affirmative action and racial policy. But these racist beliefs are of the modern racism form and not simple antiblack affect; nor are they mitigated by authoritarian, individualistic, or anti-Semitic beliefs. On the other hand, these racist convictions operate within a context where egalitarianism also operates, albeit to a lesser extent than modern racism. So, white Americans provide their responses to these survey questions based on both their egalitarian principles and on their racist ideas.

When we turned to very specific questions, however, about the status of blacks and their role in American society, a slightly different portrait of white American beliefs emerged. Instead of modern racist beliefs coexisting with egalitarian principles, we found that modern racist and simple antiblack affect were the predominant determinants of responses to these other indicators of white American beliefs about the status and role of blacks in society. This shows that when asked to think about the status of blacks, responses are formed directly by antiblack affect and by modern racial beliefs, not by any more fundamental or traditional democratic principles.

Value Conflict, Information, and Variability of Responses

Now we turn to an examination of the factors that influence the underlying variability in the responses of white Americans to questions about affirmative action, racial policies, and the status of blacks. For each set of dependent variables, we examine first the impact of the coincidence of values between egalitarianism and individualism, and then the impact of race and chronic information on response variability. In these presentations, we rely solely on graphical tools to present the effects of each factor on response variability.

In figure 6.3 we have our graphical presentation of the effect of the coincidence of egalitarianism and individualism on the variability of survey response for each of the six binary policy choices. The vertical axis represents the underlying error variance—or response variability—with low values showing low variability and high values showing high variability; the horizontal axis indicates the conflict between egalitarianism and individualism, ranging from no conflict to high conflict. (This applies to figures 6.3–6.8) The key prediction is that response variability should increase as core beliefs conflict.

We see quite mixed evidence for this predicted relationship between core belief conflict and response variability. In fact, as core belief conflict increases for five of the six measures, we see that response variability actually decreases; only for job quotas do we see response variability increasing in response to increasing core belief conflict.

Next, figures 6.4 and 6.5 provide the exact same graphical presentation of the results for core value conflict and response variability, but for the ordinal racial policy responses (figure 6.4) and the ordinal responses about the status of blacks in society (figure 6.5). We see the same pattern of weak and inconsis-

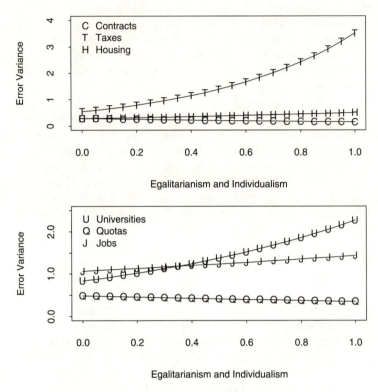

FIGURE 6.3. Effects of value conflict in binary probits

tent effects in these results as well. In only one case (housing) do we find that increasing core belief conflict leads to increased response variability. In three of the cases for the ordinal questions about blacks (advantage, knives, and racist) we see the predicted relationship between core belief conflict and response variability, but none of these relationships is of any sizable magnitude. Thus, we can reject one of the two key preconditions for ambivalence in racial policy and attitudes about blacks: that core belief conflict leads to increased response variability.

Next, we turn to a similar graphical presentation of the results for the effects of both race and chronic information on response variability. We are looking for two quite different types of effects of information on response variability: a positive relationship would provide evidence for ambivalence, while a negative relationship between information and response variability would provide evidence for uncertainty. We test for these effects by graphing the effects of each type of information on the underlying response variability for each set of models.

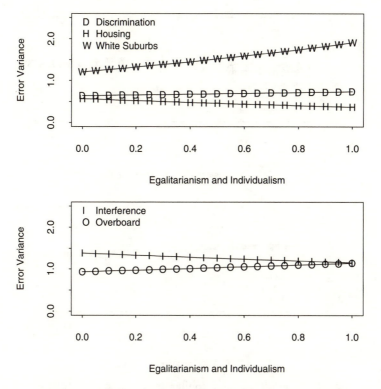

FIGURE 6.4 Effects of value conflict in ordinal probits (race)

We begin by looking at the effects of information on response variability in the binary racial policy results (figure 6.6). In these information figures, the vertical axis is the same as it was in the value conflict figures—response variability—while now the horizontal axis is either race (top two panels) or chronic information (bottom two panels).

In the top two panels of figure 6.6 we find that race information has an inconsistent and small impact on response variability in the binary racial policy variance models. Thus we conclude that race information does not systematically influence response variability in these aspects of racial policy. But in the bottom panels we see strong evidence for uncertainty. In each of the models chronic information has a strong and negative impact on response variability.

Similar results for the ordinal racial policy questions are given in figure 6.7. Once again, race information does not have a consistent or substantial impact on response variance, but chronic information has a negative impact in four of the five cases (the one exception being white suburbs). While the negative effect is not as strong as for the binary racial policy questions, it still is apparent

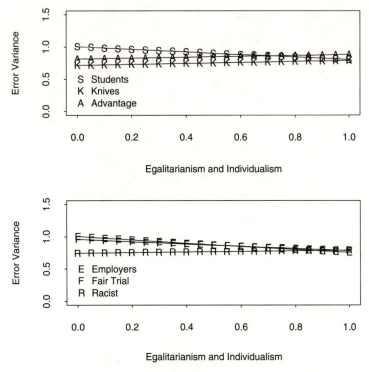

F<small>IGURE</small> 6.5 Effects of value conflict in ordinal probits (blacks)

from these results that uncertainty and not ambivalence is the process leading to response variability, since as chronic information goes up, response variability goes down, in all but one of the cases in figure 6.7.

Our last illustration of the relationship between information and response variability is figure 6.8. These are the graphs showing the effects of information on the underlying response variability for the questions about the status of blacks. The two top panels again show that race information has an inconsistent and weak impact on the underlying variability of responses about the status of blacks in American society. By contrast, the bottom two panels tell a different story about the role of chronic information. In each of these six cases we see the same negative and modest impact of chronic information on response variability. Again, as chronic information increases, response variability decreases. This provides strong support for the claim that response variability in questions about the status of blacks, just as in the questions about affirmative action and racial policy, is basically a function of uncertainty and not ambivalence.

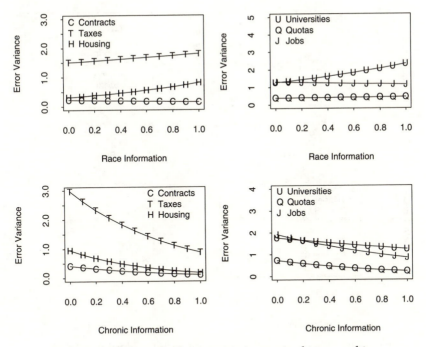

FIGURE 6.6 Effects of information in interactive binary probits

AMBIVALENCE OR UNCERTAINTY?

This chapter has presented considerable data about the fundamental determinants of white American opinions regarding affirmative action, about racial policies, and about the status of blacks in society. In the course of discussing this array of quantitative evidence, we have attempted to advance both the important themes of this book as well as our scholarly understanding of the dynamics of public opinion on race.

One of the most important contributions concerns the role of core beliefs in determining the choices Americans make when faced with these different aspects of racial politics. There has been a great deal of debate in the literature about which core beliefs are the most important determinants of public opinion about racial matters, and here our analyses shed considerable light on this persistent and puzzling research controversy. The debate has long centered on the relative importance of modern racism in public opinion about racial matters, in contrast to the importance of a set of other important core beliefs: antiblack affect, individualism, egalitarianism, anti-Semitism, and authoritarianism. There is no question that our results here provide some ammunition to

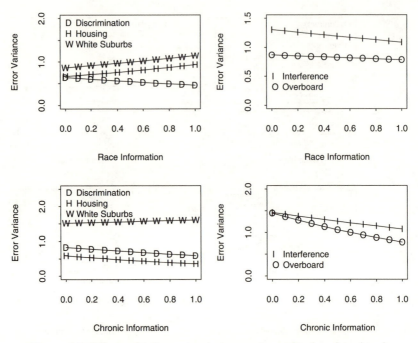

FIGURE 6.7 Effects of information in interactive ordinal probits (race)

those who believe that modern racism is the most important predictor of racial opinions; across all of our empirical models, it is clear that our modern racism measure is the strongest and most consistent predictor of this wide array of opinions concerning racial politics.

But we did find that other core beliefs were also important determinants of opinions about racial matters, particularly, egalitarianism, which was a consistent predictor of ideas about affirmative action and policies designed to alleviate racial inequality. In addition, antiblack affect was a strong predictor of beliefs about the status and role of blacks in society. Thus public opinion about racial questions, while dominated by modern racism, cannot easily be devolved into discussions about only one underlying core belief. Racial opinions in America are much more complicated than that.

Yet when we come to the other aspect of our analyses of the public opinion of race in America, we find that the one thing that different sides of the debate over the role of modern racism agree about is incorrect. Scholars arguing about the importance of modern racism as a core determinant of racial opinions all seem to agree that attitudes about racial policy are clearly influenced by question wording in public opinion surveys, leading them to assert that ambiva-

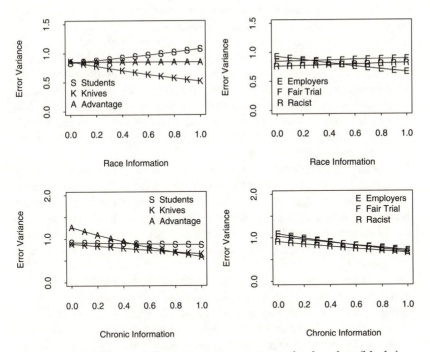

FIGURE 6.8 Effects of information in interactive ordinal probits (blacks)

lence characterizes the attitudes of white Americans about racial policy. In our work we have carefully drawn a distinction between ambivalence and uncertainty: ambivalence is a condition whereby more information leads to more response variability *and* where core belief conflict also leads to more response variability; uncertainty, on the other hand, is a state whereby more information leads to a reduction in response variance.

When it comes to the public opinion of racial matters, the evidence strongly indicates that white Americans are not ambivalent. It simply is not the case that both more information and core belief conflict lead to more response variance. Instead, more information leads to a reduction in response variance. Thus, we conclude that, as some have noted (see, for example, the Shipler, and Sniderman and Piazza quotes that began this chapter), one of the most important things about public opinion on racial issues is that white Americans are poorly informed about these issues. This is no great surprise, since few white Americans have direct experience with racial inequality, with affirmative action policies, or, in fact, with many blacks.

What is surprising about this strong and systematic finding, though, is that it centers not on how well-informed white Americans are about issues of race and racial policy; instead we have shown repeatedly that chronic and not do-main-specific political information influences variability in racial survey re-sponses. There is no doubt that white Americans are poorly informed about these issues, as was shown by Nadeau, Niemi, and Levine (1993), who found that only a stunningly low 15 percent of Americans know the extent of the black population in the United States. Since their findings indicate that in-formedness about blacks is closely tied to general political information, it is possible that our measures of chronic and domain-specific information are simply measuring very closely related phenomena. In any case, this is a ques-tion that calls for additional analysis.

In the end, if attitudes of white Americans about racial issues are uncertain, and not ambivalent, some might conclude that these attitudes can be easily changed. After all, if we could reduce the underlying variability in people's thinking by supplying them with more information, maybe that would solve the dilemma of racial strife in America. But information should not only make Americans more certain; it should also move their opinions to a point of consensus.

Unfortunately, the situation is not that simple. Reducing the variability in an individual's thinking about racial issues does not necessarily lead to any consensus about a single "correct" direction in which racial policies should go. Even if the attitudes of white Americans became less variable, it would be difficult to ascertain whether they became more fixed in an attempt to alleviate racial inequality or in a desire to end those *policies* that alleviate racial inequal-ity. Thus, there is no simple answer to the politics of race in America.

CHAPTER 7

Equivocation

THE THIRD form of response variability to be discussed in this book is equivocation. We take equivocation to literally mean "speaking in two voices," to emphasize two distinct predispositions, but where those predispositions are mutually reinforcing rather than contradictory. Furthermore, the mutually reinforcing predispositions act to *reduce* response variability, so equivocation, produced by coincident predispositions, leads individuals to have more firmly fixed opinions than individuals who do not have mutually reinforcing predispositions.

As we have argued in chapters 4 and 5, the mere presence of two predispositions does not necessitate internalized conflict. Respondents might consider two predispositions to be mutually reinforcing, as, perhaps, a respondent might be concerned for both the quality and equality of human life. The former is a core value called *humanitarianism*, while the latter is the familiar *egalitarianism*. Over many domains of politics, one would expect that both egalitarianism and humanitarianism would guide respondents in the same direction, and that sharing a high degree of both should lead them to be even more fixed in their opinions. Indeed, it is difficult to even conjure up a situation in which egalitarianism and humanitarianism lead the respondent in opposite directions.

Are there other value sets that appear to be mutually consistent? Perhaps both racism and anti-Semitism would lead respondents in similar ways, since both can be construed as negative affective evaluations of social out-groups. Perhaps both pro-business values and anticommunist predispositions would likewise work in a mutually reinforcing way. One can easily imagine combinations of predispositions that might lead to equivocation in American public opinion.

There are also predisposition pairs that, although perhaps logically contradictory, are experienced by respondents as mutually reinforcing. Recall the content analysis that Rokeach (1973) conducted of the writings of democratic socialists: these writers regarded egalitarian and libertarian impulses as complimentary, when many democratic theorists would see the impulses in tension.

Some logical contradictions are less obvious to the public than to political elites. We have previously written about advocates for public policies who do not see cutting tax revenues and achieving balanced budgets as contradictory; some analysts of racial policy (e.g., Sniderman and Carmines 1997) argue that affirmative action policies undercut egalitarianism and freedom simultaneously.

In this chapter, we consider one example of equivocation, namely, the attitudes that Americans maintain about the Internal Revenue Service. We show that Americans expect this bureaucracy, and probably others, to be responsive, honest, and equitable, even if these goals are logically contradictory. The reinforcement of these coincident predispositions, furthermore, leads individuals to have lower response variability, or in other words, to have more firmly fixed survey responses. In our conclusion, we discuss what this result means for American opinions about both the IRS and the federal government.

ATTITUDES TOWARD THE IRS

An exploration of American attitudes toward the Internal Revenue Service provides important opportunities to contribute to an unusual combination of research domains: public opinion and public administration. We employ a survey commissioned by the IRS and conducted in 1987 to determine what it is about the IRS specifically, and bureaucracies in general, that makes them both such unpopular entities in contemporary American public opinion.

The word *bureaucracy* is usually considered so negative that virtually every recent major scholarly consideration of the performance of bureaucracy begins with an acknowledgment of the poisonous connotation of the word (e.g., Downs 1967; Goodsell 1985; Niskanen 1971). Of course, with "anger at Washington bureaucrats" a popular account for electoral change in both the 1992 and 1994 elections, and with levels of trust in government at record lows (Stanley and Niemi 1995), it seems clear that the American public is increasingly dissatisfied with nonelected federal officials. This is at the same time that U.S. bureaucrats deliver services with an efficiency unmatched by equivalent public servants in virtually every other government (Goodsell 1985), and when the actual number of civilian federal employees is now at a twelve-year low (Stanley and Niemi 1995).

Why is it that "bureaucracy" has become so odious a word at a time when the federal bureaucracy provides such high delivery of service with fewer personnel? Scholars of public administration speculate that Americans hold bureaucracies in disfavor because they have such high and competing expectations about their performance (see especially Wilson 1967, 1989; but also see Goodsell 1985; Perrow 1987). Citizens expect bureaucracies to be equitable and fair, to provide all citizens with the same treatment under the law; they also want bureaucracies to be flexible, to acknowledge the variations in conditions that might make for differential application of the law. Responsiveness competes with not just equity, but also with efficiency. Bureaucracies could maximize their efficiency by treating all inputs similarly, but only at the expense of the recognition of individual variation. Bureaucrats—especially those that handle taxpayer money—should be honest, but Americans do not object

when bureaucrats cut us some slack on our own (presumably minor) violations. Wilson wrote in 1967:

> Obviously the more a bureaucracy is responsive to its clients—whether those cli-
> ents are organized by radicals into Mothers for Adequate Welfare or represented
> by Congressmen anxious to please constituents—the less it can be accountable to
> presidential directives. Similarly, the more equity, the less responsiveness. And a
> preoccupation with fiscal integrity can make the kind of program budgeting re-
> quired by enthusiasts of efficiency difficult, if not impossible. (5)

If scholars of public administration are correct, competition between expectations of equity, responsiveness, and honesty should abound in the attitudes of
Americans toward the federal bureaucracy. One purpose of this chapter is to
examine the roles of these expectations and predispositions, which determine
attitudes about the federal bureaucracy.

While it is conceivable that specific values (statements about desirable end
states, or the means to accomplish them) may pertain to evaluations of bureaucracy, in this chapter we argue that another form of predispositions, which
we call *expectations*, are appropriate. By expectations we mean beliefs about
probable results from engaging with a specific political actor (here, the IRS).
Americans may "value" honesty, fairness, and responsiveness—indeed, this is
a perfectly reasonable interpretation of these largely positive goals for bureaucracy—but it is more accurate to think of these as expectations about what
bureaucracies will or will not accomplish.

It is far from evident, however, that there really is competition between
expectations about bureaucratic performance. People may believe in equity,
honesty, and efficiency, but only as they apply to other individuals. When it
comes to their own treatment by bureaucracy, Americans want responsiveness
and see no problem when they also expect efficiency. They have remarkable
abilities to contextualize every potential policy problem, and that such abilities
should come to bear in attitudes about those who deliver policy would hardly
be surprising. Citizens want bureaucracies to meet these goals, but they do not
see the problematic implications that are so obvious to public administration
scholars. Further, if these expectations are really competing, there is no particular reason to expect systematic bias in the mean response (i.e., depressing
attitudes toward bureaucracy). As this book proposes, competing expectations
about public policy and public figures should affect the heterogeneity of individual response, not the mean (Alvarez and Brehm 1995, 1997).

Specific to this present research problem, while scholars of public administration are convincing in their arguments about how bureaucracies cannot
achieve all expectations at the same time, it is an open question whether citizens also see these expectations as competing and irreconcilable. In fact, we
demonstrate below that coincident expectations about responsiveness and
honesty lead respondents to be equivocal in their attitudes about the per-

formances of IRS employees. Thus, while many Americans hold high expectations for the IRS, they do not necessarily see these expectations as conflictual. Instead, they want the IRS to achieve both responsiveness and honesty simultaneously.

The instructiveness of this research goes both ways. The particular domain of attitudes toward bureaucracy should yield insights about public opinion not obtainable by the study of attitudes about other questions. Unlike attitudes toward much of public policy, real experience means that attitudes could be governed more by interest than by symbol. We all have experience dealing with bureaucracies, on a nearly daily basis; our attitudes concerning public policy problems such as racial integration or abortion could be present without experience, merely a result of the potent symbolic content of these policy problems. Further, the particular area of the present chapter is one where citizens have concrete incentives to acquire domain-specific information. The better informed a respondent is about changes in tax policy, the more that respondent should be able to minimize his or her own tax burden, and to minimize the risks of sanction for failure to appropriately complete tax returns. Hawthorne and Jackson (1987) demonstrate that material self-interest affects opinions on tax policy, one of very few areas where scholars have been successful in demonstrating direct effects of material self-interest on opinions. If there is ever a research area where highly domain-specific information should matter more than chronic informedness, it is probably in attitudes toward taxation, and to those who enforce tax law.

No U.S. bureaucracy is more emblematic of the disjunction between actual performance and public opprobrium than the Internal Revenue Service. Voluntary tax compliance rates in America exceed those of every other Western democracy (Long and Swingen 1991). IRS employees process more tax returns than any tax officials in the world. But the IRS and its employees fare very poorly in comparison not just to other federal bureaucracies but also to other financial institutions (Harris 1988). We demonstrate that these potentially contradictory expectations matter in determining American attitudes about the performance of IRS employees, in particular expectations about responsiveness and honesty. We will also show that chronic information and coincident expectations determine attitude variability, though in unexpected ways.

A MODEL OF ATTITUDES ABOUT THE IRS

To understand the way expectations influence attitudes about the IRS, we use the approach established in earlier chapters. The essence of the model is that attitudes are formed by values or expectations. But individuals have differing levels of variability in their attitudes (due to ambivalence or equivocation induced by competing expectations or uncertainty produced by a lack of information), and this ambivalence or uncertainty can be modeled as the variance of each attitude.

Our model requires that we have data for attitudes about the IRS, people's expectations about IRS activities, and their informedness about the IRS. The Internal Revenue Service commissioned the Harris Associates survey organization to conduct a nationwide survey of taxpayers in July and August of 1987, the first year the Tax Reform Act went into effect, referred to as the 1987 Taxpayer Opinion Survey (TOS). The purposes of the study were varied, including general questions on tax reform, views about tax evasion, and experiences with and attitudes toward the IRS. Our interest here is to explore the latter topic, and the survey instrument contains several truly unique features.[1]

We use one set of these questions to develop eight measures of attitudes about the IRS from the 1987 TOS as dependent variables in our analysis. The survey asked respondents to state whether they agreed or disagreed (on a 6-point scale, where 6 represented "strongly agree" and 1 represented "strongly disagree") with the following statements:

- Honesty: The IRS employees are honest—you could never bribe them.
- Knowledgeable: IRS employees are just as knowledgeable as any private tax expert.
- Equitable: I am confident that the IRS would never try to take more money from me than they should.
- Accurate: You can depend on the IRS to keep accurate tax records.
- Snooping: That the IRS automatically withholds some of my income and even gets copies of my W2 forms and interest statements sometimes makes me feel they are always nearby and watching.
- Check own: When it comes to investigating their own people, the IRS is as thorough as they are with everyone else.
- Integrity: IRS employees have an unusual amount of honesty and integrity.
- Reasonable: IRS procedures and practices are fair and reasonable ones that respect the rights of taxpayers.

Those eight statements give us the eight dependent variables we use below (we refer to each by the name given to the variable on the left).

Figure 7.1 displays histograms of each of the eight scales. Somewhat surprisingly, the IRS employees fare reasonably well on most of these measures. Respondents were more inclined to agree than disagree that IRS employees are honest, knowledgeable, and provide accurate information, and the differences are pronounced. The advantages of IRS employees are slightly less pronounced when it comes to being seen as reasonable, and likely to investigate violations of their own. The one dimension in which the IRS comes out poorly concerns the sole negative question, where respondents are slightly more likely to agree than disagree that they feel the IRS is always watching. Our purpose here is to account for variation on each of these eight scales by how strongly the respon-

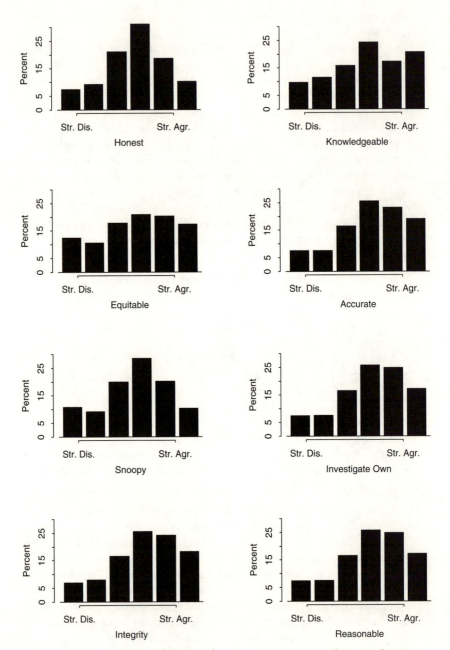

FIGURE 7.1. Attributes of IRS employees, 1987 Taxpayer Opinion Survey

TABLE 7.1
Measurement Model for Scales for Attitudes toward IRS and Taxes

Question	Loading
Fairness of Tax System	
Do you feel [federal income tax system] is fair?	1.00
As a result of Tax Reform Act of 1986, are tax laws more fair?	0.54
TRA ensures same income pays same tax?	0.60
TRA ensures each group pays fair share?	0.88
TRA ensures wealthy pay progressive share of tax?	0.74
Honesty	
Honesty of IRS staff compared to other federal government agencies	1.00
Honesty of IRS staff compared to other financial institutions	0.90
Responsiveness	
IRS employees very willing to help	1.00
IRS employees willing to act in taxpayer's best interest	0.73
Helpfulness of IRS staff compared to other federal government agencies	0.93
Helpfulness of IRS staff compared to other financial institutions	0.87

Note: Cell entries are unstandardized factor loadings.

dent feels the IRS meets each of three potentially competing expectations: honesty, responsiveness, and fairness.

Next, we use a measurement model approach to develop scales for expectations of fairnesss, honesty, and responsiveness. Specifically, we apply a confirmatory factor model that constrains each indicator to load on one latent variable alone, frees the covariances among the latent variables, and fixes the unique errors to have zero covariances. Table 7.1 details the confirmatory factor results (goodness-of-fit index of .84).

First, our measure for fairness comes from seven questions in the 1987 TOS, which all measure the fairness of the federal income tax system, or of the Tax Reform Act of 1986. We wish to be blunt about the limits of the measure for fairness. This measure concerns the fairness of the tax system, not of the members of the IRS (unlike the next two measures for honesty and responsiveness). The potential logical contradiction falls between the fairness of the IRS and the responsiveness of IRS officials: one cannot have a system that is flexible (with respect to the problems that individual citizens might have with the tax code) and still treats each individual in an identical, equitable way. The fairness of the IRS officials is closer to the idea of "procedural fairness" explained by Scholz and Pinney (1995) and Tyler (1990), and is indeed closer to the original formulation of the contradiction by Wilson (1967).

Nonetheless, the measure of the fairness of the tax system is a useful proxy for the procedural fairness of the IRS officials. Contemporary political rhetoric routinely confuses attitudes about taxation with attitudes toward the IRS. In the 1996 presidential debates over tax simplification, advocates of the flat tax, such as Robert Dole and Steve Forbes, claimed that it would eliminate the IRS as Americans currently know it. Since much of the attitudes of citizens about IRS officials is symbolic (i.e., not grounded in actual contact with IRS officials, but grounded in the submission of IRS returns), we think it is a reasonable proxy for procedural fairness to use citizens' attitudes about the tax system. We should still temper our conclusions with regard to the equivocal attitudes Americans hold toward the IRS in the potential conflict between fairness and responsiveness, since we do not have the direct measurement of responsiveness.

The second measure is for the honesty of the IRS staff, and it is constructed from responses to two questions, both focused on the honesty of the IRS staff as compared to other public and private employees. There are two indicators that compare assessments of the honesty of IRS employees relative to other federal government agencies and to other financial institutions. The loading for the freed factor is quite high, suggesting a coherence of the two indicators. Honesty is the one dimension that respondents rated IRS employees above other agencies and other financial institutions.

Last, we measure the responsiveness of the IRS with four questions. These four questions focus on the willingness of IRS staff to assist taxpayers and on the helpfulness of the IRS staff relative to other public and private employees. (An alternative interpretation of this scale—and these indicators—would be flexibility or simply helpfulness).

After construction of the scales, we rescale each of the three to 0–1 bounds, where 0 is the observed minimum for each scale, and 1 is the observed maximum. Thus, a maximum on any of our scales only refers to the maximum observed among the TOS respondents, not to a logical extreme score on all measures. What a high score means is that the respondent finds the IRS to be quite honest, flexible, or fair. We do not have any measures of whether respondents find honesty, responsiveness, or fairness to be desirable; it is logically possible that a respondent could consider, for example, IRS officials to be quite honest, and that honesty is not a particularly valued feature. (It is even conceivable that some respondents might consider IRS officials to be honest, and this honesty to be a problem!) But we do wish to argue that these three scales measure respondents' predispositions or expectations about the IRS; given an

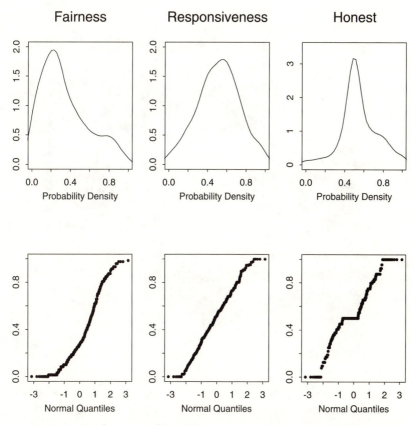

FIGURE 7.2 Scales for sense of the fairness, responsiveness, and honesty of IRS
Employees, 1987 Taxpayer Opinion Survey

arbitrary future encounter with the IRS, respondents who score high on these
scales would be expecting that the IRS officials are honest, fair, or flexible.

Figure 7.2 presents the kernel density plots and the quantile-quantile plots
for these three scales. Quite clearly, most of the respondents to this survey had
a rather low impression of the fairness (in the sense of equitability) of the IRS,
since this distribution is skewed to the low end of the scale. On the other hand,
the respondents seemed to hold that the IRS was reasonably responsive and
reasonably honest. The measure for fairness diverges from normal at the low
and upper end of the distribution; the measure for responsiveness also diverges
from normal in the tails, but to a slightly lesser degree; the measure for honesty
is quite sharply single peaked, with more observations found at the mode than
one would expect in a normal distribution.

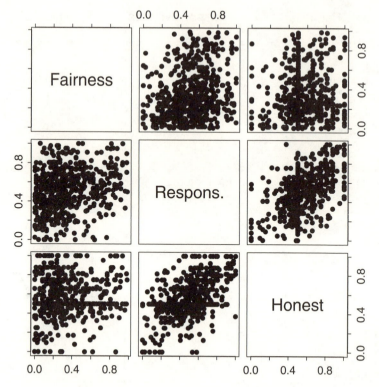

FIGURE 7.3 Scatterplot matrix for sense of the fairness, responsiveness, and honesty of IRS employees, 1987 Taxpayer Opinion Survey

Figure 7.3 provides the scatterplot matrix for these same three scales. Plainly, the potential for a high degree of coincidence in the expectations is strong. The relationship between fairness and responsiveness is weakly linear, where those who thought the IRS was fair were about as likely to think the IRS was responsive. The relationship between responsiveness and honesty is much more strongly linear. (There is no discernible pattern for fairness and honesty.) There are quite a few individuals who fall along the main diagonal, which is where our coincidence measure is strongest.

In addition to these measures of predispositions or expectations, we also employ four control variables in our choice models. Two of these control variables measure respondent contact with the IRS: respondent-initiated contact and IRS audits of the respondent's previous tax returns. We also use dummy variables to control for racial and gender differences in attitudes about the IRS.

Third, we need a measure of how informed each respondent is about tax policy for the model of the response variance. In this case, we use the quiz

TABLE 7.2
Domain-Specific Information Scale for Tax Policy

Aspect	Changed?	How?	% Correct
Dollar amount of the exemption for yourself, spouse, or dependents	Yes	Increased[1]	44.7
Personal exemption on a child's return	Yes	Eliminated[1]	14.1
Standard deduction on a child's return	Yes	Increased[1]	11.3
Deduction for being over age 65 or blind	Yes	Restricted[2]	17.2
Credit for child care expenses	No	(na)[2]	17.4
Exclusion of dividends of $100 / $200	Yes	Eliminated[1]	28.9
Tax on capital gains	Yes	Increased[1]	12.9
Tax on fellowships or scholarships' room and board	Yes	Reduced[2]	18.5
Taxable aspect of unemployment compensation	Yes	Increased[1]	19.2
Unreimbursed employee business expenses	Yes	Reduced[2]	25.2
Unreimbursed meals and entertainment expenses	Yes	Reduced[2]	39.0
IRA deductions	Yes	Reduced[2]	30.5
Deduction for married couples when both work	Yes	Eliminated[1]	33.8
Deduction for contributions to charity for those who do not itemize their deductions	Yes	Reduced[2]	34.2
Deduction for medical and dental expenses	Yes	Reduced[2]	18.6
Deduction for state and local income taxes	No	(na)[2]	34.3
Deduction for interest on consumer debt and credit cards	Yes	Reduced[2]	40.1
Deductions for other miscellaneous itemized items	Yes	Reduced[2]	25.3
Penalty for failure to pay	Yes	Increased[1]	17.8
Investment tax credit	Yes	Eliminated[1]	16.9
Need to report tax-exempt income	Yes	Increased[1]	12.5

Note: Columns "Changed?" and "How?" denote correct responses to the question: "As you may know, Congress revised many aspects of the Federal income tax law last year. Most of the changes they made are effective for the 1987 tax year. Here is a list of different aspects that are built into our income tax system. Some have been changed and some have remained the same. For each, tell me whether—from what you've read or heard—it has changed or remained the same. If you don't know about some of these, just say so. (Has it been increased, been reduced or restricted, or been eliminated?)" Column "% Correct" reports the percentage of respondents who correctly identified whether the aspect had changed (but not necessarily how). *Sources:* [1] *Summary for Individuals;* [2] *Highlights of the 1987 Tax Reform Act,* two IRS documents.

about tax policy, first discussed in chapter 3 and displayed in table 7.2. These twenty-one questions create a domain-specific information scale (the soft information measure). The soft information scale simply records whether the respondent was aware that the particular aspect had changed, in some way. Thus, our domain-specific information measure really is designed to assess the degree to which a respondent crossed the lowest threshold of informedness about the TRA (whether the twenty-one aspects of the tax code changed).[2]

It is clear from table 7.2 that nineteen out of the twenty-one items changed in one direction or another. So a naive respondent who simply assumed that everything had changed would have been correct on 90 percent of these questions. Table 7.2 also gives the percentages of TOS respondents who correctly ascertained whether the aspect had changed. We see that nearly half of the respondents knew that the dollar amount of the exemption had changed; the percentage of respondents who knew about the changes to other aspects of the code were substantially less than this. So even familiarity with whether an aspect changed (the soft information scale) proved to be a strong test of informedness about the code.

Figure 7.4 presents the kernel density plot and quantile-quantile plot of the soft information scale. One truly striking feature is that the vast majority of respondents scored extremely low on this scale, even when a guess that everything had changed would have yielded an extremely high score. In fact, only 2 percent of the respondents exceeded this score. We also wish to note that this scale generates respondents who scored at both extremes, from those who answered none of the questions correctly to those who answered only one of the questions incorrectly.

This measure of domain-specific informedness is, in our view, truly unusual for attitudes toward public policy concerns. Consider Zaller's (1992) book, which explores the respondent's levels of political informedness, in this case, constructed as a measure of "general, chronic awareness." Zaller writes:

> In using this sort of measure, I will be assuming that persons who are knowledgeable about politics in general are habitually attentive to communications on most particular issues as well.
>
> This measurement strategy is less than ideal. More narrowly focused measures of awareness—devoted exclusively, say, to intellectual engagement with foreign policy issues or race policy issues, and used exclusively in connection with reception of information concerning foreign or race policy issues—would be preferable to general awareness measures. However, such domain-specific awareness measures are rarely carried on opinion surveys and none are available for the cases I examine in this study. (43)

Likewise, Luskin (1987) constructs a measure of general political informedness by tallying respondents' correct relative placement of the parties on a battery

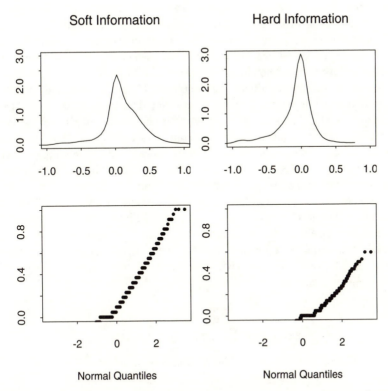

FIGURE 7.4 Distribution of information scales, 1987 Taxpayer Opinion Survey

of eleven issues. Although the measure is composed of domain-specific information, he explicitly aims for a more comprehensive notion of "information
holding," presumably because (as argued earlier in the essay), "ideology as high
sophistication is comprehensive" (863).

Despite the regular dependence of many scholars on chronic informedness
as the means to assess how respondents incorporate messages about politics,
it is possible that highly domain-specific information could matter more than
chronic informedness. If the models maintain that respondents' ability to
counter-argue against counterpartisan information (to "resist" in Zaller's
model) hinges on the store of information that the respondent possesses, it
makes more sense that the respondents' arguments be grounded in the specific
domain of the communication, and not simply their chronic connection to
elite discourse. But this is a testable question, and we do want to allow for
the possibility that chronic information matters, so we use the respondent's
education level as a measure of chronic informedness or political sophistication
in our model. This will allow us to examine whether domain-specific informa-

tion indeed outweighs chronic informedness in our models, or whether neither matters. Finally, in order to attain measures of coincident (and thus potentially contradictory) expectations, we make operational three different measures, one for each pair of expectations (fairness and responsiveness, fairness and honesty, and responsiveness and honesty).

We expect that if an individual expects the IRS to achieve a characteristic more than other individuals, that persons should be more likely to rate the performance of IRS employees positively. The effects of contacts with the IRS should be negative, while the other two control variables should have positive effects on beliefs about the IRS (whites and males should have more positive assessments of the IRS than nonwhites and females). In the variance model, though, we expect the coefficients on education and information to be negative. This means that the more information people have about the 1987 TRA, or the greater their level of educational attainment, the lower the variance in their beliefs. If respondents are ambivalent, we expect the signs on the variance model coefficients to be positive; but if respondents are equivocal, then we expect that the same coefficients will be negative. We now test these hypotheses in the next section.

EXPECTATIONS AND EQUIVOCATION

Choice Model

Tables 7.3 and 7.4 present the marginal effects computed for the models of attitudes toward the IRS. (The actual estimates for the heteroskedastic ordered probit model estimates and standard errors are provided in an appendix on our website at www.pupress.princeton.edu/alvarez). We provide two sets of estimated effects: for the choice component of the model (the top panel), and for the variance component of the model (the second panel). The bottom panel gives summary statistics for the model, the sample size of each estimated model, and the results of the test for the presence of heteroskedasticity in each model. In this first subsection of results, we turn to the choice model estimates and estimated marginal effects. The next subsection addresses the variance model results.

First, the eight models we estimated all fit the sample data reasonably well. The percentages of cases correctly predicted range from just over 30 percent to just over 50 percent, which demonstrates that we are classifying cases relatively accurately with our model. We also provide a second summary statistic, the "percentage reduction in error" (PRE), which gives the percentage increase in predictive power relative to a null model (only constants). These range from a low of about 6 percent (the "snooping" and "integrity" models) to a high of

TABLE 7.3
Marginal Effects from Heteroskedastic Ordered Probit Estimates

	Accurate	Equitable	Honesty	Integrity
Choice Model				
Responsiveness	−.19	−.29	−.07	−.16
	.33	.30	.15	.20
Fairness	−.01	−.09	−.02	−.04
	.01	.09	.05	.05
Honesty	−.12	−.23	−.17	−.16
	.21	.24	.35	.20
Male	.01	−.00	.02	−.00
	−.02	.00	−.05	.00
White	.04	.01	.01	.02
	−.07	−.01	−.01	−.02
IRS contact	.03	.03	−.00	.01
	−.06	−.03	.00	−.01
Audit	.01	.02	−.03	−.01
	−.02	−.02	.06	.01
Variance Model				
Soft information	−.07	.29	.01	−.06
Education	−.08	−.16	−.06	−.20
Fairness vs. responsiveness	−.03	.10	.00	.02
Fairness vs. honesty	.05	−.04	−.17	.07
Responsiveness vs. honesty	−.32	−.34	−.20	−.31
Log-Likelihood	−935.4	−962.8	−945.5	−844.9
% Correct	33.5	34.3	32.7	40.8
PRE	11.5%	21.6%	12.2%	6.9%
Het. Test	27.0**	26.2**	12.4**	28.9**
N	606	601	578	586

Note: Marginal effects for coefficients in the choice model are the estimated effects of each variable on the probability of choosing the low category, followed by the probability of choosing the high category. Marginal effects for coefficients in the variance model are the estimated effects of each variable on the magnitude of the estimated error variance. ** indicates significant at $p < .05$.

TABLE 7.4
Marginal Effects from Heteroskedastic Ordered Probit Estimates

	Knowledgable	Check Own	Reasonable	Snooping
Choice Model				
Responsiveness	−.27	−.18	−.39	.08
	.36	.06	.30	−.15
Fairness	.01	−.04	−.10	.04
	−.02	.33	.07	−.09
Honesty	−.07	−.16	−.14	−.00
	.09	.07	.11	.01
Male	−.00	−.00	.01	−.01
	.00	.30	−.01	.01
White	.06	.03	.05	−.00
	−.07	.00	−.04	.00
IRS contact	.04	.01	.03	.03
	−.05	−.06	−.03	−.07
Audit	.02	−.02	.02	−.01
	−.03	−.03	−.01	.01
Variance Model				
Soft information	−.01	.13	−.11	.05
Education	−.11	−.03	−.19	−.32
Fairness vs. responsiveness	−.04	−.04	−.11	−.19
Fairness vs. honesty	−.04	.17	.08	.08
Responsiveness vs. honesty	−.23	−.44	−.22	−.10
Log-Likelihood	−988.2	−889.0	−900.1	−1007.2
% Correct	31.6	51.7	40.1	31.3
PRE	16.0%	33.4%	15.2%	5.6%
Het. Test	17.2**	16.2**	24.2**	11.2**
N	598	559	606	601

Note: Marginal effects for coefficients in the choice model are the estimated effects of each variable on the probability of choosing the low category, followed by the probability of choosing the high category. Marginal effects for coefficients in the variance model are the estimated effects of each variable on the magnitude of the estimated error variance. ** indicates significant at $p < .05$.

27 percent ("the accurate" model). Again, these fit statistics show that our heteroskedastic ordinal probit model fits the sample data relatively well.

Of course, care is needed when interpreting ordered probit models. First, as is usually the case in discrete choice models, the coefficient estimates obtained are not directly related to the marginal effects of each independent variable on the choice probabilities. This means that additional steps are useful to make these results easily interpretable. Second, the ordered nature of our dependent variables can yield a further complication. Say we are interested in the marginal effect of an increase in one of the independent variables on the predicted probabilities of choosing each category. An increase in the independent variable in question implies a decrease in the probability of the lowest category being chosen, and an increase in the probability of the highest category being chosen. But for the middle categories, the results can often be ambiguous, since an increase in the value of an independent variable can lead to a decrease or an increase in the probabilities of middle categories being chosen. We thus examine the probabilities of choosing "strongly disagree" and "strongly agree," each of which defines the end points of our dependent variables.

So we present in Tables 7.3 and 7.4 the estimated marginal effects of each right-hand side variable on the probability of choosing strongly disagree in the upper row for each independent variable, followed by the probability of strongly agree in the lower row. The correct signs for these probability estimates are that those for the probability of a strongly-disagree response should be negative (increasingly positive expectations should lead to a lower probability of a strongly-disagree response), while those for the probability of a strongly-agree response should be positive (increasingly positive expectations should lead to a higher probability of a strongly-agree response).

Beginning with the estimated results for the choice component of the model, note that in general the three expectation measures perform as expected. With only three exceptions, the estimated marginal effects indicate that as individuals place greater weight on each dimension of bureaucratic expectation, they are more likely to evaluate IRS employees positively: the probability of strongly disagreeing decreases (in the upper row), while the probability of strongly agreeing increases (lower row). Also, most of these estimates in the choice model are statistically significant, with only nine of twenty-four parameters not reaching conventional levels of statistical significance. Thus, the results presented in tables 7.3 and 7.4 demonstrate that more positive expectations lead to more positive evaluations of the IRS.

The estimated results also show that expectations about fairness have little influence on attitudes about the IRS. Only three of eight estimated coefficients for fairness are statistically significant in the choice model, and two of the insignificant coefficients are even incorrectly signed. This shows that expectations about fairness are not as strong a determinant of attitudes toward the IRS as are expectations about responsiveness and honesty. (Remember that the measure of fairness is of the tax system, not of the IRS employees per se.)

In general, we obtain the results we anticipated for the expectations measures, as shown in tables 7.3 and 7.4. For six of the eight dependent variables, we see correctly signed marginal effects (accurate, equitable, honesty, integrity, check own, and reasonable). We also see a striking difference in how strong the estimated effects of each expectation are. Clearly, the effects of responsiveness are the greatest in the choice model. Second are the effects of honesty, while the effects of fairness are virtually nonexistent in the choice model.

Variance Model

Competing expectations may also influence the variance of attitudes, not just the mean. Turning now to the bottom panels of tables 7.3 and 7.4, it is clear that significant heterogeneity exists in the responses to these questions about the IRS. All of the eight heteroskedasticity tests produce χ^2 statistics that are greater than the critical threshold of 11.07. This means that we can reject the null hypothesis of no heteroskedasticity with confidence in every one of these models.

We use the estimated results from the variance model to examine three different hypotheses. First, we want to determine if information (or the lack of information, uncertainty) influences the heterogeneity that individuals exhibit in their responses to these questions about the IRS. In addition, we partition information into domain-specific information (the soft information scale) and chronic information (the respondent's level of educational attainment).

Interpreting the estimated effects of each variable in the variance function is also not straightforward. To facilitate interpretation, we resort to a procedure different from that used for the choice function. In the lower panel of tables 7.3 and 7.4 we give the marginal effects of each component of the variance function of the estimated magnitude of the error variance.

The variance model produces mixed results for the argument that uncertainty produces variability in these survey responses. On one hand, we can reject the hypothesis that domain-specific information produces response variability: only one of the soft information estimates is statistically significant, and it is positively signed (the only coefficient of the eight models that is consistent with our measure of ambivalence). On the other hand, there is some evidence that chronic information matters here, since all eight of the coefficients on education in the variance model are correctly signed (negative) and since five of these coefficients reach statistical significance. Thus, on the basis of these results, we are unable to reject the null hypothesis that domain-specific informedness does not produce individual variability in attitudes about the IRS;

but we are able to reject the null hypothesis that greater chronic information produces greater variability in respondent attitudes about the IRS.

First, for the two information variables (soft information and education), we can see the inconsistent effects of domain-specific information on error variance, but the consistent and sizable effects of chronic information. Again, the effect of chronic information (education) in the variance models is always negative, meaning that higher education yields lower error variance. This effect often seems quite strong as well.

The next hypothesis we examine with our variance model is whether simultaneous expectations induce ambivalence (and generate higher attitude variability for respondents), or whether they induce equivocation (and generate lower attitude variability for respondents). The results in tables 7.3 and 7.4 offer insight into this question, since we see strong evidence in support of the argument that coincident expectations for responsiveness and honesty leads not to greater attitude variability for respondents, but to significantly lower variability. Seven of the eight coefficients for this simultaneous expectations term are statistically significant and negatively signed. However, the results for the other two expectation competition terms (fairness versus responsiveness and fairness versus honesty) do not demonstrate consistent effects, which means that the coincident expectation of responsiveness and honesty is the most influential of the joint expectation terms in the variance model.

The coincident expectation terms show clearly that the competition between responsiveness and honesty has the most potent effect in the variance models. All of the estimated effects are negatively signed. While the fairness-responsiveness expectation competition term is negatively signed in five of eight models, the estimated effect of this expectational competition is generally less than that for responsiveness-honesty. Last, note that the estimated effect for the fairness-honesty competition is only negatively signed in just four instances, and is not very strong.

We produce a visual demonstration of the variance effects in two sets of graphs: figure 7.5 presents the variance effects for the responsiveness versus honesty tradeoff, and figure 7.6 presents the variance effects as a function of education. Every single one of these curves is downward sloping, showing that as the respondent holds coincident expectations of responsiveness and honesty, the response variability sharply decreases. The same is plainly true for the effect of education: better-educated respondents are much less variable in their opinions than less-educated ones.

Although Wilson (1967) and others are persuasive in their arguments that bureaucracies cannot achieve high levels of responsiveness, equity, and honesty at the same time, the evidence here is that most respondents fail to see the contradiction. If they were aware of the difficulties that bureaucracies have in being both flexible and honest, for example, we would have seen positive signs

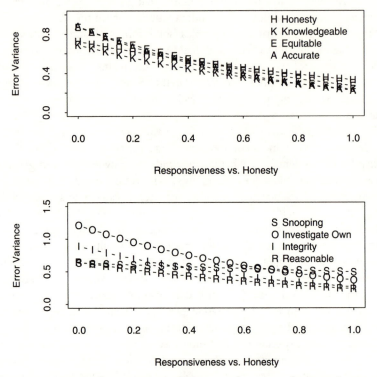

FIGURE 7.5 Estimated response variability as a function of responsiveness vs. honesty of IRS employees, 1987 Taxpayer Opinion Survey

on the simultaneous expectations; but the results are overwhelmingly the reverse. In fact, the results demonstrate that the more that respondents expect both responsiveness and honesty, the less variable and more certain they are in their opinions. In other words, with respect to responsiveness and honesty—the two expectations that most strongly shape attitudes about the IRS—our evidence demonstrates that respondents are equivocal, not ambivalent or uncertain.

The results from the variance model also demonstrate that chronic, and not domain-specific, information has a strong effect on individual belief variance. But, as tables 7.3 and 7.4 show, the effects of chronic information are generally less than those for the responsiveness-honesty interaction, indicating that individual variation in beliefs about the IRS stems not as much from a lack of chronic information as it does from the kinds of expectations people have about bureaucracies.

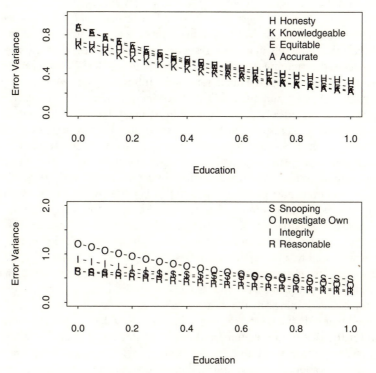

FIGURE 7.6 Estimated response variability as a function of education, 1987
Taxpayer Opinion Survey

CONCLUSIONS

Political discourse in recent years, especially in the wake of insurgent
anti-Washington and antigovernment candidates like Patrick Buchanan and
Ross Perot, shows an increasing level of ambivalence toward the institutions
of government. Some branches of the federal government, like the FBI and
the IRS, have drawn particular scorn from many elements in American society.
Although Wilson's (1967) article on the varied and competing expectations Americans have about bureaucratic performance is widely reprinted and
cited, our research here is the first attempt to employ public opinion data to
test the presence of coincident expectations. In this chapter we have begun
the first systematic effort to assess whether Americans are indeed ambivalent
about their federal government, and to examine what might produce that
ambivalence.

There are three specific conclusions to draw from our results in this chapter. First, *responsiveness and honesty are the expectations that tend to dominate beliefs about the IRS, not fairness.* We found that across the eight different dimensions of beliefs about the IRS, in general, responsiveness and honesty had the strongest effect in determining individual attitudes about the IRS. This indicates that attempts to reform both the operations of the IRS and the current tax code are not going to be easy and quick sells to the American public. On the one hand, the beliefs of Americans about the IRS are strongly related to the notion of responsiveness—as responsiveness increases in importance, so does positive evaluation of the IRS—implying that if any proposal is to be successful, it must preserve or enhance the responsiveness in the current system. But on the other hand, Americans also structure their attitudes about the IRS with beliefs about honesty; reforms must produce a system that is perceived as honest. Surprisingly, fairness is not as strong a determinant of beliefs about the IRS, although the measure of fairness is not a measure of procedural fairness, but of the fairness of the tax system. Nonetheless, changes in the tax code do not have to necessarily lead to a perception of fairness.

Second, *domain-specific information does not play a strong role in determining individual variability in beliefs.* In this respect, the findings here are dissimilar to our earlier findings in the case of beliefs about racial policy. There we showed that individual variability in beliefs is largely determined by information (or the lack of information) and not by conflicting core beliefs. Thus, in contrast to the case of opinions about affirmative action, we feel that the beliefs of Americans about their governmental institutions are not strongly influenced by the information they obtain about those institutions. In this sense, uncertainty in beliefs about the IRS are not strongly influenced by elite discourse about the IRS specifically, or the government in general.

Third, *both coincident expectations and chronic informedness influence the fundamental variability of Americans attitudes about the IRS.* In the results presented here, we portrayed Americans as having complicated beliefs about the IRS. In our earlier work, we found that competing predispositions influenced heterogeneity in beliefs about abortion policy, but not for beliefs about affirmative action. We also found that information heavily influenced beliefs about affirmative action but not abortion.

We believe that our findings on the origins of attitudes toward bureaucracy, in this case the IRS, are unique. Our results suggest that although contradictions presumptively exist across these expectations, public attitudes toward the IRS hinge primarily on only two of the three potential expectations: responsiveness and honesty take preeminence; fairness, as measured here, matters hardly at all, but note that the idea of fairness measured here emphasizes fairness of outcomes, as opposed to procedural fairness.[3]

Although both responsiveness and honesty were influential in our models, responsiveness dominates for most of the eight dependent measures. This implies that what affects whether a typical citizen expresses support for bureaucracy is his or her perception that the bureaucracy is responsive and flexible. Wilson (1967) presages the potential for political problems when responsiveness is the sole goal:

> Responsiveness is never easy or wholly desirable; if every person were treated in accordance with his special needs, there would be no program at all. (The only system that meets the responsiveness problem squarely is the free market.) But at least with clear objectives we would know what we are giving up in those cases when responsiveness seems necessary, and thus we would be able to decide how much we are willing to tolerate. (8)

In the case of attitudes about the IRS, *both* chronic information and expectation competition are important determinants of heterogenous beliefs, but in surprising ways. We have strong evidence that expectations about bureaucracy are not "contradictory" in the sense that holding high expectations on competing dimensions leads to greater response variance; in fact, exactly the opposite occurs. It may be true that bureaucracies cannot be fully flexible, fully honest, and fully equitable all at the same time, but respondents do not share the worries of public administration scholars. Our results make Wilson's arguments even more ironic. If it is true that these competing expectations hinder bureaucracies' ability to achieve high public standards and meet approval, most respondents are unaware of that fact and are more likely to be confident about their (presumably) low opinions. In only one instance did we find that the effects of chronic information were greater than expectation conflict. As we have shown, these effects, while present and important, affect the variability of attitudes about the IRS less than coincident expectations do.

Thus, the causes of heterogeneous beliefs in the case of the IRS comprise a very different case from the two cases we have examined in previous chapters. Information matters, particularly of the chronic form, which looks more like the condition we referred to as "uncertain" regarding racial policy. Competing expectations matter, too, but in such a way that they reduce rather than augment variation in opinion, unlike both the racial policy and abortion policy cases. This is a state we call *equivocation*: holding simultaneous expectations that do not contradict each other (to the respondent), while also becoming less variable in opinion with acquisition of more information.

This means that, like the debate over abortion, the political debate about the IRS (and possibly the federal bureaucracy) will be quite sensitive to how the debate is framed; in other words, the equivocation of Americans about the IRS will be influenced by the way in which politicians and elites frame their debate about this federal institution. Framing the debate as about responsiveness or honesty, or about both simultaneously, will influence how the American public thinks about the IRS.

What this chapter (and earlier ones) offers is a method for adjudicating between the three different forms of response variability. The larger question is *when* should the analyst expect each of these forms and *why*. Full exploration of this question is beyond the scope of the present analysis, but we can speculate. There are two distinct routes by which respondents would be ambivalent, uncertain, or equivocal: one, which proceeds from logical relationships among predispositions, and a second, which proceeds from the framing of elites' debates to citizens' understanding of the problem. Under some circumstances, it is entirely possible that predispositions are logically incompatible; it is logically incompatible, for instance, to protect life before birth and at the same time to allow a woman full autonomy in deciding whether to have an abortion. By this first route, respondents become ambivalent because they are seeking to reconcile incompatible predispositions. But the present study illustrates that what the analyst might consider to be a logical incompatibility, or at least a tension, between responsiveness, honesty, and fairness does not exist in mass attitudes toward the IRS.

The more plausible route to ambivalence, uncertainty, and equivocation is the second: elites frame policy choices as choices between values, beliefs, or expectations. There is growing evidence of the prominence of elite frames as setting the way in which citizens understand policy questions (e.g., Kinder and Sanders 1996). If competing elites are equally successful in propagating irreconcilable values across the public (such that many members of the public express support for both), we would expect ambivalence to be the norm. If competing elites convince separate groups of the applicability of key values, then uncertainty is more likely. If elites advocate multiple values, and the conflict between these values is never salient (or logically present), we would expect equivocation. The two routes need not be mutually exclusive. Elites might exploit the irreconcilability of widely shared mass values, leading to an interplay between mass predispositions and elite framing.

From here, our research agenda must proceed in a different direction: to step back and try to understand the processes that help shape public opinion at the macrolevel. When Americans are ambivalent in their attitudes about important aspects of public policy or their government, what has made their core beliefs salient, and what has induced citizens to realize the conflicts in their beliefs? And when Americans are uncertain in these, or other attitudes, what is the source of their uncertainty? By understanding the origins of ambivalence and uncertainty in American public opinion, we should be in a better position to explain what, if anything, can cause Americans to change their attitudes about politics.

So in the next two chapters we consider the relationship between elites and masses. First, do elites see conflict in the masses themselves? Then we ask, do elites themselves experience internalized conflict when masses do not? Both chapters explore the ramifications of ambivalence, uncertainty, and equivocation on the representative role of elites.

Part 3

MASSES AND ELITES

Mass Opinion and Representation

WE BEGAN THIS BOOK by arguing that politics is rooted in conflict: conflict over resources, public policy, even such fundamental questions as the shape and structure of a nation's government. Just as conflict between people is an important defining characteristic of politics, people are also internally conflicted about their interests and opinions relating to the same issues that shape interpersonal political struggles.

In a stable, representative democracy like the United States, how is intrapersonal conflict related to interpersonal conflict? To take an issue like abortion, which we have already argued is an issue about which Americans are deeply conflicted, how is the conflict that individual Americans feel about the issue of abortion expressed in the political system?

Generally speaking, the normative theory of representative democracy asserts that some individuals from the body politic are appointed or elected to legislative or policymaking assemblies, and the purpose of these representatives is to channel or express the opinions and interests of a larger set or class of constituents. Thus, if intrapersonal conflict is to be expressed in a representative democratic system, that conflict must be observed and acted upon by the individual's representative.

There have been many important studies, both philosophical and empirical, regarding how representatives should act on behalf of the interests or opinions of their constituents. These studies have focused on two different types of representation, *descriptive* and *substantive*. The first makes no direct linkage between the interests or opinions of constituents and representatives, other than that the representative "looks like" the constituent in some way. The descriptive "looking like" might be racial or ethnic, or it might be based on gender or religion or class. By electing a representative for descriptive reasons, the constituent is assuming that because the representative "looks like me," he or she would be more likely to share similar or identical interests or opinions.

In recent years, the normative notion of descriptive representation has received new scrutiny. As America is becoming more racially and ethnically diverse, there have been many calls for reforms that might allow for more women and minorities to be elected to legislative offices. In particular, there has been a great deal of controversy over the use of the redistricting process to draw legislative district lines producing districts that might facilitate the election of minority representatives.[1] Of course, the intention behind these efforts is to increase the descriptive representation of minorities in American politics.

But many have pointed out the problems of descriptive representation. Clearly, the mere fact that a representative is female, or Mexican American, or Catholic, does not necessarily mean that the representative will advocate pro-women, pro-Mexican American, or pro-Catholic legislative agendas. Political representation is often much more complicated than simple descriptive-based normative models imply, because many important issues in American politics do not neatly fit into white versus black, or male versus female, terms.

Even more subtle, however, is the very problem of conflict that we discussed earlier. As Bianco (1994) has noted, descriptive representation might work in a geographic area that is homogeneous, for the very homogeneity of the legislative district might facilitate the development of trust and responsiveness between constituents and representatives who look like them. But in heterogeneous districts—those that are split on racial, ethnic, or other divisions—trust and responsiveness seem impossible to achieve, and here Bianco argues that descriptive representation will fail.

This has led many scholars to look more seriously at substantive representation. Instead of evaluating representation based on a comparison of the appearance or identities of constituents and legislators, substantive representation is evaluated by the extent to which a legislator acts in the interests of constituents. As argued eloquently by Pitkin (1967), substantive representation can occur in two different—and not mutually exclusive—ways: representatives can be *trustees*, who represent the interest of constituents at a distance and only as part of a larger picture of multiple and possibly competing interests; or they can be *delegates*, directly carrying out the exact orders of constituents. Based on this distinction, an important line of empirical research has sought to measure substantive representation in many different settings.[2]

Yet even the normative notion of substantive representation still encounters three important problems. No matter whether one believes that representatives should act like trustees or delegates, they still must get information about the interests and opinions they need to implement, either directly or indirectly, into policy. In other words, for representatives to be either trustees or delegates, they must monitor the state of opinion among their constituents so as to be informed enough to act when policy proposals are under legislative consideration. If representatives are ill-informed about the opinions and interests of their constituents, they cannot adequately represent their constituents.

Equally problematic for substantive representation is the fundamental point of the earlier analyses in this book: American public opinion is plagued by uncertainty, ambivalence, and equivocation as the result of imperfect information, or competing values and predispositions. These three states of public opinion make the representative's job difficult, if not impossible, because there may not be a simple constituent interest that the representative can implement. Instead, constituents might be imperfectly informed about their interest regarding some policy issue, which means that there could be a wide range of possible actions for the representative. Or constituents might be ambivalent because of competing values, and statements they make about their own interests will be influenced by how much is at stake.

Third, the representative must engage in information collection about the interests and opinions of his or her constituents, giving rise to what we will call the "representative-as-analyst." Some representatives will engage in traditional retail politics while in office—walking precincts of their district and talking with constituents in their homes, or having town hall meetings, or participating in local social events—the purpose of which is to nonscientifically sample the interests and opinions of constituents. Other representatives will closely observe published opinion polls, or will even periodically have their own polling analyses conducted, to scientifically sample their constituents. But no matter how representatives collect data about the interests and opinions of their constituents, at some point they will try to compile their observations into some sort of summary judgment, perhaps even statistics, which will stand for the district's overall interest or opinion. At that point, the representative has engaged in exactly the same sort of aggregation of opinion that social scientists often undertake when studying public opinion—an undertaking that is known to be fraught with biases commonly called the "ecological inference problem." The ecological inferences representatives draw also greatly complicate their jobs.

Thus, while we are agnostic about the tradeoffs between descriptive and substantive representation, and we also do not take a stand in the debate over the relative merits of delegate-based or trustee-based substantive representation, our research does point to problems with political representation that have not been well-studied in past research. In fact, our representative-as-analyst has an even more difficult job than has been recognized in the past, because of three implications of our research: first, the representative must monitor or sample constituent interests or opinions; second, these same interests or opinions are likely to be uncertain, ambivalent, or equivocal; and third, the representative must be able to discern aggregated opinions or interests that might be biased.

In this chapter, we apply the results from our previous chapters to the study of political representation. We show that the representative-as-analyst does have a difficult problem. In the next section we detail the ecological inference problem, and in our analysis we show that aggregation is indeed an issue for the representative. This implies that the process of monitoring or sampling constituent opinion is not straightforward and that the representative needs to understand the underlying reasons for constituent interests or opinions.

POLITICAL REPRESENTATION AND AGGREGATION

Social scientists have long studied aggregate public opinion data, ranging from studies of the proportions of survey respondents expressing opinions about some policy, accumulated at the national, state, or congressional district level, to studies that examine the average or mean position on policy scales where the average was computed for some geographic unit. Examples of these studies of collective opinion are abundant in the literature of public opinion and political behavior.

One series of studies of aggregated public opinion has been the analysis of aggregated trends in presidential approval; both scholars and political actors see high levels of approval as an important political resource for presidents (Kernell 1986). High levels of approval are a central component of presidential power (Neustadt 1980) and influences electoral outcomes and legislative success (Brody 1991; Rivers and Rose 1985; Simon and Ostrom 1989). Since the early 1970s, a long list of articles and books have examined presidential approval from a time-series perspective. In general, these scholars have studied changes in the percentages of survey respondents who approve of the performance of the president as a function primarily of "rally events" (such as rational catastrophes and wars), economic conditions, and various time-related effects.[3]

A second major line of research examining the patterns of aggregated public opinion grew out of the early "Michigan" studies of Campbell, Converse, Miller, and Stokes (1960). They outlined two critical findings regarding mass political opinions. First, on most important political issues of the time—for example, government assistance with the provision of employment opportunities, American armed forces abroad, and government assistance for education—they found that the overwhelming majority of respondents in their survey samples had little idea of what the federal government was doing regarding each issue, where the two parties stood on each issue, or what their own opinions were on these same issues. Furthermore, since the issue positions of most citizens were weakly intercorrelated, and since they were unstable over time, these scholars also argued that there was little support for the notion of an overall ideological structuring of public opinion. There arose, as a result, a conception of the American electorate as poorly informed about issues, to the extent that many thought it impossible that people could make voting decisions on the basis of policy issues.

But these same scholars also argued that identifications with political parties—the concept of partisan identification—were strongly held by the public, that these identifications were stable over time and shaped how Americans viewed the political world around them. So, instead of seeing the American public as having an ideological view of public policy, the "Michigan" scholars argued for a partisan structuring of the polity.

Both of these findings have produced intense debate in political science. On one side are the advocates of "macropartisanship," which is essentially the study of the proportions of Democrats relative to Republicans, aggregated to the national level from various public opinion polls. The macropartisanship literature focuses on how different political and economic factors produce shifts in the partisan proportions over time (Box-Steffensmeier and Smith 1998; Green, Palmquist, and Schickler 1998; MacKuen, Erikson, and Stimson 1989, 1995). On the other side of the debate, there are those who study "macroideology," either at the state level (Erikson, Wright, and McIver 1993) or at the national level (Box-Steffensmeier, Knight, and Sigelman 1998; Stimson 1991). Much in the same line as the macropartisanship scholarship, these studies focus on explaining over-time differences (and between states, in the case of Erikson and colleagues) in the proportion of liberals to conservatives in American political life.

There have also been studies of collective American public opinion about various policy areas, most prominently in the area of racial attitudes and racial policy. A very important analysis of aggregate public opinion about racial issues is in Schuman, Steeh, Bobo, and Krysan (1997), and Page and Shapiro (1992) devote considerable attention to this subject as well. These analyses have examined the slow erosion of explicitly prejudicial political attitudes in American society but have also found that there has been little change in the willingness of Americans to support affirmative action programs for disadvantaged minority groups.

This research on racial attitudes is an important example for our purposes in this chapter, since racial politics is a problem that cuts across individual psychologies and aggregate politics. At the first level, a substantial body of scholarship argues over the determinants of individual attitudes toward racial policy, rooted in such diverse forces as racial resentment (Kinder and Sanders 1996), generalized out-group animosity (Sniderman and Piazza 1993), realistic group conflict (Bobo 1983; LeVine and Campbell 1972), or racial aversion (Gaertner and Dovidio 1986), all of which we addressed in an earlier chapter. But at the second level, scholars since Myrdal (1944) contend that the conflict between races, between holders of particular values, or between social conditions and values shapes outcomes of racial politics. These ecologies of racial politics interact with consequences for representation and for the potential of individual internalization of external political conflict. This chapter offers the argument that the problem of inference across the individual and collective political ecologies speaks not only to problems for the social scientist but also to fundamental problems of representation.

It is quite clear that Myrdal regards aggregate social conditions and cultural values as being at the root of the "Negro problem." Just a few pages into the introduction, Myrdal writes:

The Negro problem is an integral part of, or a special phase of, the whole complex
of problems in the larger American civilization. It cannot be treated in isolation.
There is no single side of the Negro problem—whether it be the Negro's political
status, the education he gets, his place in the labor market, his cultural and personality traits, or anything else—which is not predominantly determined by its total
American setting (lxxxv).

More recent efforts draw conclusions similarly from aggregate political numbers. Schuman, Steeh, and Bobo (1988) identify "principle-implementation"
gaps, where support for principles of racial equality always exceeds support
for any policies that might implement equality, as evidence for, among other
conclusions, conflict between principles at an individual level.

In this chapter, we turn our analysis to a comparison of the determinants of
public opinion about public policies at the individual and the aggregated level.
We use the same kind of inferential statistical models as we detailed earlier in
the book, but here we apply our statistical models to data at both the individual
and the congressional district level. Also, we look at public opinion at two
different points in time (1992 and 1996) and on different aspects of public
policy (affirmative action, welfare, and homosexuality). In the next section, we
discuss the complexities associated with studying public opinion at multiple
levels. We then move into our analyses of individual and collective public
opinion in subsequent sections of this chapter.

STUDYING CHOICES AT MULTIPLE LEVELS

The Ecological Inference Problem and Public Opinion

The problems of drawing inferences from aggregate politics to respondents'
internal states of mind is an obvious instance of an ecological inference problem. Gary King, in his 1997 book, provided the following definition: "*Ecological
inference* is the process of using aggregate (i.e., "ecological") data to infer discrete individual-level relationships of interest when individual-level data are
not available" (xv). As applied to the study of collective public opinion, then,
the ecological inference problem arises because scholars (like those discussed
in the previous section of this chapter) use aggregated measures of public
opinion to make inferences or claims about public opinion on the individual
level. The problem of ecological inference arises because the assumptions that
must be made when the scholar moves from aggregated public opinion statistics to arguments about individual-level behavior are often implausible and
untenable.

To make both the concept of an ecological inference more concrete, and to
underscore the problematic nature of the assumptions underlying ecological
inferences, we turn to one of the most dramatic examples of changes in Ameri-

can public opinion: the evolution of American attitudes about civil rights and racial equality. Page and Shapiro (1992) find that "the expressed attitudes of white Americans toward black Americans have undergone a great transformation over the last forty or fifty years, a change greater than on any other issue" (68). In their exposition of the changes in white American attitudes, they show that from 1963 to 1990 a sweeping transformation was under way in collective attitudes about racial issues.

Page and Shapiro then study the collective attitudes of Americans about school desegregation, broken down by education and region, thus examining the collective attitudes of highly educated white northerners, poorly educated white northerners, highly educated white southerners, and poorly educated white southerners. They conclude:

> Northern whites, for reasons dating back to abolitionism and the Civil War, were relatively quick to sympathize with the plight of blacks in the South and to apply Northern principles of legal equality to the Southern situation. (To be sure, the implementation of full social and economic equality in the North has been another matter.) Whites in the South were slower to accept the idea of black legal equality but eventually caught up, for the most part, under the influence of Northern pressure and the "new" South's own modernization, urbanization, rising education levels, generational replacement, and—probably to a lesser extent—immigration from the North. (80–81)

Using aggregated survey responses (the proportions of white Americans saying they favor different types of racial policies), they draw inferences about the processes that are driving individual white Americans to change their own minds about these important issues of public policy. At first glance, this does seem to be quite logical and conclusive, which is why many social scientists fall into the trap of the ecological inference problem.

Unfortunately, there are several important assumptions that must hold for the inferences that Page and Shapiro draw from their collective opinion data to be valid. To start with, remember that they are beginning with a single survey respondent, who is answering a series of survey questions at one point in time. They are careful to discuss their assumptions about the answers of this single respondent.

> [E]ach individual has a central tendency of opinion, which might be called a "true" or *long-term preference*, and which can be ascertained by averaging the opinions expressed by the *same individual* at several different times. If the individual's opinions fluctuate randomly around the same central tendency for a sustained period of time, his or her true long-term preferences will be stable and ascertainable, despite observed momentary fluctuations in opinion. (16)

Thus, much like the model of the survey response we have used throughout this book, Page and Shapiro see an individual's response as being composed of a central tendency and some variation around that central tendency.

They next move on to the process of aggregation.

> Moreover—and this is the key point—at any given moment, the random devia-
> tions of individuals from their long-term opinions may well cancel out over a large
> sample, so that a poll or survey can accurately measure collective preferences as
> defined in terms of the true or long-term preferences of many citizens. As a result,
> the measurement of collective public opinion is largely free of the random error
> associated with individual attitudes. (16)

So if the variances in opinions and responses among the individuals in a particular survey sample are random and not correlated with each other (the key
assumption noted by Page and Shapiro in this quote), simple aggregation of
the survey responses could produce an unbiased measure of collective opinion
at the time the survey was conducted.

But as our analyses in the previous chapters have shown time and again,
this assumption is untenable. Each of the different states of opinion we have
examined—uncertainty, ambivalence, and equivocation—imply that the variances of opinion and response for many different aspects of public opinion are
not random across individuals. Finding that measures of uncertainty, ambivalence, and equivocation *systematically and predictably* are determinants of response variability is clear evidence against the validity of this assumption. So
when we study collective public opinion, we cannot assume that the individual-level variances are random and independent from person to person, nor
can we study the simple aggregates. We need an approach similar to the one
we use for the individual-level analyses in earlier chapters, which explicitly
includes a model for a heterogeneous response—an approach we discuss and
develop in the next section of this chapter.

But before we turn to our approach for studying collective public opinion,
we should point out that these ecological inference problems are not strictly
an issue of academic interest. Ecological inference problems are much more
than mere problems for social scientists: the problem of drawing inferences
about the states of minds of aggregates speaks to a basic problem of political representation we discussed above. Aggregation is supposed to be one of
the means by which republics are able to cure the mischiefs of faction. *Federalist* 10 is quite explicit on the point: "the greater number of citizens and
extent of territory which may be brought within the compass of republican
than of democratic government . . . principally . . . renders factious combinations less to be dreaded in the former than in the latter" (Hamilton, Madison,
and Jay 83).

Aggregation of citizens' interests in republican government supposedly en-
velops a greater range of interests, reducing the likelihood of single, dominant
factions. But there is an irony of representation presaged in the same document.

Another means by which republics limit the damage of faction is that the representative should be able to distill the community interest better than the masses acting in their own self-interests. Thus the representative acting as a trustee must understand the broader scope of the constituency's interest, not just what they want across issues but also why it is that they want it.

Let us make the trustee's problem concrete in terms of racial politics. Constituents may be willing to react to policies couched as "racial preference," "affirmative action," or "quotas" without having a clear sense of what exactly these policies refer to. Should a representative regard marginals opposing quotas as dispositive of the constituency's immediate interest, much less long-term interests? The representative is in a better position to understand why it is that the constituency opposes quotas—that it is the result of a conflict with libertarian principles, or that it is a backlash of white resentment—than simply to know that the constituency opposes quotas. We return to the problem of ecological inference for representatives in the conclusion of this chapter.

Ecological Inference and Heterogeneous Opinions

In earlier chapters, we developed an inferential statistical model, with a model of the policy choice and a model of the variability around that choice. We use this particular statistical inference approach because we recognize that public opinion about policy issues is heterogeneous, since individuals differ in the amount of variability in their policy opinion. As we have seen in previous chapters, this variability stems from uncertainty, from ambivalence, or from equivocation.

But the results in earlier chapters are all based on individual-level analyses. There, we uncovered substantial evidence demonstrating time and again that individual Americans differ in both their opinions about policy issues and in their uncertainty, ambivalence, or equivocation about these same issues. The question we face in this chapter is determining what role this heterogeneity in public opinion plays in the study of collective public opinion, and to understand that, we need to move our inferential statistical model from the individual level to the aggregate level. This is the task of the remainder of this section.

In the public opinion data we examine in this chapter, all of our dependent measures of attitudes have three or four ordered categories. Here, the easiest approach (using linear regression) is clearly incorrect, since the linear regression model is based on the assumption that the difference between survey response categories is constant, for instance, that the difference between "strongly agree" (1) and "agree somewhat" (2) is the same as the difference between "agree somewhat" (2) and "disagree somewhat" (3). Additionally, other discrete choice techniques like multinomial logit would not take into account the ordinal nature of our dependent variables. Instead, we develop an aggregate heteroskedastic choice model.

Armed with our individual-level and aggregate-level heteroskedastic choice models, we can now estimate the parameters of interest at both levels. This lets us examine the determinants of individual-level public opinion just as we have done in previous chapters. It also lets us study the determinants of aggregate-level public opinion with virtually the same inferential statistical technique. We can then see exactly what the differences are in opinion at both levels. A complete discussion of these results is contained in an appendix located on our website (www.pupress.princeton.edu/alvarez).

In the remainder of this chapter, we undertake exactly this type of analysis using data drawn from two successive National Election Studies: 1992 and 1996. We use the 1992 data to study three different aspects of opinion about affirmative action, thus reproducing the analyses reported in chapter 6 on affirmative action, but with a different data source; we use the 1996 data to study opinions about affirmative action, welfare, and homosexuals. The 1996 NES data on affirmative action contain one question that is worded exactly as it was worded in 1992, allowing us to directly compare opinion on this important social issue at two different points in time at both the individual and aggregate levels. In the analyses below, we focus on the individual-level data and on the data aggregated to the U.S. House of Representatives district level. We believe that this is a very interesting level at which to study collective opinion, since these aggregates are the ones that House representatives monitor.

Before we begin to discuss the estimates of our heteroskedastic choice models, though, we examine more fully the different value measures employed in the models, beginning with a closer look at the variables we use in our estimations. We also discuss in detail the construction of the value measures for 1992 and 1996 as well as their distributions across individuals and across congressional districts. Finally, the results from our heteroskedastic choice models are presented.

INDIVIDUAL AND COLLECTIVE ATTITUDES

Our data for the analyses presented in this chapter come from the 1992 and 1996 National Election Study, pre- and post-election waves. Both data sets are ideal for present purposes, since the sample sizes are large (in 1992 there were 1,420 respondents, of whom 1,207 were white, while in the 1996 study there were 1,750 respondents, of whom 1,454 were white), and with the usual admirably efficient survey administration. Further, in the NES data from these two presidential election years, there are a wealth of policy choice variables (affirmative action, welfare, and gay rights) we can examine and very good indicators for our right-hand side explanatory variables. For purposes of the present analysis, we restrict the sample to white respondents only.

The dependent variables for our analysis of the 1992 NES data on affirmative action are responses to two questions:

- Preferential hiring of blacks: Some people say that because of past discrimination, blacks should be given preference in hiring and promotion. Others say that such preference in hiring and promotion of blacks is wrong because it gives blacks advantages they haven't earned. What about your opinion—are you for or against preferential hiring and promotion of blacks? Do you favor/oppose preference in hiring and promotion strongly or not strongly?
- Racial quotas for education: Some people say that because of past discrimination it is sometimes necessary for colleges and universities to reserve openings for black students. Others oppose quotas because they say quotas give blacks advantages they haven't earned. What about your opinion—are you for or against quotas to admit black students? Do you favor/oppose quotas strongly or not strongly?

The responses to these questions produce two dependent variables, which have four ordinal responses.

From the 1996 NES study we drew a larger collection of dependent measures, with two focused on affirmative action, two on welfare, and two on homosexuality. The questions all had four ordered responses, and we recoded each so that increasing values implied affirmative responses regarding each policy opinion.

1. Affirmative action
   - Hiring preferences: Some people say that because of past discrimination, blacks should be given preference in hiring and promotion. Others say that such preference in hiring and promotion of blacks is wrong because it gives blacks advantages they haven't earned. What about your opinion—are you for or against preferential hiring and promotion of blacks? Do you favor preference in hiring and promotion strongly or not strongly?
   - Private companies and affirmative action: Some people think that if a company has a history of discriminating against blacks when making hiring decisions, then they should be required to have an affirmative action program that gives blacks preference in hiring. What do you think? Should companies that have discriminated against blacks have to have an affirmative action program? Do you feel strongly or not strongly (that they should have to have affirmative action)?
2. Welfare
   - Welfare benefits for additional children: Some people have proposed that a woman on welfare who has another child not be given an increase in her

welfare check. Do you favor or oppose this change in welfare policy? Do you favor this change strongly or not strongly?

- Two-year limit on welfare benefits: Another proposal is to put a two-year limit on how long someone can receive welfare benefits. Do you favor or oppose this two-year limit? Do you favor the two-year limit strongly or not strongly?

3. Gay rights
  - Homosexuals and job discrimination: Do you favor or oppose laws to protect homosexuals against job discrimination? Do you favor such laws strongly or not strongly?
  - Homosexuals and the U.S. armed forces: Do you think homosexuals should be allowed to serve in the U.S. armed forces or don't you think so? Do you feel strongly or not strongly that homosexuals should be allowed to serve in the U.S. armed forces?

Thus, these dependent variables from the 1992 and 1996 NES studies allow us to examine public opinion on racial policy, welfare policy, and policies relating to homosexuality, providing different dimensions of public opinion to compare and contrast. Additionally, we have one question on preferential hiring of blacks, posed to survey respondents in both 1992 and 1996, which will allow us to examine the evolution of this one important aspect of racial policy during a time of considerable elite debate.

Individual and Aggregate Values

Our method for generating the individual-level value measures is the same as that employed previously in this book: conduct confirmatory factor analyses to generate the loadings for the scales, and then rescale the measure to 0–1 bounds. Table 8.1 displays the confirmatory factor loadings and question text for the four attitudinal scales of central interest from the 1992 NES data: racial resentment, spending preferences, economic individualism, and egalitarianism. The overall fit of the model is acceptable, with a goodness-of-fit index of .85.[4]

In general, the indicators for the scales perform quite well. Turning first to the racial resentment scale, we note that all three estimated loadings are large relative to the fixed scale and are statistically significant. Further, these measures do a reasonable job of separating the racial resentment from the policy choice: neither specific policies nor even the government are mentioned in any questions. We believe that these questions break the potential tautology in the earlier symbolic racism measures.

The indicators for spending preferences are more of a mixed bag, reflecting the mixed policy orientations of the indicators. By the magnitude of the load-

TABLE 8.1
Measurement Model, 1992 National Election Studies

Variable	Loading
Racial Resentment	
Irish, Italian, Jewish and many other minorities overcame prejudice and worked their way up. Blacks should do the same without any special favors.	1.00
Over the past few years blacks have gotten less than they deserve.	0.79 (0.03)
It's really a matter of some people not trying hard enough; if blacks would only try harder they could be just as well off as whites.	0.83 (0.03)
Generations of slavery and discrimination have created conditions that make it difficult for blacks to work their way out of the lower class.	0.70 (0.03)
Spending Preferences	
If you had a say in making up the federal budget this year, for which of the following programs would you like to see spending increased and for which would you like to see spending decreased?	
Food stamps	1.00
Welfare programs	0.71 (0.03)
AIDS research	0.52 (0.03)
Financial aid for college students	0.52 (0.03)
Programs that assist blacks	0.60 (0.03)
Solving the problem of the homeless	0.76 (0.03)
Social Security	0.42 (0.03)
Science and technology	0.06 (0.03)
Child care	0.72 (0.03)
Dealing with crime	0.27 (0.03)
Improving and protecting the environment	0.53 (0.03)

TABLE 8.1 (continued)
Measurement Model, 1992 National Election Studies

Variable	Loading
Spending Preferences (continued)	
Assisting the unemployed	0.73
	(0.03)
Poor people	0.88
	(0.03)
Public schools	0.55
	(0.03)
Aid to big cities	0.60
	(0.03)
Economic Individualism	
Which comes closer to your own opinion?	
One, the less government the better; or two, there are more things that government should be doing.	1.00
One, we need a strong government to handle today's complex economic problems; or two, the free market can handle these problems without government being involved.	0.78 (0.03)
One, the main reason government has become bigger over the years is because it has gotten involved in things that people should do for themselves; or two, government has become bigger because the problems we face have become bigger.	0.66 (0.03)
Egalitarianism	
Our society should do whatever is necessary to make sure that everyone has an equal opportunity to succeed.	1.00
We have gone too far in pushing equal rights in this country.	0.80 (0.03)
This country would be better off if we worried less about how equal people are.	0.81 (0.03)
It is not really that big a problem if some people have more of a chance in life than others.	0.69 (0.03)
If people were treated more equally in this country we would have many fewer problems.	0.67 (0.03)
One of the big problems in this country is that we don't give everyone an equal chance.	0.76 (0.03)

Note: Cell entries are unstandardized factor loadings; standard errors are in parentheses.

ings, one would interpret the spending preferences measure as dealing most explicitly with domestic policy preferences as expressed by the Democratic party. The only two anomalous loadings are those for science and technology and dealing with crime, arguably part of a more Republican vision for spending (and we do not include foreign policy or defense spending in the analysis). The pattern is hardly novel; Jacoby (1994) finds similar dimensions to policy spending preferences.

The estimates for the remaining scales, economic individualism and egalitarianism, likewise suggest that we have good measures for the latent scales. All loadings are large and statistically significant. The composition of the scales very closely resembles Feldman's seminal 1988 analysis of core values and welfare policy.

For the 1996 NES data, we again conduct confirmatory factor analyses to generate the loadings for the scales, and then rescale the measure to 0–1 bounds. Table 8.2 displays the confirmatory factor loadings and question text for the four value scales from the 1996 NES data: racial resentment, spending preferences, economic individualism, and egalitarianism. The overall fit of the model is reasonable, with a goodness-of-fit index of .79. Thus, the model fits almost as well as we saw for the 1992 NES confirmatory factor analysis.

Most important, our confirmatory factor analysis using the 1996 NES data differs significantly with regard to one of the value measures, racial resentment. In the 1996 NES data, there was a new battery of items that were included to provide specific measures of resentment against blacks and Hispanics. This battery consists of three sets of 7-point ratings, asking respondents to rate both blacks and Hispanics on whether they are hardworking or lazy, intelligent or unintelligent, and trustworthy or not trustworthy. Examination of the estimates in table 8.2 shows that each of these different items correlate highly with the latent measure of racial resentment.

The other value measures differ in only minor ways to those used for the 1992 NES data. In general, the spending preferences, economic individualism, and egalitarianism measures from the 1996 NES data are quite similar—both in terms of the survey questions used to construct each measure and in the correlations between these questions and the underlying latent values they are intended to measure—to the results from the 1992 NES data. We are confident that we have comparable, high-quality measures of these four values for both 1992 and 1996.

Distributions of Values

In Figures 8.1 and 8.2 we present graphs of the distributions of each of the four value measures (figure 8.1) across the individual survey respondents in

TABLE 8.2
Measurement Model, 1996 National Election Studies

Variable	Loading

Racial Resentment

Now I have some questions about different groups in our society. I'm going to show you a 7-point scale on which the characteristics of the people in a group can be rated. In the first statement a score of 1 means that you think almost all of the people in that group tend to be "hard-working." A score of 7 means that you think most people in the group are "lazy." A score of 4 means that you think that most people in the group are not closer to one end or the other, and of course, you may choose any number in between.

Where would you rate blacks?	1.00
Where would you rate Hispanic Americans?	0.67
	(0.03)

The next set asks if people in each group tend to be "intelligent" or "unintelligent."

Where would you rate blacks?	0.94
	(0.02)
Where would you rate Hispanic Americans?	0.88
	(0.02)

Do people in these groups tend to be "trustworthy" or do they tend to be "not trustworthy"?

Where would you rate blacks?	0.89
	(0.02)
Where would you rate Hispanic Americans?	0.83
	(0.02)

Spending Preferences

If you had a say in making up the federal budget this year, for which of the following programs would you like to see spending increased and for which would you like to see spending decreased?

Food stamps	1.00
Welfare programs	0.62
	(0.03)
AIDS research	0.63
	(0.03)
Solving the problem of the homeless	0.75
	(0.03)
Financial aid for college students	0.56
	(0.03)

TABLE 8.2 (continued)
Measurement Model, 1996 National Election Studies

Variable	Loading
Spending Preferences (continued)	
Social Security	0.52
	(0.03)
Improving and protecting the environment	0.55
	(0.03)
Public schools	0.67
	(0.03)
Dealing with crime	0.34
	(0.03)
Child care	0.76
	(0.03)
Poor people	0.80
	(0.03)
Economic Individualism	
Which comes closer to your own opinion?	
One, the less government the better; or two, there are more things that government should be doing.	1.00
One, we need a strong government to handle today's complex economic problems; or two, the free market can handle these problems without government being involved.	0.69
	(0.03)
One, the main reason government has become bigger over the years is because it has gotten involved in things that people should do for themselves; or two, government has become bigger because the problems we face have become bigger.	0.69
	(0.03)
Egalitarianism	
Our society should do whatever is necessary to make sure that everyone has an equal opportunity to succeed.	1.00
We have gone too far in pushing equal rights in this country.	0.58
	(0.03)
One of the big problems in this country is that we don't give everyone an equal chance.	0.69
	(0.03)
This country would be better off if we worried less about how equal people are.	0.55
	(0.03)
It is not really that big a problem if some people have more of a chance in life than others.	0.52
	(0.03)
If people were treated more equally in this country we would have many fewer problems.	0.69
	(0.03)

Note: Cell entries are unstandardized factor loadings; standard errors are in parentheses.

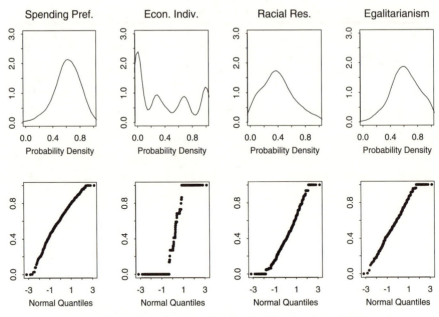

FIGURE 8.1. Distribution of individual-level values, 1992

our sample and the bivariate distributions of these same measures (figure 8.2). These figures are similar to others we have presented in earlier chapters.

Beginning with the individual-level univariate distributions, we see that in 1992 the spending preferences measure had a relatively symmetric distribution, with most respondents falling just above this measure's midpoint. Economic individualism, on the other hand, has a very bimodal distribution in the individual-level data, with many respondents being clustered at each end of this scale. Racial resentment, though, shown in the third panel of figure 8.1, has a relatively symmetric distribution, with the central tendency just below the midpoint. Last, the distribution of egalitarianism looks a great deal like the distribution for spending preferences, except for the fact that the egalitarianism measure has a slightly less symmetric look.

The bivariate distributions of these individual-level measures, given in figure 8.2, are simple to interpret. Beginning with the spending preference measure (whose bivariate distribution with each successive value measure is given in the first row and first column), there seems to be little relationship between spending preferences and economic individualism, but there are positive correlations between spending preferences, racial resentment, and egalitarianism. Next, moving to economic individualism, it is clear that this value is relatively

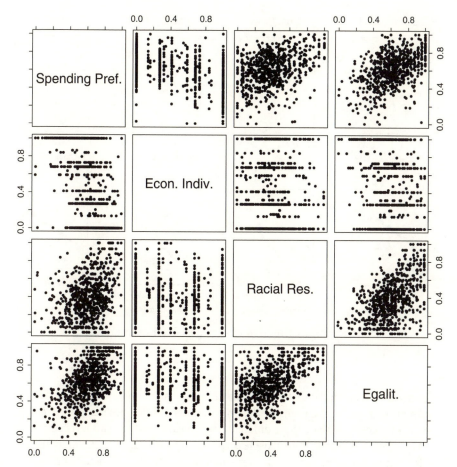

FIGURE 8.2. Bivariate distributions of individual-level values, 1992

uncorrelated with all of the other value measures. Last, there is also a positive correlation between racial resentment and egalitarianism.

But when we aggregate these value measures to the congressional district level, do we find that they have the same univariate and bivariate distributions? To examine this question, we provide identical graphs for the 1992 value measures, but for the distributions of the aggregated measures. These graphs are given in figure 8.3, which provides the univariate distributions, and figure 8.4, which provides the bivariate distributions.

Comparison of the univariate aggregate distributions to the univariate individual distributions (figures 8.3 and 8.1) shows that three of the value mea-

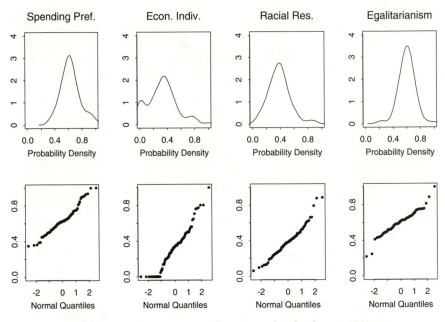

FIGURE 8.3. Distribution of aggregate-level values, 1992

sures have very similar distributions at each level: spending preferences, racial resentment, and egalitarianism. The only important difference that is apparent when we compare these three different value measures at the two levels is that the aggregated distributions have less variance in them than do the individual distributions; in other words, the distributions in figure 8.3 of spending preferences, racial resentment, and egalitarianism are narrower than in figure 8.1. But the economic individualism distributions are quite different at each level. The individual-level distribution of economic individualism was bimodal, with most respondents being either at the low end or the high end of this measure. We see in the 1992 aggregate distribution, however, that now economic individualism has a clear unimodal distribution, with the central tendency being below the midpoint of the 0 to 1 scale.

Additionally, when we compare the aggregate-level bivariate distributions (figure 8.4) with the individual-level bivariate distributions (figure 8.2), we see that while there are obviously far fewer data points to show in the bivariate distributions of the aggregate-level value measures, the patterns there are similar to what we found for the individual-level value measures. There seem to be slight positive intercorrelations for spending preferences, racial resentment,

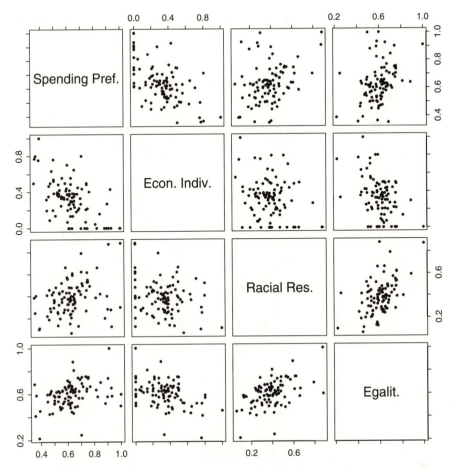

FIGURE 8.4. Bivariate distributions of aggregate-level values, 1992

and egalitarianism. But economic individualism seems to be uncorrelated with any of the other value measures.

Now we can compare the distributions of the 1992 values, at both individual and aggregate levels, to the same values in 1996. We begin by looking at the individual-level value measures from the 1996 NES data, presented in figure 8.5 (univariate distributions) and in figure 8.6 (bivariate distributions).

A direct comparison of the individual-level value measure distributions from 1996 with those in 1992 (in figure 8.1) shows both stability and change in these distributions in this four-year period. The stability seems confined to the spending preference measure; in 1996 this measure again has a relatively

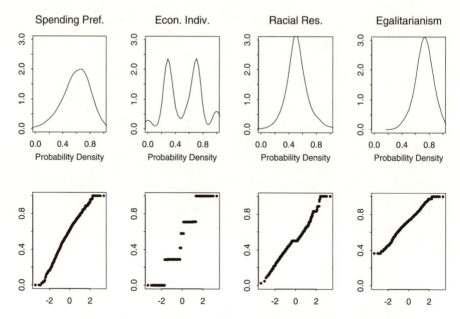

FIGURE 8.5. Distribution of individual-level values, 1996

symmetric distribution, centered just above the scale's midpoint. There seems to have been little change in American values for spending preferences in this four-year period.

On the other hand, we see evidence of change in the economic individualism, racial resentment, and egalitarianism value measures over the same period. Economic individualism is again bimodal in 1996, but with the two primary modes having moved considerably closer to the center of the scale. Racial resentment, on the other hand, is still unimodal, but now with a much tighter distribution centered slightly above the midpoint of the scale in 1996. Egalitarianism still has a central tendency above the midpoint of the scale, but the variance narrows considerably between 1992 and 1996. Thus, we see that in some ways the distributions of individual values in just this four-year period have changed in some important ways.[5]

We also see considerable change in the interrelationships of the different value measures, as shown in figure 8.6. Once again, economic individualism is relatively uncorrelated with the other value measures. But in 1996, spending preferences and racial resentment are much more independent of each other than they were in 1992. Spending preferences and egalitarianism in 1996 have a negative relationship, while racial resentment, and egalitarianism are uncor-

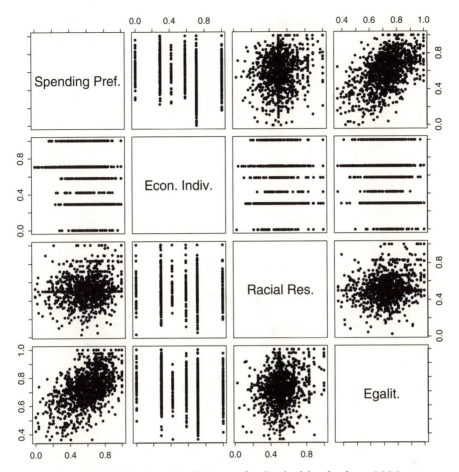

FIGURE 8.6. Bivariate distributions of individual-level values, 1996

related in 1996. Thus, while we saw slightly positive interrelationships in 1992 between spending preferences, racial resentment, and egalitarianism, in 1996 we see that these value measures are much more independent, with the only exception being spending preferences and egalitarianism, which now has a negative relationship.

The last two graphs are figures 8.7 and 8.8, which present the univariate distributions of the aggregated values for 1996 and their bivariate distributions for the same year.

Beginning with figure 8.7, it is clear that the aggregate-level value measures are very similar to the individual-level value measures in 1996. The primary

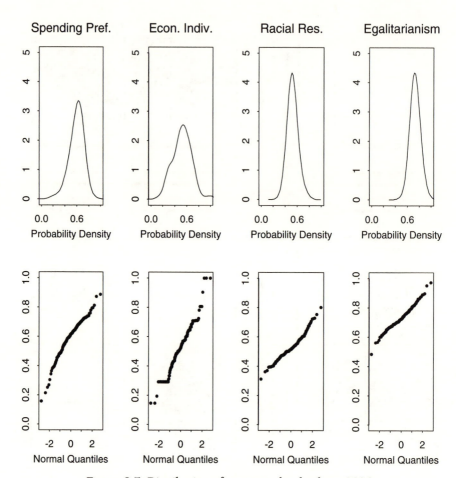

FIGURE 8.7. Distribution of aggregate-level values, 1996

difference is that the 1996 aggregate-level value measures generally have a narrower distribution than the individual-level measures. We also see that the bi-modality of the economic individualism measure is vastly reduced in the aggregated economic individualism measure, where we see a much flatter and unimodal distribution of aggregated economic individualism.

Compared with the aggregated value measures from 1992 (figure 8.3), the aggregated distributions of spending preferences are virtually identical. In 1996, though, we see that the distribution of economic individualism, racial resentment, and egalitarianism has shifted slightly to the higher end of the scale. These aggregated changes indicate that from 1992 to 1996, at the con-

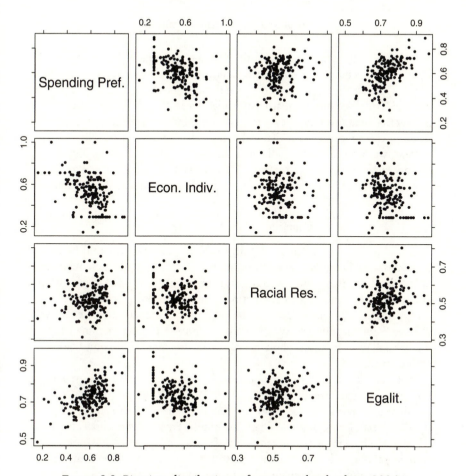

FIGURE 8.8. Bivariate distributions of aggregate-level values, 1996

gressional district level, spending preferences were constant, but the values of economic individualism, racial resentment, and egalitarianism all shifted slightly toward the upper end of each aggregated value scale.

Last, the bivariate distributions of the aggregated value measures in 1996 are given in figure 8.8. Most of the aggregated value measures show little, if any, intercorrelation. There is a weakly positive relationship between the spending preferences and egalitarianism measures, similar to what we found in the individual-level distributions in figure 8.6. Thus, these value measures are, in general, independently distributed in the aggregate-level data in 1996, just as they are in the individual-level data in this same election year.

Control and Information Variables

In addition to the scales measured through the confirmatory factor approach, we need other controlling variables and a measure for information. For the former, we include the self-placement of the respondent on the liberal-conservative ideology scale and the standard party identification scale, each fixed to -1 (strong Democrat/extreme liberal) to 1 (strong Republican/extreme conservative) bounds. These measures are identical in both the 1992 and 1996 NES data.

Next, we need measures to determine whether ambivalence, equivocation, or uncertainty are operative as regards the variability of opinions about these three aspects of racial policy. To begin, we need to measure competition among the expressed values, as before

$$\text{Competition } (v_1, v_2) = 1 - |v_1 - v_2|$$

This means that respondents who prize both values equally would be in the highest state of potential competition among the values, while those who prize only one of the two values would be in the lowest state. If respondents are ambivalent, the sign on the competition estimates will be positive and significant; if respondents are equivocal, the sign on the competition estimates will be negative and significant. We thus have a simple way of determining whether the variability in opinions about racial policy are shaped by equivocation or ambivalence.

To tackle uncertainty, though, we use a measure of chronic informedness. For the chronic information scale from the 1992 NES data, we simply include a count of the number of accurate answers to factual questions describing the political job of Dan Quayle, William Rehnquist, Boris Yeltsin, and Tom Foley: who has the final responsibility to decide if a law is constitutional or not; whose responsibility it is to nominate judges to the federal courts; and which party controls the House and Senate. The chronic information scale from the 1996 data uses slightly different survey questions, with a count of the number of correct answers to factual questions describing the political job of Al Gore, William Rehnquist, Boris Yeltsin, and Newt Gingrich. Despite these minor differences in the two chronic information measures in 1992 and 1996, we are confident that they both are adequate measures of the extent to which survey respondents are politically informed.

INDIVIDUAL AND COLLECTIVE OPINIONS

Now that we have fully elaborated on the problem of analysis of aggregated public opinion data, our model of it, and the specification and variations of our models using data from the 1992 and 1996 NES, we will present the results

TABLE 8.3
Effect of Values on Choices in 1992

	Individual Level		Congressional Level	
	Preferential Hiring	Racial Quotas for Education	Preferential Hiring	Racial Quotas for Education
Racial Resentment				
Low	.93	.82	.92	.79
High	.19	.10	.12	.13
Difference	−.74	−.73	−.81	−.65
Economic Individualism				
Low	.68	.51	.78	.53
High	.76	.52	.41	.48
Difference	.08	.01	−.38	−.05
Egalitarianism				
Low	.78	.69	.77	.79
High	.67	.41	.61	.32
Difference	−.11	−.29	−.15	−.47
Spending Preferences				
Low	.86	.69	.97	.57
High	.59	.40	.28	.49
Difference	−.28	−.29	−.69	−.09
Liberal-Conservative Placement				
Liberal	.71	.52	.69	.52
Conservative	.74	.49	.51	.53
Difference	.03	−.03	−.17	.02

of the secondary analyses from our heteroskedastic choice models. We begin by examining the effects of the different value measures in the choice component of our model, and then turn to an exploration of the variance component of our model.

Choices and Values

We begin our discussion of the choice function results in table 8.3. Here we present the individual-level results from the 1992 NES data in the second (preferential hiring of blacks) and third (racial quotas for education) columns; the congressional-level results are in the fourth (preferential hiring of blacks) and fifth (racial quotas for education) columns. For each choice function variable (the first column), we compute the probability that respondents in the survey would give the high category for the dependent variable if they scored low on the choice function variable. We next recompute the same probability, but changing the choice function variable to the high value, and then we compute the difference between these two probabilities.

At the individual level, we find clear evidence that racial resentment is the primary factor structuring beliefs about these two aspects of racial policy at both levels of aggregation in 1992. For each of the three dependent measures, racial resentment is the strongest predictor of choice, affecting beliefs about both preferential hiring of blacks (−.74) and racial quotas for education (−.73). The effects of racial resentment at the congressional level are slightly stronger on preferential hiring of blacks (−.81), but slightly weaker on racial quotas for education (−.65). In any case, citizens without racial resentment are strong supporters of these policies at both levels of aggregation, while those who harbor strong racial resentment are quite likely to oppose these racial policies.

We also have evidence that egalitarianism and spending preferences play some role in determining racial policy choices at both levels of aggregation in 1992, but not as strongly as racial resentment. Egalitarian values and spending preferences have less than half of the effect on racial policy choice at the individual level as does racial resentment. Thus, while they are important predictors of racial policy choices in 1992, they are dwarfed in magnitude by racial resentment. Both egalitarianism and spending preferences, though, generally have strong effects at the congressional level, in three of four cases (the only exception being spending preferences in the racial quotas for education model) having a stronger estimated effect than at the individual level.

We present our results of the effect of values on policy choices from the 1996 NES data in an identical manner, but in three different tables: table 8.4 provides our estimates of the effect of values on racial policy choices; table 8.5 presents the estimated effect of each value measure on welfare policy choices; and table 8.6 shows the effect of values on choices about the two questions on policies regarding homosexuals. We discuss each set of results in turn.

Beginning with the effect of values on racial policy choices in 1996 (table 8.4), we again find that, generally, racial resentment plays an important role in determining whether citizens support preferential hiring of blacks and whether companies should be required to have affirmative action policies. This effect of racial resentment on racial policy choices is important at the individual level in regard to both preferential hiring and company affirmative action plans, but at the congressional level it is important in only the preferential hiring model. We also see that egalitarianism plays an important role, at both levels, in determining racial policy choices in 1996. In fact, other than at the individual

TABLE 8.4
Effect of Values on Racial Policy Choices in 1996

	Individual Level		Congressional Level	
	Preferential Hiring	Private Companies	Preferential Hiring	Private Companies
Racial Resentment				
Low	.84	.58	.87	.06
High	.63	.21	.44	.00
Difference	−.21	−.36	−.43	−.06
Economic Individualism				
Low	.71	.36	.61	.01
High	.77	.38	.75	.02
Difference	.07	.03	.13	.01
Egalitarianism				
Low	.97	.95	.98	.60
High	.65	.13	.43	.00
Difference	−.20	−.82	−.55	−.60
Spending Preferences				
Low	.75	.69	.55	.57
High	.76	.19	.77	.00
Difference	.01	−.50	.22	−.57
Liberal-Conservative Placement				
Liberal	.75	.37	.71	.01
Conservative	.76	.34	.82	.01
Difference	.01	−.03	.11	.00

level in the preferential hiring model, we find that in 1996 egalitarianism has a stronger effect than did racial resentment. Spending preferences, though, play a strong role when it comes to beliefs about company affirmative action plans, at both levels, but only have an important effect on preferential hiring beliefs at the congressional level.

We can also compare the preferential hiring results in 1996 with those from 1992. Recall that in 1992 we found that racial resentment was by far the most important predictor of choices regarding preferential hiring at both the individual and congressional levels, and that both egalitarianism and spending preferences played some role in determining beliefs about this one racial policy. In 1992, spending preferences were about twice as strong in their estimated effect on beliefs about preferential hiring than egalitarianism.

In 1996, however, egalitarianism becomes about as strong a determinant of beliefs about preferential hiring as racial resentment, both at the individual and congressional levels. At the same time, spending preferences drop substantially as a strong predictor of preferential hiring beliefs at the individual level, while having a reasonable effect at the congressional level. The differences between the 1992 and 1996 results in this one aspect of beliefs about racial policies is interesting because it suggests that an important change in the determinants of beliefs about preferential hiring occurred in this four-year period. That is, beliefs about preferential hiring seem to have become much less structured by racial resentment by 1996 and much more determined by egalitarianism. This could be the result of changes in the way in which political elites discussed the issue of hiring preferences for blacks, since the political environment in 1996 did include a substantial discussion of this issue in the presidential election. Both major-party presidential candidates in 1996 took positions on the use of hiring preferences for minorities, in part because of Proposition 209 on the California ballot and in part because of discussions in Washington about the elimination of hiring preferences or "quotas" in the federal government. Much of this political rhetoric in 1996, furthermore, revolved around whether such hiring preferences provided equal treatment, thus tapping directly into egalitarian values.[6] Another possibility, suggested by Kinder and Sanders (1996), is that the rhetoric of those opposed to affirmative action has shifted from one of complaints of undeserved advantages to reverse discrimination, with an accompanying reversal of the effect of egalitarianism.

Next, we turn to the effect of values on welfare policy choices, presented in table 8.5. There we give the estimated effect of each of the value measures on beliefs about whether a woman on welfare should receive additional welfare benefits if she has another child while on welfare, and whether there should be a two-year limit placed on welfare benefits.

First, looking at the individual-level results, we consistently see that racial resentment, egalitarianism, and spending preferences all have roughly the same effect on welfare policy choices. Repondents scoring low on racial resentment, low on egalitarianism, and low on spending preferences are likely to support both welfare benefits for women who have additional children while on welfare and no time limits on welfare benefits. Changing these values to their opposite extremes produces almost identical changes in the probability that a hypothetical individual would support each policy.

But when we move to the congressional level, we still see a relatively consistent effect of these three values. At the congressional level, racial resentment has strong effects on both welfare policy choices, as does egalitarianism, whereas spending preferences have a weaker, and inconsistent, effect.

TABLE 8.5
Effect of Values on Welfare Choices in 1996

	Individual Level		Congressional Level	
	Additional Children	Time Limits	Additional Children	Time Limits
Racial Resentment				
Low	.74	.74	.73	.88
High	.40	.40	.65	.19
Difference	−.34	−.34	−.42	−.69
Economic Individualism				
Low	.53	.53	.36	.50
High	.61	.61	.65	.59
Difference	.08	.08	.29	.10
Egalitarianism				
Low	.84	.84	.95	.75
High	.44	.44	.26	.46
Difference	−.39	−.39	−.70	−.28
Spending Preferences				
Low	.76	.76	.40	.68
High	.43	.43	.58	.45
Difference	−.33	−.33	.19	−.23
Liberal-Conservative Placement				
Liberal	.58	.58	.53	.56
Conservative	.63	.63	.66	.65
Difference	.05	.05	.13	.08

Finally, we present in table 8.6 the estimated effect of each value on the two questions about policies relating to homosexuals. At the individual level, we again see racial resentment, egalitarianism, and spending preferences as important factors explaining beliefs about policy relating to homosexuality and job discrimination and their place in the U.S. military. But clearly egalitarianism plays the strongest role in explaining beliefs about these two public policy issues, with estimated probability differences at least twice those for racial resentment and spending preferences.

When we turn to the congressional-level results, we see roughly the same type of pattern in the estimated effects of each of these three value measures.

TABLE 8.6
Effect of Values on Homosexuality Policy Choices in 1996

	Individual Level		Congressional Level	
	Job Discrimination	Military Service	Job Discrimination	Military Service
Racial Resentment				
Low	.32	.40	.59	.56
High	.12	.10	.06	.07
Difference	−.20	−.31	−.53	−.49
Economic Individualism				
Low	.17	.18	.16	.29
High	.22	.23	.28	.17
Difference	.05	.05	.12	−.12
Egalitarianism				
Low	.77	.63	.85	.63
High	.08	.11	.09	.13
Difference	−.69	−.52	−.76	−.50
Spending Preferences				
Low	.39	.29	.33	.40
High	.11	.16	.16	.14
Difference	−.28	−.13	−.17	−.26
Liberal-Conservative Placement				
Liberal	.21	.22	.24	.25
Conservative	.33	.38	.36	.44
Difference	.12	.16	.12	.19

Again, egalitarianism is the value most strongly predictive of beliefs about homosexuality and job discrimination or service in the U.S. armed forces. But here, racial resentment becomes a much stronger predictor of these beliefs, becoming almost as strong a factor as egalitarianism. Spending preferences have roughly the same effect at the congressional level that they did at the individual level.

So what conclusions can we draw from this series of individual- and congressional-level results about what values drive each set of policy choices? First, and most important, we have seen that three of our value measures generally seem to dominate choices in each policy area: racial resentment, egalitarianism, and spending preferences. Second, we found that there were important differences in which value measure played the strongest role in different policy areas, with racial resentment being the strongest value in the 1992 racial policy models, egalitarianism playing the strongest predictive role in the 1996 racial policy models and in the homosexual policy models, and with each of the three values having roughly the same effect in the welfare policy models. Third, in most cases, we tended to see that the values that were important predictors of policy choices at the individual level were also important predictors at the congressional district level.

Information and Variability

Now that we have analyzed the effect of values on policy choices, at the individual and aggregate levels in both 1992 and 1996, we need to focus our attention here on the determinants of variability in these choices across these citizens at both levels of aggregation. Our specification of the respondents' variance function was discussed earlier and is similar to what we have used in previous chapters. We are primarily interested in finding whether the variability in citizen opinions are driven by uncertainty, ambivalence, or equivocation.

We include in the variance function for each policy choice, at both levels of aggregation in 1992 and 1996, our usual measure of chronic information. Here we will look for evidence of uncertainty, ambivalence, and equivocation using graphical methods. Our procedure parallels what we have done in earlier chapters; provide a graph of the error variance for a hypothetical or modal citizen in our sample for each policy choice at each level of aggregation, for the range of our information, and for value competition measures. The first set of these results are provided for the 1992 NES racial policy measures (figure 8.9).

If uncertainty is a primary force determining the variability in citizen policy choices, we expect to see the lines in each of the graphs slope downward. That is, citizens who are poorly informed (who score close to 0 on the chronic information scale) should have high error variability, while citizens who are well informed (and who score close to 1 on the chronic information scale) should have low error variability. This is exactly what we see in figure 8.9, which displays the results for individuals on the left, and those for aggregates on the right.

In these figures, we graph the hypothetical error variance at a particular level of chronic information using an A for hiring preferences and a Q for company affirmative action policies. Beginning with the effects of uncertainty at the individual level in 1992 (figure 8.9, left), we find strong and consistent evidence of uncertainty. Both lines in this figure slope downward, and it is clear that the effects of uncertainty are especially pronounced for hiring preferences at the individual level in 1992.[7] Thus we see strong and consistent

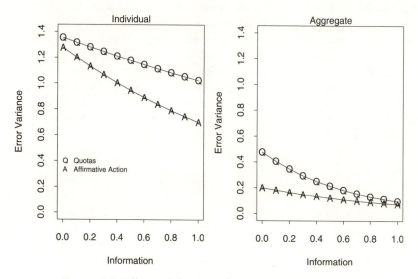

FIGURE 8.9. Effects of chronic information at the individual and aggregate levels, 1992

evidence of uncertainty at the individual level for racial policy choices in 1992—a result that is very similar to those presented in earlier chapters on uncertainty.

Furthermore, as figure 8, 9 (right) shows, the effects of uncertainty also exist at the aggregate level. In both cases, aggregates with higher proportions of poorly informed citizens have more policy choice variability; aggregates with higher proportions of well-informed citizens have much less policy choice variability. This effect of uncertainty, though, is much stronger at the aggregate level for company affirmative action policies than for hiring preferences, leading us to support the hypothesis that uncertainty drives racial policy choice variability at both the individual and the aggregate level in 1992.

Is the role of uncertainty as strong in the 1996 results? We again examine the effect of chronic uncertainty on policy choice variability using our graphical approach. This time we will present the results for each policy area in a separate panel of a graph. Figure 8.10 shows the effects of uncertainty on error variability for the two racial policy questions in the top panel, for the two questions about welfare policy in the middle panel, and for the questions about homosexuality policies in the lower panel.

Beginning with the individual-level effects of uncertainty in figure 8.10 (left), we see that generally the results are in the direction we expect. That is, uncertainty seems to affect the variability of policy choices at the individual level,

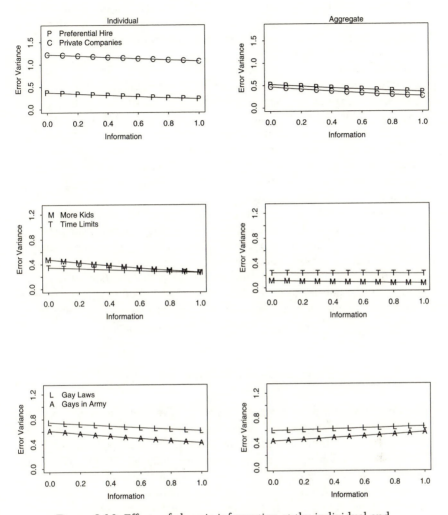

FIGURE 8.10. Effects of chronic information at the individual and aggregate levels, 1996

with poorly informed citizens having high variability and well-informed citizens having low variability.[8] Thus, we again see uncertainty effects in the directions we expect in the 1996 results, just as we found in the 1992 results discussed above.

Moving to the aggregate level (figure 8.10, right), we again see uncertainty results in the direction we expect for the racial policy choices, which are in the top panel of this figure. These uncertainty effects show that in regard to racial policy choices, uncertainty influences variability at both the individual and aggregate levels.[9] This parallels the results we found in the 1992 NES data on racial policy choices as well.

But in the other two policy domains, welfare policy (middle panels) and gay rights (lower panels), we see uncertainty effects that are not as strong or consistent. Regarding the aggregate effects of uncertainty on welfare policy choices in 1996, the effects of uncertainty are correctly signed (negative), with the effect of uncertainty being stronger for the question concerning whether welfare benefits should continue for women who have more kids while on welfare (M in the figure).[10] As for the two questions on policies relating to homosexuals, we find that uncertainty actually has an effect that runs counter to our expectation (being positive).[11]

Regarding the effects of uncertainty on policy choice variability, we reach three conclusions. First, we find strong evidence that uncertainty characterizes racial policy variability, at both levels (individual and congressional districts), in both 1992 and 1996. Second, we also have consistent evidence that uncertainty is operative in 1996 regarding variability in choices about welfare and homosexuality policies at the individual level. Third, we do not find strong or consistent support for the hypothesis that uncertainty structures choices at the aggregate level in the areas of welfare or homosexuality policy.

VALUE CONFLICT AND VARIABILITY

We now turn to the other two possible sources of variability in public opinion: ambivalence and equivocation. Recall that from our value competition measure, if we see a positive relationship between value competition and error variability, we will have evidence of ambivalence; if the relationship is negative, we will have evidence of equivocation. We start with the results from 1992, which we give in figure 8.11. Both of these graphs are organized just as the graphs discussed in the last section, except that for each pair of policy choices, we will present three different panels; each panel will graph one set of value competition measures (racial resentment and egalitarianism, racial resentment and individualism, and egalitarianism and individualism).

Beginning with the individual-level value competition results for the two racial policy choices in 1992 (figure 8.11, left), we see that there is potential evidence for ambivalence (racial resentment and egalitarianism for both policy choices, and racial resentment and individualism for only the company affirmative action model). Of these three possibilities, however, only one is statistically significant: racial resentment and individualism in regard to policies relating to private company affirmative action programs. Furthermore, we find little

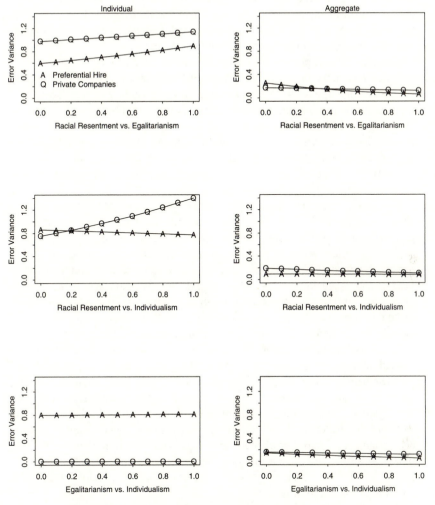

FIGURE 8.11. Effects of value conflict at the individual and
aggregate levels, 1992

evidence of any relationship between egalitarianism and individualism competition and error variability.

Turning next to the value competition results at the aggregate level (figure
8.11, right), a much more consistent picture emerges. First, we see that each
of the value competition measures does have a negative effect on error variability, which is evidence of equivocation. But most of the estimated magnitudes

seen in this figure are quite weak, except for the effect of racial resentment and egalitarianism in the aggregated model for hiring preferences. In fact, this is the only statistically significant estimate of value competition we observe in the 1992 aggregated models of racial policy variability.

Thus, the general picture that emerges from the 1992 results on the determinants of variability in racial policy opinions at both levels of aggregation is relatively uncomplicated. We find strong and consistent evidence of uncertainty as the major driving force behind policy choice variability at both levels of aggregation. There is also some evidence of equivocation, based on the competition between racial resentment and egalitarianism, when we look at the aggregated variability for hiring preferences, but we find no evidence of value competition effects on policy variability in the aggregated choices regarding private company affirmative action policies.

Next, we turn to the value competition results from the three sets of policy choice variables in the 1996 NES data at the individual level. We present three graphs for each pair of issues: the two racial policy questions in figure 8.12, the paired welfare policy choices in figure 8.13, and the two questions about gays in figure 8.14. In each of these figures, the interaction between racial resentment and egalitarianism is shown (in the top panel at the individual level on the left, and at the aggregate level on the right); the interaction between racial resentment and individualism is in the middle panel; and the interaction between egalitarianism and individualism appears in the lower panel.

Let us look at value conflict in the context of racial policy in 1996, at the individual and aggregate levels. In figure 8.12 we see at the individual level (the left panels) weak support for value conflict producing equivocation for preferential hires; these effects are strongest between racial resentment and egalitarianism, and egalitarianism and individualism. There is also some evidence of ambivalence in the case of conflict between racial resentment and egalitarianism concerning private company affirmative action plans, where we have a positively sloped line. Because the line is based on a statistically insignificant coefficient estimate, we cannot be certain that this possible instance of ambivalence is different from 0.

Turning to the results for value conflict at the aggregate level in racial policies (right panels of figure 8.12), we see significant contrasts to the individual-level results. At the aggregate level, the conflict between racial resentment and egalitarianism produces no ambivalence or equivocation, which is different from what we observed at the individual level. We also find that the conflict between racial resentment and individualism at the aggregate level induces equivocation in the case of private company contracts, but ambivalence in the case of hiring preferences; both of these effects, while of modest magnitude, are statistically significant. And last, we see a marked contrast in the lower right graph, which shows a decided clash between egalitarianism and individualism in the case of hiring preferences, producing strong evidence of equivocation. While equivoca-

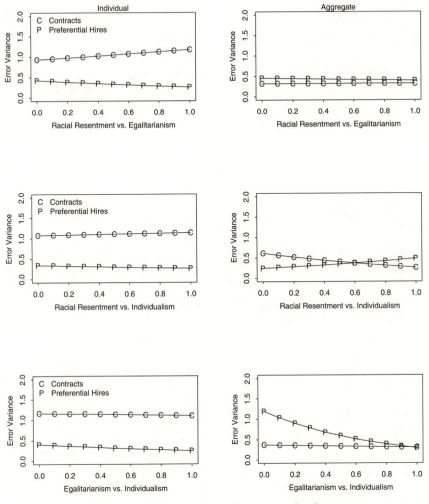

FIGURE 8.12. Effects of value conflict on racial policy, 1996

tion is also present at the individual level in the clash between egalitarianism and individualism, it is much stronger at the aggregate level.

We next examine the two questions about welfare policy in 1996 in figure 8.13. At the individual level, there are signs of value conflict producing equivocation in all six of these graphs, although the magnitudes are obviously weak. The equivocation results are all statistically significant for the two-year limit on welfare, and the equivocation-inducing clash between racial resentment and individualism is statistically significant for the more-kids results.

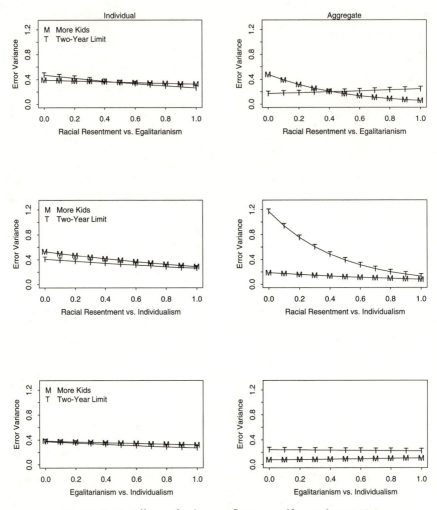

FIGURE 8.13. Effects of value conflict on welfare policy, 1996

At the aggregate level, on the other hand, we see some more dramatic results. Again, there is strong evidence of equivocation in three cases. First, racial resentment and egalitarianism conflict to produce equivocation in the case of whether women who have more children should get welfare benefits. Second, we find that the conflict between racial resentment and individualism produces very strong equivocation in responses about the two-year limit on welfare, and weaker equivocation for the more-kids analysis. All of these three equivocation effects are statistically significant in the aggregate level models.

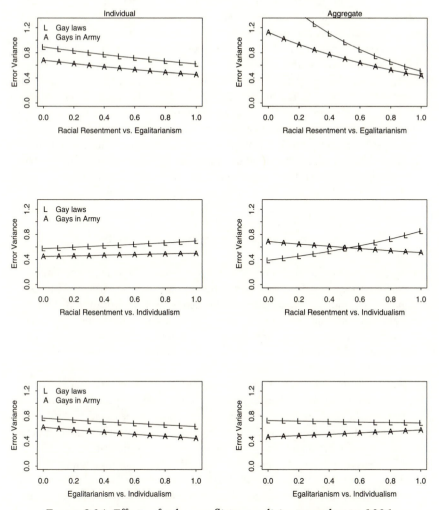

FIGURE 8.14. Effects of value conflict on policies toward gays, 1996

Last, there are the two questions about policies toward gays in 1996 (figure 8.14). Again, we find evidence for equivocation in policies about gays at the individual level: racial resentment and egalitarianism conflict to produce equivocation about laws to protect gays from discrimination; egalitarianism and individualism conflict to yield equivocation about gays in the military.

At the aggregate level, we see more signs of equivocation. The conflict between racial resentment and egalitarianism produces equivocation for both laws to protect gays from discrimination and gays in the military. On the other hand, we do find that the clash between racial resentment and individualism produces statistically significant evidence for ambivalence at the aggregate level in the context of laws to protect gays from discrimination.

The results presented in this section should sound a note of caution to most previous discussions about political representation. The representative-as-analyst must observe and monitor constituent opinion if he or she is to be responsive to voters in the district. But the evidence we have presented here shows that if the representative pays attention only to aggregate-level opinion, he or she may be led astray. Aggregate opinion, at least regarding the policy measures we examined in 1992 and 1996, differs from individual-level opinion in many ways, and, most important, information and value conflict operate differently as well. While we sometimes see reinforcing patterns of value conflict at both levels, we also see conflicting patterns across levels.

VALUES, OPINIONS, AND REPRESENTATION

This chapter has extended our two major arguments about the importance of values in structuring American public opinion and the importance of understanding the roles that uncertainty, ambivalence, and equivocation play in explaining the variability of those opinions. We have shifted the focus from earlier chapters—which examined individual-level public opinion—to the level of aggregated public opinion, a level of analysis that has seen considerable scrutiny in recent years.

Substantively, we have demonstrated repeatedly that aggregated public opinion about policy choices is like individual public opinion: the choices citizens make are structured by their deeply held values, and in both, the variability of these choices are determined by uncertainty and by the competition or conflict between values that produce either equivocation or ambivalence. Across the different policy issues studied, furthermore, we found considerable evidence to support the hypothesis that variability in public choices, at both the individual and aggregate levels, is fundamentally driven by uncertainty and equivocation.

Methodologically, we have also shown repeatedly that in each domain of public policy—racial policy, welfare policy, and policies about gays—the problems of ecological inference loom large. Unfortunately, researchers in many areas of public opinion analysis, especially in the politically controversial area of opinions about racial policies, have ignored the problems of ecological inference in their studies using aggregated public opinion (Myrdal 1944; Schuman, Steeh, and Bobo 1985; Page and Shapiro 1992). We have demonstrated that some of the important assumptions made by research using aggregated public opinion are false and that there are great complexities in the comparison of individual public opinion and aggregated public opinion.

These results also have important implications for political representation. If we assume that representatives (in our case, congressional representatives) are simple aggregate political analysts, our findings show that their task of understanding the desires of their constituents is complicated, because the representative-as-analyst observes aggregated opinion that may seem more fixed given additional information and if certain types of value conflict or competition are induced. But the representative-as-analyst may have no clear idea why these aggregates they observe adhere to the policy choices they make.

Our research paints a very pessimistic portrait of what we have called the representative-as-analyst. Whether delegate or trustee, the representative-as-analyst must monitor or sample the opinions and interests of constituents. As has been shown, the individual-level opinions a representative observes are not necessarily identical to the aggregate-level opinions also observed. Aggregation of opinions or interests, an inevitable and easy task for the representative-as-analyst, might lead them astray in their efforts to understand the needs and desires of constituents.

This is a disturbing and controversial conclusion. Because if we believe that political representatives choose between being the delegate of their constituents' preferences or being the trustee of their constituency's collective interest in the longer run, then the representative-as-analyst is in a difficult and perhaps impossible position. The delegate may be able to discern what his or her constituents want in terms of public policies, but the trustee will need to know why constituents want a particular policy. In a political environment where code words and phrases ignite passionate arguments and provoke value conflict, where few citizens have detailed understandings of what affirmative action or limits on welfare benefits actually mean, the representative-as-analyst needs to know whether his or her constituency opposes a policy on grounds that are repugnant or on grounds that are principled. By observing aggregates only, the representative will fail to appreciate what is driving constituent opinion and how those attitudes might be changed for the collective good.

Do Elites Experience Ambivalence
Where Masses Do Not?

THE NOTION that policy choices are riven by a conflict between fundamental core beliefs and values permeates the literatures on public opinion (e.g., Alvarez and Brehm 1995, 1997, 1998; Hochschild 1981; McClosky and Zaller 1984), public policy (e.g., Baumgartner and Jones 1993), and democratic theory (e.g., Tocqueville 1969). The clash of egalitarian and libertarian principles or moral traditionalism and democratic ideals permeates larger debates on affirmative action, abortion, the legitimate scope of government, and the U.S. role in the post–Cold War world. This has been a central theme of our book.

Given the scope and ubiquity of these fundamental value and belief clashes, it is easy to see why scholars of public opinion have long conjectured that Americans are divided over policy choices, producing ambivalence. But we contend that internalized conflict rarely produces ambivalence, since it entails the simultaneous presence of irreconcilably conflicting predispositions. The detection of ambivalence in surveys requires that the matters be of sufficient salience to the respondent to summon multiple predispositions at the same time, that the issues be important enough so that the respondent feels some investment in the choice for it to be "conflictual," and that the terms of the choice preclude compromise. Thus far in our analyses, only the issues of abortion and euthanasia meet these conditions for the detection of ambivalence in the mass survey response. Even in these two policy areas, the choice has to be one where a single value does not overwhelm the policy choice. We have thus shown that while ambivalence does occur for some public policy choices, it happens less frequently than either uncertainty or equivocation.

But elites may experience the pain of value and belief conflict when masses do not, for many reasons. Because elites are in the position of making choices about the implementation of policy, the salience of the consequences of policy choices may be considerably more marked for elites than for masses. The terms of a policy debate may be held by conflicting groups, even when the conflict does not reside in internal deliberation. Elites may experience internalized conflict in their role as representatives of the conflicting groups. They may be more conflicted over the policy choice because they understand the irreconcilability of the choices better, or because they are more aware of the risks associated with different policy choices. So for elites, internalized conflict might be an inevitable part of their decision making in some policy areas.

In this chapter, we conduct what we consider to be an acid test of the proposition that elites may experience value and belief conflict when masses do not, in an examination of the differences between the responses of a civilian masses and military elites over two categories of military policy choice: the level of acceptable casualties in military conflict, and the scope of civilian control of the military. This examination is possible because identical questions were asked in simultaneously conducted surveys of the two groups. Although it is possible that masses may comprehend the tensions undergirding the policy choices, we think it unlikely. As Lippmann (1922) observed, foreign policy is a distant matter for most citizens: "At almost all other times, and even in war when it is deadlocked, a sufficiently greater range of feelings is aroused to establish conflict, choice, hesitation, and compromise. The symbolism of public opinion usually bears, as we shall see, the marks of this balancing of interest" (153). But such choices about the acceptable levels of casualties for varying forms of conflict, or of the proper levels of military independence and autonomy from civilian oversight, are literal matters of life and death for military officers.

Lippmann provides one eloquent comparison of the differences between elites and masses with regard to casualties sustained in World War I:

> In the Great War previous calculations were upset to an extraordinary degree, for "out of every nine men who went to France five became casualties." The limit of endurance was far greater than anyone had supposed. But there was a limit somewhere. And so, partly because of its effect on the enemy, but also in great measure because of its effect on the troops and their families, no command in this war dared to publish a candid statement of its losses. In France the casualty lists were never published. In England, America, and Germany publication of the losses of a big battle were spread out over long periods so as to destroy a unified impression of the total. Only the insiders knew until long afterwards what the Somme had cost, or the Flanders battles; and Ludendorff undoubtedly had a much more accurate idea of these casualties than any private person in London, Paris, or Chicago. (153–54)

Do civilians have even the remotest clue as to the levels of casualties sustained in real combat? Do civilians have a sense of the levels of casualties that are typical for engagements overseas?

This chapter begins with a discussion of the two kinds of dependent variables we deploy in the analysis reported below, and is followed by a look at the predispositions that affect respondents' choices. Next, we present the results of our inferential approach to identifying ambivalence in variable response, demonstrating that while the opinions of elites are better crystallized, these opinions are also subject to tensions not experienced by the mass survey respondents. Finally, the broader implications of these differences in the extent of internalized conflict between elites and masses is examined.

TOUGH CHOICES ABOUT THE MILITARY

To test our model, we need data for the attitudes of military elites and the civilian masses about issues of civilian control and their casualty tolerance for different foreign policy objectives. Under the direction of Peter Feaver and Richard Kohn, the Triangle Institute for Security Studies (TISS) commissioned Princeton Survey Research Associates to conduct a nationwide survey of civilians and the military in the fall and winter of 1998, referred to as the "Survey on the Military in the Post-Cold War Era" (SMPCWE). The survey focused on the "civil-military culture gap" (Feaver 1999a, 1999b; Feaver and Gelpi 1999a, 1999b), and included general questions about domestic and foreign policy, attitudes about civilian and military culture, the role and performance of various domestic institutions, civilian control of the military, and casualty tolerance for selected foreign policy objectives. This survey contains several truly unique aspects that allow for the exploration of a broad range of topics.[1] Our interest here, however, is to explore aspects of the latter two topics.

We use two sets of these questions to develop five measures of attitudes about the scope of civilian control of the military and three measures of acceptable casualty levels from SMPCWE as dependent variables in our analysis. On the first set of measures, the survey asked respondents to state whether they agreed or disagreed (on a 4-point scale, where 4 represented "strongly disagree" and 1 represented "strongly agree") with the following statements:

- Civilians decide use: In general, high-ranking civilian officials rather than high-ranking military officers should have the final say on whether or not to use military force.
- Civilians decide type: In general, high-ranking civilian officials rather than high-ranking military officers should have the final say on what type of military force to use.
- Domestic politics decides: When civilians tell the military what to do, domestic partisan politics rather than national security requirements are often the primary motivation.
- In war, military should control: In wartime, civilian government leaders should let the military take over running the war.
- Civilian control safe: Civilian control of the military is absolutely safe and secure in the United States.

These five statements give us the five dependent variables on civilian control of the military that we use below.

On the second set of measures, the survey asked respondents to indicate the number of American deaths they consider acceptable for several foreign policy objectives. The question was put in historical context and asked: "When American troops are sent overseas, there are almost always casualties. Forty-three

Americans were killed in Somalia, 383 in the Gulf War, roughly 54,000 in Korea, 58,000 in Vietnam, and 400,000 in World War II. Imagine for a moment that a president decided to send military troops. In your opinion, what would be the highest number of American deaths that would be acceptable to achieve the following goals?"

- Congo: To stabilize a democratic government in Congo.
- Iraq: To prevent Iraq from obtaining weapons of mass destruction.
- Taiwan: To defend Taiwan against invasion by China.

These three statements give us the three dependent variables we use below on casualty tolerance.

Figure 9.1 displays histograms of each of the five scales on civilian control. The most notable divergence of the attitudes between military elites and civilian masses is in response to whether civilians should decide about the use of force (upper left panel). Whereas the military elites tend to strongly agree, the civilian masses do not seem to have well-formed opinions about this question or to have even thought much about the issue. On the three statements focusing squarely on civilian control, we see that while the military elites clearly believe that civilians should decide whether to use force (civilians decide use), they tend to also believe that once the decision to employ force has been taken, the military should run the war (in war, military should control) and decide the type of force used (civilians decide type). These findings are not surprising, given the indoctrination of the military and the seminal influence of Huntington's (1957) work on civilian control in military education. He argued strongly for civilian control, but also for the use of military expertise.[2]

The findings that the military elites disagreed that civilians should decide the type of force used but agreed that in war the military should have control fit with the work of Feaver (1999a, 1999b) on the rules of engagement and Huntington (1957). Somewhat surprisingly, however, whereas the civilian masses did strongly agree, the military elites did not strongly agree that the military should have control in war. It is perhaps also surprising that a majority of the civilian masses favored letting the military both decide the type of force and run the war. It seems more than likely that the wide dissemination of the "lessons of Vietnam" and the strong subsequent sentiments against politicians "micromanaging" the war are responsible. The phrasing of the question on whether civilian control is absolutely safe may have left some ambiguity about its meaning for respondents. Some may well have interpreted the question as meaning the possibility of a military coup, while others may have interpreted it as asking whether civilian control is a good idea. Both the civilian masses and the military elites, however, seem to have similar attitudes about this statement.

Figure 9.2 displays kernel density plots of each of the three scales of acceptable casualty levels.[3] While the distribution of the levels of acceptable casualties is weakly bimodal for the civilian masses, it is always strongly bimodal for the

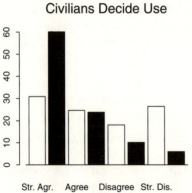

Civilians Decide Use

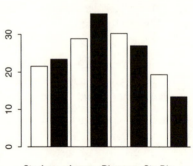

Civilian Control Safe

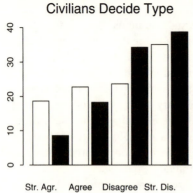

Civilians Decide Type

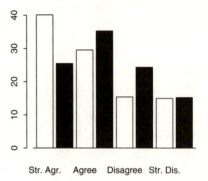

In War, Military Should Control

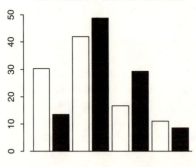

Domestic Politics Decides

■ Military Elites

□ Civilian Masses

FIGURE 9.1. Scope of civilian control of military, military
elites vs. civilian masses

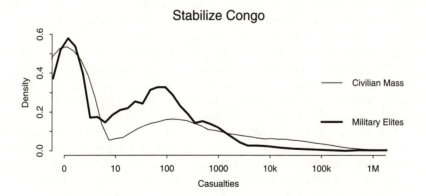

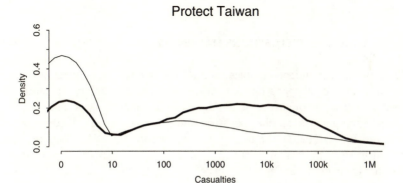

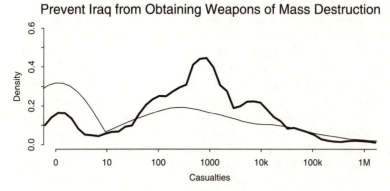

FIGURE 9.2. Kernel density plot of acceptable casualty levels,
military elites vs. civilian masses

military elites. It is striking how, for the civilian masses, the mode of acceptable casualties across the different foreign policy objectives is consistently at 0. For the military elites, however, the mode is 0 only for the issue of stabilizing Congo. Perhaps somewhat surprisingly, on average, one military elite respondent for each of the three foreign policy objectives stated that he was willing to accept higher numbers of casualties. As the reader will shortly discover, when one controls for the predispositions of the respondents, the military elites actually prefer fewer casualty levels than the civilian respondents.

Next, we turn to our primary goal in this chapter: to account for variations in each of these eight scales by how strongly the military elites and civilian masses simultaneously perceive a threat to American national security, are moral traditionalists, and hold pro-military attitudes. In the next section we discuss how we operationalize each of these concepts, examine other methodological details of our analysis, and present and discuss the results.

WHICH PREDISPOSITIONS MATTER FOR MILITARY POLICY?

Both types of dependent variables used in this chapter—acceptable levels of casualties and the proper scope of civilian control of the military—potentially invoke a cluster of predispositions. Although the model proposed here does not explicitly incorporate the "postures" and "core values" identified by Hurwitz and Peffley (1987), the basic principles are the same. Respondents are guided in their choices by relatively simple heuristics that could produce a reasonably coherent foreign policy belief system. In this section, we consider four specific predispositions: a sense of the dangerousness of the world, moral traditionalism, pro-military affect, and the trustworthiness of different political actors. In addition, there are a number of plausible controls to introduce.

We continue with our general method of employing scales derived from confirmatory factor analysis. Table 9.1 displays the factor loadings for three of the predispositions we employ in this chapter, for threat (dangerousness of the world), moral traditionalism, and pro-military affect.

We expect that perceptions of the dangerousness of the world should affect both one's willingness to expend high levels of casualties for different foreign policy purposes and the autonomy one would accord to the military. Those who perceive the world to be a dangerous place may be more willing to accept high casualty rates for American forces. Likewise, those who see a dangerous world may be loathe to restrain the U.S. military, or to defer to civilian political control. At least since Walt (1987), one theoretical school in international relations has argued that people and states balance against threat, not against power. The perception of high threat to national security makes Americans more disposed to support a more active foreign policy where American troops are put into danger. In the current unipolar world, no other power comes

TABLE 9.1
Confirmatory Factor Analysis Loadings for Scales

Variable	Loading
Threat	
First, I would like you to evaluate the seriousness of the following possible threats to American national security. Please tell me how serious you think each possible threat is.	
The emergence of China as a great military power	1.69
A large number of immigrants and refugees coming to the United States	1.00
The decline of standards and morals in American society	1.89
Economic competition from abroad	0.85
Terrorist attacks on the United States	0.70
Moral Traditionalism	
Prayer in public schools should be allowed.	1.00
The decline of traditional values is contributing to the breakdown of our society.	1.20
Civilian society would be better of if it adopted more of the military's values and customs.	0.72
American society would have fewer problems if people took God's will more seriously.	1.14
All Americans should be willing to give up their lives to defend our country.	0.55
Pro-Military Affect	
Most members of the military have a great deal of respect for civilian society.	1.00
Most members of civilian society have a great deal of respect for the military.	0.94
I would be disappointed if a child of mine joined the military.	−0.15
I have confidence in the ability of our military to perform well in wartime.	1.92
I expect that ten years from now America will still have the best military in the world.	2.12

Note: Cell entries are loadings from a confirmatory factor analysis using unweighted least squares.

close to the United States in military and economic might (excluding perhaps Russia's nuclear capabilities). While there exists no clear and immediate danger to America's power position, attention among both the public and the government has shifted to other more indirect threats to America's national security, including unconventional warfare, terrorism, and the potential dangers from conflicts in other parts of the world.

The confirmatory factor analysis relies upon five questions with a common stem: "I would like you to evaluate the seriousness of the following possible threats to American national security. Please tell me how serious you think each possible threat is":

- The emergence of China as a great military power
- A large number of immigrants and refugees coming to the United States
- The decline of standards and morals in American society
- Economic competition from abroad
- Terrorist attacks on the United States

The range of the "threats" invoked by the five questions obviously ranges from strictly domestic (decline of morals) to foreign (China as a military power), and from economic (competition from abroad) to military (terrorist attacks). Nonetheless, the loadings are all large and close to 1, implying that the components of the scale track a common dimension.

A general positive affect for the military should affect both of our classes of dependent variables. Those who have a high regard for the military should presumably wish to see lower levels of casualties for any engagement. Feaver and Gelpi (1999a, 1999b), however, suggest that people with a pro-military affect will understand the dangers and risks of the use of force and therefore understand that casualties may be uncontrollable. They also propose a second argument, citing General Colin Powell, that if people dislike the military and do not understand it, they may be less sensitive to casualties. Likewise, those who have a high positive affect toward the military may eschew civilian control, preferring that the military be autonomous. We rely on five questions, each measured as a 5-point Likert scale:

- Most members of the military have a great deal of respect for civilian society.
- Most members of civilian society have a great deal of respect for the military.
- I would be disappointed if a child of mine joined the military.
- I have confidence in the ability of our military to perform well in wartime.
- I expect that ten years from now America will still have the best military in the world.

All of the loadings but two are close to 1 (the exceptions being disappointment about a child joining the military, which has a tiny negative loading, and the statement about the best military, which has a loading of 2), again implying a strong common scale.

We also expect that moral traditionalists may be more willing to incur high casualties and to defer to the military. Moral traditionalism involves deference to authority, strong moral foundations, and emphasis on religiosity. This deference to authority should be more likely to lead to support for the military over elected political leaders. As Hurwitz and Peffley (1987) argue, "clearly, one's willingness to endorse a militaristic posture should be related to one's values regarding the 'rightness' of military solutions" (1109). Moral traditionalists should be more accepting of casualties for what they perceive to be "just wars." Moral attitudes, thus, should affect whether the respondents endorsed particular foreign policy objectives to the point where they would be willing to sacrifices American lives. Moral traditionalism also feeds back into expectations and considerations about domestic political institutions and issues of civilian control.

The five items for the moral traditionalism scale are all measured on a 5-point Likert scale:

- Prayer in public schools should be allowed.
- The decline of traditional values is contributing to the breakdown of our society.
- Civilian society would be better off if it adopted more of the military's values and customs.
- American society would have fewer problems if people took God's will more seriously.
- All Americans should be willing to give up their lives to defend our country.

With the exception of the last item, the indicators all scale close to one, implying a common underlying factor.

We display the univariate distribution plots for these first three, continuous scales (threat, moral traditionalism, and pro-military affect) in figure 9.3. All three of these scales are skewed toward the high end, implying that the respondents find the world a threatening place, they are moral traditionalists, and they hold a high degree of positive affect toward the military.

The fourth and final predisposition that we employ in this analysis concerns the confidence one has in the institutions that provide oversight of the actions of the military. Unlike the prior predispositions, we measure each of the oversight measures separately, since there is no particular reason to expect a single, common component. Here, we look at confidence in the military, the executive, and the press, and general social trust. The greater confidence one has in the military, the more one should be willing to defer to the military in matters of policy. The greater confidence one has in the executive, the more that one should be willing to accede to civilian control. The greater confidence one has in the press and in people generally, the more one may find civilians appropriate controls over military choices.

Three of these predispositions may come in conflict with one another, the possibility of which is apparent in the bivariate distribution plots in figure 9.4.

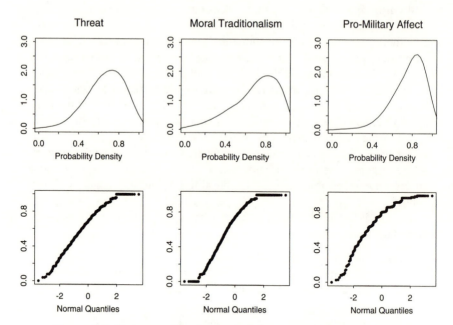

FIGURE 9.3. Univariate distributions of threat, moral traditionalism,
and pro-military affect

The extent to which one sees a dangerous world but still holds a high affect for
the military may be conflictual: on the one hand, the threats of the world may
lead one to commit troops for their resolution, putting them in harm's way,
while at the same time, one feels an affinity for the troops at risk. The threatening
nature of the world may also conflict with moral traditionalism: one postulates
that the world is a disorderly and violent place, while the latter values traditional
order and deference. Figure 9.4 demonstrates that there are, in fact, quite a large
proportion of respondents who score equivalently on all three predispositions.

Second, we include several variables to pick up attitudes on the trustworthiness of the relevant domestic institutions and actors. These variables come
from four questions in the survey on general social trust (Brehm and Rahn
1997; Yamagishi and Yamagishi 1994): Confidence in the military, confidence
in the executive, and confidence in television (Jordan and Page 1992). One
might be more willing to place civilian politicians in control over the military
if one regards those civilians as trustworthy. Likewise, the greater confidence
one has in the military itself, the more likely that one would accord it autonomy
from civilian control.

Third, we ask three questions in the survey dealing with variables for immediate connections to the military, such as personal experience in the military

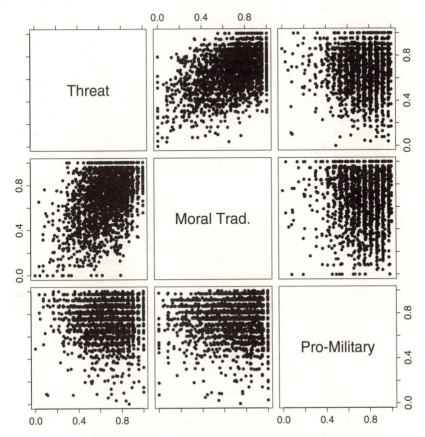

FIGURE 9.4. Scatterplot matrix of threat, moral traditionalism, and pro-military affect

or reserves and whether the respondent has family members in the military. If Huntington is right, we might expect considerable fluctuations in the numbers of casualties that members of the military and their families find acceptable for the three foreign policy objectives. He argues that "the military man" wants to avoid war and "has no concern with the desirability or undesirability of political goals as such. He is, however, concerned with the relation between political goals and military means since this directly affects the military security of the states" (Huntington 1957, 68.) Respondents who have served in the military or have family members in the military might thus be more sophisticated in their evaluation of the relation between any particular foreign policy objective and overall American national security.

Fourth, we employ three important control variables in our choice models, age and dummy variables for gender and race, and the respondent's education level as a measure of chronic informedness or political sophistication.

Fifth, and most important, we test for differences in responses between the civilians and the military elites in two different ways. One way we control for systematic differences is by including a dummy variable for elites in the choice component of our models, which allows for differences in their responses. The second way is more fundamental to the analysis in this chapter, which is that we hypothesize that there are systematic differences in the underlying variability of mass and elite attitudes about military policy. To allow for these differences in response variability, we include an interaction term in the variance component of our models.

Finally, there is one difference between our analysis presented below and the analyses reported in previous chapters of this book that should be noted. Two types of dependent variables are used in this chapter: three continuous measures of acceptable levels of casualties and five ordinal measures of the proper scope of civilian control of the military. We examine the impact of our value and belief measures, and our operationalizations for uncertainty, ambivalence, and equivocation, for the five ordinal measures using the same heteroskedastic-ordered probit model we have used in earlier chapters.

But our treatment of the continuous measures of acceptable levels of casualties is different than anything we have done thus far. These dependent variables are unusual because they can actually be thought of as "count" variables (in this case, counts of the appropriate number of casualties in three different scenarios). Dependent variables of this nature require the use of statistical distributions appropriate for count variables (King 1989). So, given a count variable that is hypothesized to be heterogenous, the negative binomial distribution is appropriate, (according to King 1989, 52, 128). There is a technical discussion of the heterogeneous negative binomial model in an appendix on our website, www.pupress.princeton.edu/alvarez. We present those results first, in the next section, followed by the heteroskedastic ordinal probit results. Thereafter, we deviate from our past practice of presenting and discussing only the estimated marginal effects, since we are here also interested in examining the statistical differences between mass and elite survey responses.

INFERENCES ABOUT RESPONSE VARIABILITY

Acceptable Casuality Levels

Table 9.2 presents the heterogeneous negative binomial estimates of the models for acceptable casualities in the Congo, Taiwan, and Iraq.[4] The pattern of coefficients is quite similiar across the three distinct scenarios for military engagement.

TABLE 9.2

Choice Component of Heterogeneous Negative Binomial Estimates for Models of
Acceptable Casualty Levels

Variable	Stabilize Dem. Govt. in Congo	Defend Taiwan	Prevent Mass Dest. by Iraq
Constant	10.14	10.45	12.66
	(0.72)	(0.67)	(0.58)
Threat	0.64	0.47	0.05
	(0.56)	(0.48)	(0.41)
Pro-military	−0.98	−1.16	−1.24
	(0.58)	(0.55)	(0.47)
Moral traditionalism	−0.26	−0.49	0.43
	(0.46)	(0.37)	(0.31)
Elite?	−4.36	−1.26	−1.33
	(0.43)	(0.42)	(0.31)
White?	0.17	−0.19	0.13
	(0.22)	(0.21)	(0.18)
Male?	0.58	1.91	0.39
	(0.21)	(0.22)	(0.17)
Age	0.03	0.02	−0.001
	(0.01)	(0.01)	(0.01)
Social trust	−0.05	0.22	0.21
	(0.11)	(0.09)	(0.07)
Confidence in military	−0.05	−0.06	−0.83
	(0.27)	(0.36)	(0.27)
Confidence in executive	0.001	−0.41	−0.01
	(0.24)	(0.12)	(0.11)
Confidence in TV	0.10	−0.38	−0.09
	(0.16)	(0.11)	(0.09)
Military service?	−0.61	0.66	−0.16
	(0.24)	(0.24)	(0.18)
In reserves?	−0.20	−0.27	−0.25
	(0.23)	(0.23)	(0.17)
Family in military?	0.14	0.33	−0.34
	(0.16)	(0.15)	(0.13)
N	1677	1677	1677

Note: Cell entries are maximum likelihood estimates of heterogeneous negative binomial model; standard errors are in parentheses. *Source:* Triangle Institute for Security Studies Survey on the Military in the Post–Cold War Era.

Of the three scales that we employ in this analysis, only the pro-military scale affects the respondent's assessment of levels of casualties to a statistically significant degree. Not surprisingly, those with high regard for the military generally set the limit on casualties much lower than those without such high regard. Moreover, this lesser tolerance for casualties is exactly inverse to the mean level of casualties for each scenario. Those who see the world as a threatening place are, in each of the three models, willing to incur higher levels of casualties, but the estimate is never significant.

Military elites, in general, want significantly lower casualties than the civilian masses. (Compare this result to the difference in the kernel density plots.) This may stem from multiple causes. For one, they are personally closer to the men and women who would be engaged in the scenarios, and such personal attachment should manifest in a lower ceiling on acceptable casualties. Military elites may also better comprehend how many casualties are typically incurred for different scenarios. But in any event, it is clear that the military are considerably less tolerant of casualties than are the civilians.

Next, most of the "confidence" measures are negative, and several of these negative estimates are statistically significant. Those with high confidence in the military, the executive branch, or TV generally set limits on casualties much lower than those who do not express such confidence. These results are especially pronounced for confidence in the military in the Iraq equation, and for both confidence in the executive branch and in TV in the Taiwan equation.

Turning to the control variables, we find one clear result: men are more willing to incur casualties than are women, although the magnitude of the coefficient is rather small. The pattern for the other demographic controls is somewhat inconsistent across the three models.

But the most interesting portion of this first analysis appears in table 9.3, which presents the variance component of the heterogeneous negative binomial model. The results strongly imply that civilian masses experience equivocation, while military elites are ambivalent. The sign on the coefficient for education (for masses) is negative, as is the sign on the coincidence of threat and pro-military affect, and of threat and moral traditionalism. Better-informed civilians have lower response variability. In addition, those respondents who perceive the world to be a threatening place, hold the military in high esteem, and are moral traditionalists are also less variable in their responses. As with our analysis of attitudes toward the IRS, the implication is that masses see no difficulty in accomplishing all three of these key predispositions.

The pattern for elites, on the other hand, is quite different. Elites are themselves much less variable in their attitudes about acceptable casualty levels: the sign on the dummy variable for elites is negative and sizable. The signs on the education term and the coincidence measure (for threat and pro-military affect), however, are positive and strong. The implication is that the effect of

TABLE 9.3

Variance Component of Heterogeneous Negative Binomial Estimates for
Models of Acceptable Casualty Levels

Variable	Stabilize Dem. Govt. in Congo	Defend Taiwan	Prevent Mass Dest. by Iraq
Constant	3.07	3.77	3.12
	(0.55)	(0.56)	(0.48)
Education	−.05	−.04	−.41
	(0.26)	(0.26)	(0.22)
Coincidence (threat, pro-mil.)	−.44	−.75	−.82
	(0.46)	(0.48)	(0.41)
Coincidence (threat, moral trad.)	−.10	−.58	−.28
	(0.48)	(0.50)	(0.43)
Coincidence (moral trad., pro-mil.)	.30	.25	.58
	(0.44)	(0.45)	(0.39)
Elite	−1.46	−2.47	−1.76
	(0.62)	(0.63)	(0.55)
Elite × Education	1.29	1.17	.72
	(0.31)	(0.30)	(0.27)
Elite × Coincidence (threat, pro-mil.)	.57	.56	.68
	(0.53)	(0.54)	(0.47)
Elite × Coincidence (threat, moral trad.)	−.02	.56	.32
	(0.55)	(0.56)	(0.49)
Elite × Coincidence (moral trad., pro-mil.)	−.49	.15	−.51
	(0.50)	(0.50)	(0.44)
N	1677	1677	1677

Note: Cell entries are maximum likelihood estimates of heterogeneous negative binomial model; standard errors are in parentheses. *Source:* Triangle Institute for Security Studies Survey on the Military in the Post–Cold War Era.

additional information for elites *increases* response variance, as does the coincidence of perceptions of threat and a pro-military affect.

Figure 9.5 shows the variance results in a more graphical format. The dark lines present the estimated variance for respondents with zero coincidence of the threat/pro-military predisposition, while the light lines present the estimated variance for respondents with perfect coincidence of the predisposition.[5] Note that the variance for masses generally exceeds that for elites (the sole exception is for highly educated elites in the Congo scenario). This suggests that elites have more crystallized attitudes toward acceptable casualties, much as one would expect. The lines, however, are sloped in opposite directions for

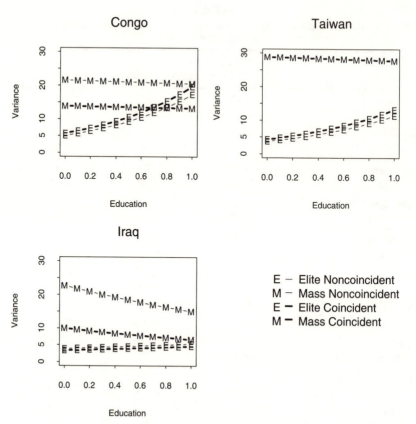

FIGURE 9.5. Variance in models of acceptable casualties, military elites vs. civilian masses

masses and elites. As masses become better informed, the variance in their attitudes about casualties decreases, whereas as elites become better informed, their variance increases. The effect of the joint coincidence of predispositions is also opposite for masses and elites. When masses hold both predispositions, the effect is to reduce variance; when elites hold both predispositions, the effect (slightly) increases variance. By the criteria we have set out in this book, masses are equivocal about military casualties, while elites are ambivalent.

Civilian Control of Military Policy

The second wave of analysis of attitudes regarding military policy concerns civilian control of the military. Table 9.4 presents the estimated marginal effect

TABLE 9.4
Estimated Effects of Predispositions on Support for Civilian Control of the Military

Variable	Civilians Decide Use		Civilians Decide Type		Civilian Control Safe		Domestic Politics Determines		In War, Military Control	
Threat	−.24	.09	−.24	.09	.23	−.18	.15	−.09	.19	−.12
Pro-military	.12	−.05	.12	−.05	.06	−.04	−.14	.08	.01	−.01
Moral traditionalism	−.10	.04	−.10	.04	.17	−.13	.08	−.05	.23	−.15
Elite?	.26	−.10	.26	−.10	−.003	.002	−.15	.08	−.16	.10
White?	.06	−.02	.06	−.03	.03	−.02	.04	−.02	.02	−.01
Male?	.16	−.06	.16	−.06	.07	−.06	−.001	.001	.04	−.03
Age	−.003	.001	−.003	.001	.002	−.002	.003	−.001	.002	−.002
Social trust	.02	−.01	.02	−.001	−.002	.002	−.01	.07	−.02	.02
Conf. in military	.06	−.02	−.02	.04	.06	−.05	.01	−.005	.04	−.03
Conf. in executive	.05	−.02	.02	−.05	−.02	.01	−.04	.02	−.01	.004
Conf. in TV	−.06	.03	.01	−.01	−.003	.003	−.01	.01	.025	−.02
Military service?	.17	−.06	−.02	.04	−.11	.08	−.03	.02	−.004	.002
In reserves?	−.03	.01	−.004	.01	.03	−.02	.03	−.02	.04	−.03
Family in military?	−.003	.001	−.01	.02	.01	−.01	.01	−.001	−.01	.004

Note: Entries are the predicted marginal effects for the probability that the individual strongly agrees (left) or strongly disagrees (right).

of each variable on the probability of strongly agreeing (left column in each pair) and strongly disagreeing (right column in each pair).[6]

Examination of these results shows that attitudes about civilian control of the military are driven by different factors for both elites and masses than were attitudes about acceptable casualty levels. Unlike in the models for acceptable casualties, perceptions of a dangerous world and moral traditionalism carry considerable weight in these models of support for principles of civilian control. Those who find the world to be a threatening place are more likely to disagree that civilians should decide whether to use the military, more likely to agree that domestic politics determines use of the military, and more likely to support the idea that the military should control its own behavior during war. They are also more likely to concur with the idea that civilian control of the military is safe. Moral traditionalists believe much the same things: that domestic politics determines military use, that the military should control itself during war, and that civilian control is safe. Pro-military affect, on the other hand, only matters for one of the measures of support for principals of civilian control; here, those who have high regard for the military are more likely to *disagree* with the claim that domestic politics determines military use.

Military elites differ somewhat from civilian masses. Elites are more likely to agree that civilians should decide whether to use military force, more likely to disagree that domestic politics determines the use of the military, and more likely to disagree that the military should control itself during war. Military elites scarcely differ from civilian masses on whether civilians should decide the type of intervention or whether the concept of civilian control is safe. These results might seem curious at first glance. Why should the military elites, more so than civilian masses, prefer that civilians control the behavior of the military? We can think of two distinct reasons. One is that the U.S. military has long been indoctrinated with the value of supporting civilian control of the military. A second is that the U.S. military may prefer that others, specifically civilian politicians, be responsible for the policy choices leading to war, saving responsibility for the execution of the war for themselves.

The variance component of the heteroskedastic ordered probit estimates tells a similar story to the models for acceptable casualties. With the exception of one question, the effect of additional education reduces variance for the civilian masses. Further, the effect of the coincidence of threat and a pro-military affect likewise reduces variance. The masses are, by the criteria of this book, equivocal: additional information reduces response variability, and the simultaneous presence of what might be conflicting predispositions also reduces varience. Like the models for casualty levels, elites are (except for the question of whether civilian control is safe) less variable in general in their response, although the effect of additional education and the coincidence of the predispositions increases variance.

Figure 9.6 presents the graphs of estimated variance of the five different civilian control choices, for masses and elites, and for high and low levels of the coincidence of threat and pro-military affect. All of the curves presenting the estimated variance for the military elites are upward sloping, indicating that additional information increases response variability. Three of the curves for the civilian masses are downward sloping (for civilians deciding use, civilians deciding type, and domestic politics determines), indicating that additional information increases response variability. The effect of the coincident predispositions is pronounced for the masses: in every one of the five graphs, those respondents in the civilian masses who have coincident predispositions have lower response variability.

CONCLUSIONS

The opinions of the military elites in this study are quite clearly better crystallized than those for the civilian masses. Although the present analysis cannot

Civilians Decide Use

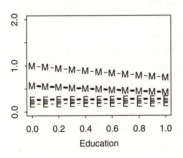

Civilians Decide Type

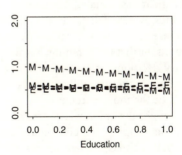

Civilian Control Safe

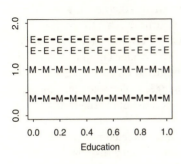

Domestic Politics Determines

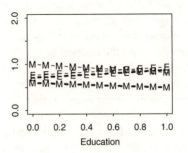

In War, Military Control

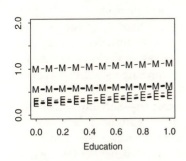

E – Elite Noncoincident
M – Mass Noncoincident
E – Elite Coincident
M – Mass Coincident

FIGURE 9.6. Variance in models of scope of civilian control of military, military elites vs. civilian masses

ascertain whether it is because the former group is "military" or "elite" that there is less variance, the result should not be surprising. These officers must, on a regular basis, make decisions about putting troops in a position to incur casualties, while civilians do not. Whether the source of the crystallization is that these are military people who are accustomed to making such weighty decisions, or that their training has produced more crystallized thinking about military decisions, is not especially pertinent for the present tests, since the claim here is that the differences between military elites and civilian masses should be the most extreme.

Although elite opinion is better crystallized, it is also evident from the analysis in this chapter that elites may also experience internalized conflict over these policy choices where masses do not. Those in the civilian sample who are better educated have less response variability than those who have less education. The reverse holds for the military elites: the better educated they are, the more variable their response. This is a condition, which we have argued throughout the book, that is consistent with internalized conflict, or ambivalence. This finding, too, perhaps should not be a surprise. That the mass public has equivocal opinions about foreign policy is entirely consistent with arguments in the public opinion literature since at least Walter Lippmann. But the finding that elites may have more internally conflicted opinions suggests that elite opinion is not impervious to important changes in context: elites may be more variable in their opinions than masses, but because of internalized tension over the policy choice, not because of any vacuity to their belief systems.

Our broader findings should also be placed within the context of what has been a dominant consensus among public opinion scholars: that the mass public is volatile in its attitudes toward foreign policy. The most famous formulation of the volatility of public opinion about foreign affairs was by Gabriel Almond (1950): "Perhaps the gravest general problem confronting policy-makers is that of the instability of mass moods, the cyclical fluctuations which stand in the way of policy stability" (239). Our results are certainly consistent with the idea that masses exhibit greater variance in response than decision-making elites, but also adds the important qualifier that elites, too, may be volatile in their opinions, if those conditions implicate competing values that cannot be rectified.

But what is important about our work in this chapter—and throughout this book—is that not only can we show that elite and mass attitudes about foreign and military policy are volatile, we can also show why they are volatile. By developing our theoretical model of uncertainty, ambivalence, and equivocation in public opinion, and by developing inferential statistical methods to test this model, we can show which policy areas are characterized by which condition. This moves us well beyond the usual hand-wringing about the volatility and instability of American public opinion to a clearer understanding of the determinants of this volatility.

Unfortunately, our results also demonstrate the great difficulty facing foreign and military policymakers (and perhaps, more generally, domestic and foreign policymakers). On one hand, the policymakers themselves can face difficulty making consistent and coherent policy decisions given the ambivalence that arises from their own value and belief conflicts. But on the other hand, the gulf that separates the determinants of policy choices and their variability between policymakers and the mass public will make it difficult for these policy decisions to necessarily be consistent with public beliefs, and also for policymakers to be able to communicate the reasons for their decisions to the mass public.

These two dilemmas will make military and foreign policymaking difficult and complex in a democratic society. Perhaps this is not a bad situation, given that military policy decisions in the post–Cold War era always involve an immediate risk of putting American lives at stake and a low, but not trivial, risk of escalation into large-scale, worldwide military confrontation. Given the stakes, instead of bemoaning and belittling the instability of mass opinion and the gulf between elite and mass opinion, perhaps we should reconceptualize these dilemmas and understand them as yet another important kind of "check" in our democratic system of government.

CHAPTER 10

Politics, Psychology, and the Survey Response

The subject we have been examining in this book is the variability of survey responses, or the range of potential responses to a survey question. First proposed by Achen (1975) and developed into a full theory of survey response by Feldman and Zaller (1992), the idea of response variance is powerful: survey respondents do not carry around fixed opinions, but instead, may offer a range of opinions. Our object has been to demonstrate that this range of opinions can yield useful information about what influences the most likely response (the central tendency, or the result of the choice model), and how variable the responses may be (the variance model).

But equally important, the other major theme of our research has been the role that predispositions, core values, and expectations play in the survey response. In each of the examples studied, we found that predispositions fundamentally shape how people answer survey questions, which leads us to infer that values and predispositions are a critical determinant of American public opinion.

In a departure from most research on public opinion, though, we do not contend that a single or very small set of predispositions "matter" in the survey response. This sets us firmly in opposition to the vast majority of research on public opinion, which has tended to assume that either a single predisposition (like ideology) or a very small set of predispositions (like egalitarianism and economic individualism) structure how Americans think about politics.

Rather, we have shown that a lot of different predispositions matter in our studies, both for the responses people give to questions about important public policies and for their underlying variability in their responses. This opens up an entirely new line of research for public opinion scholars, since we have clearly shown that a multiplicity of predispositions go toward forming public opinion, with some being more important for some policies than others, and with some likely suspects not mattering at all. While this complexity of predispositions might seem daunting, we argue that it should breathe fresh new life into long-lasting debates about the political opinions of Americans.

So the purpose of this concluding chapter is to recapitulate and integrate the main elements of our theory of survey response. We begin by addressing the complexity of predispositions we have uncovered, before turning to larger issues of political representation and public opinion.

A PROFUSION OF PREDISPOSITIONS

We considered many forms of predispositions in this study, including values, group attachments, affective relationships with groups, and expectations. Core values, in particular, play an especially important role in shaping public opinion. In several chapters, we discussed egalitarianism and individualism, two highly prized American concepts, and we demonstrated that these two values significantly affect attitudes about racial policy (chapters 6 and 8). But not all values are virtuous; we also showed that authoritarianism and racism affect the same set of policies.

Values are only one form of the predispositions that circulate in public opinion. Group attachments, affective relations with groups, and expectations differ from core values in the weight of affect and emotion over cognition. The heated debate about racial policy exemplifies the difference. Whether it is dubbed modern racism, symbolic racism, affective racism, or racial resentment, we demonstrate in chapter 6 that this affective relationship of whites toward blacks determines attitudes about affirmative action in universities, jobs, housing, taxation, and other policy areas, and indeed in the stereotypes whites hold about blacks. Further, we show that these attitudes dominate over values, lending support for the idea that espousal of the values is a mask for more emotionally grounded opinions.

Group attachments can take a much more positive role, as we show in chapter 9. Both the civilian masses and the military elites present a high degree of positive affect toward members of the military. This creates real tensions for military elites in deciding how many troops could be plausibly sacrificed for American foreign policy interests, although it appears not to create the same tensions for the mass public.

Expectations about the performance of political actors comprise another set of predispositions that differ from core values. In chapter 7, we demonstrate that the logically competing expectations that Americans hold about the performance of the Internal Revenue Service strongly shape their evaluations of that agency. For more than thirty years, public administration scholars have been pointing to the logical tensions between expecting agencies to be simultaneously equitable, honest, and responsive; the public plainly has not understood that.

What does this profusion of predispositions imply about American mass belief systems? For one, the sheer number and diversity of these beliefs creates a problem for both the public and the scholar of public opinion. If the public understands and evaluates policy and politics by way of these predispositions, they will know which ones are relevant when, why, and with what consequence. Some predispositions have enduring links to policy areas: respect for both the dignity of human life and for a woman's right to choose will probably always be competing ideologies in the abortion debate. Other predispositions have a more complex relationship with policy: egalitarianism is a core value that can be invoked on both sides of the debate over racial policy. Some policy problems are new enough that the mass public may not yet know what to make of the choice.

But while the profusion of predispositions might seem to make the study of public opinion much more difficult than it has been in the past, we believe that the profusion of predispositions actually will make the study of public opinion much more interesting and relevant. If the study of public opinion could be reduced to a single or simple set of predispositions, it would be neither academically nor politically interesting. But by uncovering the complexity of predispositions, we are much closer to the roots of the *politics* of public opinion.

The complexity of predispositions is leading us back to an explicitly political theory of the survey response. As we argued in chapters 8 and 9, politicians both influence and respond to the ways in which the profusion of predispositions influences public opinion. We are thus bringing politics back into the study of public opinion, and giving politicians and political elites a prominent position in our research. This runs counter to many recent research efforts in the public opinion literature, where there is little if any role for politics and political elites.

Because all of this complexity argues that what happens at the doorstep or over the phone is that the survey respondent *constructs* answers to the questions asked by the interviewer. But if these are "doorstep opinions," they are not created out of thin air or "made up as they go along," but constructed using a toolkit of predispositions. Which predispositions are relevant and how they influence the survey response is both a psychological and a political process. Our research makes clear that politicians and political elites must play important roles in our theories of the survey response and public opinion.

Turning in a different direction, though, we must reemphasize that our arguments about the profusion of predispositions has other important implications for the study of public opinion. For one, the range and complexity of predispositions also argues against an expectation of a consistent left-right political ideology. This is certainly a point for empirical studies of public opinion. Instead of single dimensional ideologies, perhaps it is more useful to seek multiple ideologies that can wax and wane in their prominence, influenced by the political process. In the end, we have shown that American public opinion is complex, dynamic, political, and simply too interesting for simplistic unidimensional orderings to dominate.

Perhaps, too, this is normatively appropriate. As philosophers of both the nineteenth century (Condorcet) and the twentieth (Berlin, Rawls, and Lukes) hold, insistence on the dominance of one value over others precludes sensible choices, limits the responsiveness of government, and creates false priorities.

THE PROMINENCE OF INFORMATION

The problem, alluded to above, with all these predispositions is which ones matter when? Uncertainty about politics and policy choices abounds. We are, of course, uncertain about the future consequences of policy choices. What will happen to the U.S. budget deficit, or to the economy itself, should the government pass massive tax cuts? Will China mobilize its military against Taiwan? But perhaps more important, we are uncertain about politics and policy because they are ambiguous; the meaning of political debates and the consequences of policy must be understood in terms of diverse predispositions.

These ideas stem from some of the earliest systematic studies of public opinion, the work conducted by Berelson and his colleagues (1954). They argue that *political information* serves three functions: it activates predispositions, it reinforces standing predispositions, and it (perhaps only rarely) converts predispositions. There is an intimate link between the profusion of predispositions and exposure to political information, which can take several forms. Sometimes it is domain specific, relevant only to a narrow scope of the political debate. In the discussion about abortion policy, for example, we considered how information specifically pertinent to abortion issues, subjectively assessed by the respondent, mattered for their policy choices. In attitudes about the performance of the IRS, we examined how much respondents knew about changes to tax law. On other occasions, political information should be better thought of as a chronic condition, reflecting how exposed people are to elite political discourse. And sometimes, political informedness is revealed through the acquisition of education.

What recurs throughout this book and our multiple examinations of diverse policy areas is that chronic political information matters more than domain-specific policy information. Regarding attitudes about racial policy and the IRS, examples where we have solid measures of both domain and chronic information, we demonstrate clearly that it is chronic information that is most responsible for activation of predispositions.

What does the dominance of chronic over domain-specific information say about mass opinion? One implication might be that the terms of policy debate happen at the elite level, not among masses, and that masses rely upon elites to structure the terms of political debate. This is the idea of "framing," and there is considerable support for framing effects in several policy areas (Gamson and Modigliani 1979; Kinder and Sanders 1996). But the manipulation of frames is constrained: elites do not create predispositions, they activate them, and plausibility provides a limit.

Another implication is that exposure to elite discourse conditions people to learn the "right" answers to survey questions. A standard finding from the public opinion literature on tolerance and democratic values is that people with more years of education more consistently express more tolerant beliefs than those people with fewer years of education (McClosky 1964; Prothro and Grigg 1960). In the mid 1970s, Mary Jackman (1978) argued that what is really at work is that better-educated people have learned the social norms about tolerance, but are not, in fact, any more tolerant than those people with fewer years of education.

The research discussed in chapters 5 and 9 provides some refutation of the hypothesis that education affects how people present themselves, not what they truly believe. In chapter 5, we show that information about abortion only makes certain policy choices more difficult. Chapter 9 demonstrates that information works differently for military elites than for civilian masses, such that better-informed civilians have more crystalized beliefs than do less-informed ones, but that the reverse is true for military elites. If acquiring information is supposed to make it easier to answer hard questions merely by learning the "right" response, then these relatively rare conditions of ambivalence indicate it is not always so.

Information of both forms is clearly a heterogeneous phenomenon. Whether it is subjectively assessed, measured by years of education, or assessed by virtue of some kind of quiz, respondents vary considerably in their levels of informedness.

AMBIVALENCE, UNCERTAINTY, AND EQUIVOCATION

What happens when the respondent activates more than one predisposition? Our argument is that simultaneous consideration of multiple predispositions only rarely induces internalized conflict. Instead, the dominance of a single predisposition, or mutual reinforcement of two or more predispositions, is a much more likely scenario.

Consider the issue of race. Despite conjectures from multiple scholars, race remains an area where a single predisposition, racism itself, tends to dominate policy choice. In both chapter 6 (at the individual level) and 8 (at the aggregate level), we find consistent evidence for uncertainty as the characteristic form of response variance in issues of race. The key effects were the prominent role of information in the variance function without an effect of coincident predispositions, even though such predispositions play a strong role in shaping choice about racial policy.

Perhaps, given the long literature on the politics of race, this should not be that surprising. After all, the issue of race is the one area where Phillip Converse (1964) consistently found that masses tended to retain their issue positions from survey to survey. By our terms, the low level of response variance might be termed a setting for certainty, rather than uncertainty.

Even under conditions with such little uncertainty, it is important to remember that attitudes can systematically change. Kinder and Sanders (1996) document the effect of the change in the position taken by opponents of affirmative action from one of "unearned advantages" to one of "reverse discrimination": the meaning of egalitarianism changed from one that would lead egalitarians to support affirmative action to one that would lead them to oppose it. Indeed, even over the earlier period studied by Converse, Gerber and Jackson (1993) show that both parties and voters changed their preferences on race.

The dominance of uncertainty in the present climate of attitudes on race may not have been the condition of earlier eras. It is entirely possible that those citizens who were living in the era of major civil rights change did experience a conflict between egalitarianism and overt racial ideologies. The longer-run dynamics of public opinion change may weave in and out of internalized conflict.

Equivocation, the scenario whereby coincident predispositions tend to reinforce one another, may be a common phenomenon. We identified two settings in this book, in evaluations of the Internal Revenue Service (chapter 7) and foreign policy (among masses, in chapter 9). This leads us to anticipate that equivocation, based on the simultaneous effects of egalitarianism and humanitarianism, might also be relevant in many other domains of public opinion (including welfare policy) and in attitudes toward other areas of government.

It is of course possible for multiple predispositions to contradict each other, putting respondents on the horns of a dilemma. Indeed, it was our initial expectation as we began this work (Alvarez and Brehm 1995) that ambivalence would be a much more common condition, where respondents would realize the difficult trade-offs in policy choices, or would simultaneously experience opposite emotions when evaluating key political figures.

As it turns out, our initial expectations were not altogether accurate. The conditions whereby respondents experience internalized, or personal, conflict about survey questions make it unlikely to find it often. Ambivalence necessitates simultaneous deliberation over multiple and conflicting predispositions, where no trade-offs are possible. There were just three settings that met these conditions—abortion, euthanasia, and (among military elites) limits of casualties and civilian control—and it is perhaps no accident that all three of these settings involve life-and-death conditions.

Is this rarity a product of the survey setting? Possibly so, since respondents are asked to proceed from question to question in relatively quick order, without necessarily having the opportunity to deliberate. Without that opportunity, meeting the condition of summoning predispositions simultaneously is probably unlikely.

What this suggests is that other settings might demonstrate real internalized conflict that the survey setting does not. Settings that require the respondent to mull over choices, and to explain the logic of a choice, could produce ambivalent responses. Authors employing intensive interviewing techniques (e.g., Hochschild 1981; Chong 1993) found the public to be more conflicted about policy areas such as welfare, which we found to be conditions of equivocation. Part of realizing the logical contradictions between predispositions may just be that it requires hard thought. Indeed, when we contrast those who rarely think about the consequences of war (civilian masses), with those who think about the consequences of war throughout most of their waking day (military elites), we see a difference between an equivocal public and a conflicted military elite.

So which is the better characterization of the likelihood of ambivalence in the mass public? It all depends on the reference point. If the point is to consider what ordinary people in ordinary conditions think about the major issues of the day, we think the survey setting is a more accurate portrayal. We know that for the most part, people do not deliberate over matters of politics. If the point is to highlight what happens to ordinary people when compelled to act in much the same way as their representatives, then the deliberative nature of the intensive interview is the most appropriate.

CONSEQUENCES FOR POLITICAL REPRESENTATION

There is, of course, a group of citizens whose duty it is to deliberate over policy, namely, representative elites. The problem of representation, while not the central concern of our research here, has lurked in the background of our discussion of public opinion. Our research does have many implications for the study of representation, however, since the problem of democratic representation is typically formulated as the question of popular control over the actions of elected representatives (Dahl 1956; Pitkin 1967).

The democratic control problem, furthermore, has usually been cast in two different ways. On one hand, representatives might be only weakly controlled by their constituents and thus should have a broad range of discretion in their policymaking activities. On the other hand, representatives might be sharply constrained by their constituents and thus should be tightly bound by the desires of their constituents in policymaking. In chapters 8 and 9, we approach both problems that such representatives confront in each of these two distinct directions, paralleling the traditional division of the roles of the representative into "delegates" and "trustees."

Chapter 8 considers what happens when elites look to masses, treating representatives as if they were examining poll results in order to make judgments about how to vote on policy. The delegate would simply need to know what the marginals were in support of or opposition to the matter at hand. We suggest that the trustee would need to know why the constituency favors or opposes the issue.

The consistent and strong finding is that the polity appears to be much more certain than the individuals who comprise it. This makes the representative-as-delegate's job somewhat easier, as they only need to monitor the aggregate views of their constituents and act according to the wishes of the majority. If the aggregate's wishes are more certain, that reduces the amount of potential error for the representative-as-delegate.

But the complexity of predispositions makes the job of the representative-as-trustee more problematic. A representative-as-trustee needs to understand why constituents hold the opinions they hold, which means also understanding the complexity of predispositions of their constituents. It is not enough to simply monitor the aggregate opinions of the constitutents; the representative should consider the motivations underlying the aggregate opinion. So when multiple predispositions help shape opinions, and the interaction of the predispositions introduces variability into responses and opinions, the trustee must try to understand both the opinions and the role of predispositions in influencing those opinions.

But it is also possible, as we show in chapter 9, for military elites to find themselves on the horns of a dilemma. Because of their role as representatives of competing groups, or because the salience of the issues is more visible to them, or because of (perhaps) a better understanding of the consequences, representatives may be more conflicted about policy choices than those they represent. The elites displayed better crystalized belief systems, in the form of lower response variance, but this variance rises sharply with years of education, and with reflection on multiple predispositions (pro-military affect and a sense of a dangerous world).

The picture we are drawing of the process of democratic representation, though, is more convoluted than the simple model of democratic control, which is usually discussed in the literature on representation. Most scholars view democratic control as the extent to which citizens constrain their representatives; to recast this in terms of our study, representation is usually viewed as the extent to which citizens' opinions are used by policymakers in their deliberations.

But that is too simplistic a perspective on democratic representation because it ignores the critical fact that political elites act to influence the views of their constituents. Whether they do it through their campaign activities, through media relations, in speeches, or now on the Internet, politicians and other elites do try to alter the set of predispositions that frame policy debates. They try to change the ways in which predispositions interact, or to eliminate the interaction, and they try to change the policy opinions themselves.

So through these feedback mechanisms, politicians and elites try to change the predispositions and opinions of constituents. The eventual reciprocal causal relationship between mass and elite behavior, in our view, is a major contributor to the complexity of American public opinion and one of the main reasons we have brought politics back into our theories of survey responses, public opinion, and, ultimately, representation.

CONCLUDING THOUGHTS

We have come full circle in our thinking about why responses change over time. To be sure, mass opinion can be fickle; with inadequate political information, especially of a chronic form, mass opinion can swing back and forth, with respondents appearing to hold contrary opinions at different times. On a few, rare occasions, when respondents face difficult choices between incommensurables, it is the more thoughtful and sophisticated ones who may be the most variable. In the mass surveys, this usually happens in the areas of abortion and euthanasia, easily among the most controversial and salient issues in politics. But there are other subjects such as race, where opinion is far from fickle, and other issues, such as the (perhaps) unreasonable expectations people have about government, when the contradictions not only elude the public but even characterize a greater desire for unachievable aims.

For those of us who teach, write, and think about politics, we have many times been aghast at the public's apparent lack of knowledge about the hard choices faced by the polity, where only a few may understand how difficult the choices may be. Many observers then sharply criticize the public, and political elites, for how poorly informed they appear about important political issues.

But the problem of public opinion requires deeper study and analysis. While many citizens, and even elites, might perform poorly on the types of political "pop quizzes" that often appear on public opinion surveys, and while their responses might sometimes seem fickle, we hope that our research has demonstrated that neither lack of information nor response variability necessarily implies a public incapable of reasoning about politics.

Rather, predispositions, core values, and expectations can and do provide structure to public opinion. These fundamental beliefs may not act uniformly across issues, and in many cases they come into sharp conflict or even reinforce each other. The complexity that results from the impact of multiple and competing fundamental beliefs, then, mirrors the complexity of the polity's problems and the many ways in which political elites constantly attempt to influence the public's thinking about political issues.

Given the complexity of these difficult political problems, it should come as no surprise that the public's thinking about these issues is also complex. Opinion surveys ask citizens about complex issues in relatively simple terms; drawing upon their predispositions and their available stores of political information, citizens attempt to develop a response. Surveys elicit easy answers to these hard choices, revealing not just one opinion, but potentially many. The challenge facing both politicians and political observers is what to make of the complexity of American opinion.

Notes

Chapter 1
A Fickle Public?

1. That Custred and Wood used the Sniderman and Piazza research is documented in Chavez (1999, 20).

2. These data are from the Los Angeles Times poll, Study 386, "California Issues, October 1996." Altogether, 1,551 California adults were interviewed by telephone for this survey; detailed results are available at www.latimes.com/news/timespoll.

3. The Gallup Poll conducted telephone interviews with 998 American adults on March 30 through April 2, 2000. The full survey results are available at www.gallup.com.

4. See Feldman (1988) or Kinder and Sears (1981) regarding individualism. The idea of a core set of beliefs as the monopoles under which diverse arrays of opinions might be understood takes root in several important works. Feldman's article demonstrated that attitudes toward economic individualism structure appraisals of welfare and economic policy, and further affect evaluations of how well elites administer these policies. Hochschild (1981) explores how attitudes about the fairness of capitalism undermine support for redistribution of wealth, even among the poor. Kinder and Sanders (1996) show that support of racial policy reflects dominant elite discourse, such that egalitarians who are invited to think about racial policy in a frame of racial resentment are more inclined to support policy, whereas those who are invited to think about racial policy in a frame of reverse discrimination are more likely to oppose policy. Stenner (1996) shows that authoritarian predispositions lead to greater intolerance, but only when authoritarians perceive political threat.

Chapter 3
Why Does Political Information Matter?

1. Another important body of research that attacked the issue knowledge of Americans was produced by Campbell et al. (1960) in *The American Voter*. For a discussion of this literature see Alvarez 1997.

2. For examples of this research in recent American presidential elections, see Alvarez and Nagler 1995, 1998.

3. In this example, we present the uncertainty curves as unimodal and single-peaked, which is appropriate for policy domains that can be captured by single preferences, or by multiple preferences that condense down to single dimensions. An important exception to this representation would occur when respondents hold *nonseparable preferences* over multiple domains. For example, a respondent might prefer that the United States not commit its military to overseas actions, but if the country does, then it should free the military from constraints on the rules of engagement. If the respondent were asked to summarize his or her opinions on the extent to which the military should be involved in overseas actions, this would be better represented as a bimodal uncer-

tainty curve. Dean Lacy (1993; Lacy and Niou 1998) is the author of the seminal treatments of the problem of nonseparable preferences in opinion and voting.

4. We return to the specific topic of beliefs about affirmative action in chapter 5, where we demonstrate that there is considerable uncertainty about changes in affirmative action policy, despite the claims of some in the literature that beliefs about affirmative action are somewhat ambivalent. Our evidence in chapter 5 is quite conclusive on this point: in general, a single, dominant predisposition influences beliefs about affirmative action, and there is little support for the notion that beliefs about affirmative action are ambivalent due to conflicting predispositions.

5. Under the assumption that the citizen's earlier belief, the new information, and their new updated beliefs all have conditional distributions that are normally distributed, we can write the mean and variance of the citizen's updated beliefs (Alvarez 1997):

$$B_t = \frac{\mu_{t-1} B_{t-1} + \mu_t^I I_t}{\mu_{t-1} + \mu_t^I} \tag{3.1}$$

$$\mu_t = \mu_{t-1} + \mu_t^I \tag{3.2}$$

where B_t stands for a person's belief at time t, μ_t stands for their certainty about that attitude, I_t stands for some new information, and μ_t^I the certainty about that information.

6. Using the mathematical notation from the Bayesian learning model, this is a situation where μ_{t-1} is small—they have uncertain predispositions—which, when combined with very certain new information, will produce a very certain posterior belief (i.e., μ_t will be much larger than μ_{t-1}).

7. For political predispositions, Lazarsfeld et al. focused on social-economic status, religious affiliation, and region of residence. The researchers combined these different indicators into one scale they called the Index of Political Predispositions. They used this IPP to differentiate Republicans from Democrats, so in effect it was a way to measure partisan predispositions.

8. There is a long literature on both sides of this debate. Some who have found evidence for issue publics include Glasgow (1999); Rabinowitz, Prothro, and Jacoby (1982), RePass (1971); and Rivers (1988). On the other side is the important research of Niemi and Bartels (1985) and Delli Carpini and Keeter (1996).

9. There is also the question about how the researcher can determine the level of domain-specific information held by a survey respondent. The distinction is usually made between subjective and objective approaches to the measurement of political information (Alvarez 1997). Subjective approaches ask survey respondents to tell the interviewer how well informed they think they are about the particular issue; the most widely used subjective information items are the certainty questions (Alvarez and Franklin 1994). Objective approaches ask survey respondents batteries of questions, to which there are factual answers. We use objective information measures in our work.

10. We determined the correct answer in each case by consultation with one of two IRS documents, the *Summary for Individuals* or the *Highlights of the 1987 Tax Reform Act*.

11. We are limited by the availability of comparable survey questions in our ability to develop identical models for both affirmative action and IRS information levels. In general, we have tried to specify models for these two different domains so they are as similar as possible.

Chapter 5
Ambivalent Attitudes: Abortion and Euthanasia

1. More detailed discussion of the variables used in our analysis is an appendix on our website at www.pupress.princeton.edu/alvarez.

2. The logic we use here in our measure of elaboration is consistent with the Petty and Cacioppo (1986) "elaboration-likelihood model," or ELM: "Elaboration refers to the extent to which a person scrutinizes the issue-relevant arguments contained in the persuasive communication" (7). One measure of elaboration, which we tend to underuse as political scientists, is the degree to which respondents are able to elucidate answers to open-ended questions.

3. We use the same fear-of-God scale that we used in the previous section (see figure 5.4.).

Chapter 6
Uncertainty and Racial Attitudes

1. The survey was a telephone interview based on random-digit dialing using a stratified two-phase sample selection procedure. The first phase of the procedure sampled from known area codes and prefixes, appending a four-digit random number to generate a complete ten-digit telephone number. The second phase drew disproportionately from sample strata containing at least one known residential number, while drawing also from strata where there was no known residential number. Known residential numbers were drawn from a tape created by Donnelly Marketing Services. See Casady and Lepkowski 1991 for further details of the sampling methodology. The target population consisted of all English-speaking adults over eighteen years of age, residing in households with telephones, within the forty-eight contiguous states. The total sample size was 2,223, with a response rate of 65.3 percent (a response rate in excess of typical rates for telephone surveys).

2. McConahay (1986) prefers the term "modern" racism, with the explicit idea that the underlying racial attitudes are possible only in the period of the post–civil rights movement, and because "old-fashioned" racism might also be symbolic (i.e., not grounded in realistic group conflict). Kinder (1986) prefers the term "symbolic" racism, since the "traditional" American values invoked by the idea are hardly modern. Neither label is perfect. We opt for "modern" racism in the context of the specific questions, since all refer (obliquely) to policies only in practice since the 1960s.

3. The "anger" variables are scaled from 0 (doesn't bother) to 10 (extremely angry), while the first question is scaled in the reverse, from 1 (too much attention) to 5 (not paying enough attention). Considering the range of the indicators, the indicators load roughly equally on the underlying scale, with estimated factor loadings of −0.27 (anger about giving blacks and other minorities special advantages) and −0.34 (anger about spokesmen for minorities who are always complaining); the attention-to-minority problems indicator has been constrained to a coefficient of 1.0.

4. Each of the indicators is a response on a 10-point scale to a question of the form "How about X? On a scale from 0 to 10, how important is that to you?" where 0 denotes "one of the least important things" and 10 denotes "one of the absolutely most important

things." (This scale is *not* reversed.) The confirmatory factor analysis estimates loadings of 1.00 for "preserving the traditional ideas of right and wrong," 0.91 for "respect for authority," 0.74 for "following God's will," 0.71 for "improving standards of politeness in everyday behavior," 0.76 for "strengthening law and order," and 0.78 for "respect for American Power." This scale thus omits at least six aspects of the F scale: anti-intraception, superstition, power and toughness, destructiveness and cynicism, projectivity, and sex. One might consider the "respect for American power" question to tap into the "power and toughness" aspect of the F scale.

5. Two of the questions are of a similar form to those used for the authoritarianism scale (in fact, part of the same battery of questions): "self-reliance" and "emphasizing individual achievement." "Self-reliance" is fixed at 1, and "emphasizing individual achievement and excellence on the job" scales at only 0.30. Likewise, "(how about) government officials interfering and trying to tell us what we can and can't do with our own lives" scales at only 0.15.

6. The confirmatory factor loadings for the anti-Semitism scale are 1.00 for "most Jews are ambitious and work hard to succeed," 0.85 for "most Jews are more willing than other people to use shady practices to get ahead in life," 0.90 for "most Jews believe that they are better than other people," 0.76 for "most Jews in general are inclined to be more loyal to Israel than to America" and 0.86 for "most Jews don't care what happens to people who aren't Jewish."

7. Each of the indicators for the antiblack stereotyping scale is a response to a question of the form "How about X? On a scale from 0 to 10, how well do you think that it describes most blacks?" where the scale ranges from 0 ("very inaccurate") to 10 ("very accurate"). Since this scale is ultimately reversed, each of the factor loadings represents a score in a problack direction. The factor loadings for the antiblack stereotyping scale we construct are: aggressive or violent (1.00), lazy (0.87), boastful (0.63), irresponsible (0.77), and complaining (0.68). We have replicated our analysis with a second scale for antiblack stereotyping, where the measures include both positive and negative stereotypes. This alternative scale has some serious defects in that the positive and negative attributes appear to load better on separate scales than on a single scale.

8. Although there were many variations in question format, we found few statistically significant interaction effects. That is, the effect of the different question wordings (denoted here by dummies) only shifted the base probability and did not interact with any of the scales to an appreciable degree.

9. This also raises issues about selection bias, as the respondents who mailed back this survey might not be a representative sampling of the entire respondent pool. While we recognize the possibility of selection biases, we do not attempt any correction for selection. Nor do we see any appreciable differences in the results we obtain for these particular questions, which indicates that selection biases, if present, are minimal in their effects on our analyses.

10. The ideological placement is to control for the possibility that ideology as a core belief structures racial opinions; this, of course, runs counter to the early literature (Converse 1964, 1970; McClosky 1964; Prothro and Grigg 1960) but is more in line with later work (Aberbach and Walker 1973; Carmines and Stimson 1989; Kinder and Rhodebeck 1982; Nie, Verba, and Petrocik 1979; Sniderman and Hagen 1985). Personal financial status is intended to control for the possible impact of self-interest on racial beliefs (Kinder and Sanders 1996).

11. It is conceivable that conflict among the other scales might also lead to greater response variability. Previous work, in fact, included all possible combinations of scales in a similar test. None of the results to follow vary significantly from the results of the fully saturated test. We prefer the simpler test of conflict between egalitarianism and individualism since it is one based on the standing literature. We can think of no similarly motivated reason to expect conflict among any other pair of values.

12. We also included ideological strength in the variance function in order to control for a similar effect such that individuals with stronger ideological beliefs might be less fixed in their opinions. As the reader will note in this chapter, this effect did not materialize. Additionally, we examined different variations where we included ideological beliefs in the variance function, since liberals may be more variable in their opinions about racial policy than conservatives, and found no support for this hypothesis. Another variation of this model was explored wherein we scaled ideological self-placement to reflect extremism (i.e., extreme liberals and extreme conservatives score at the maximum, moderates at the minimum), and there was again no effect of ideology on variance.

Chapter 7
Equivocation

1. The survey data are available through the Interuniversity Consortium for Political and Social Research (ICPSR # 8927) as a Class IV release. This means that much of the details of the study information must be obtained through government documents, or through the Harris Organization. As best as we can tell at this time, the survey was administered as a face-to-face interview to 2,003 respondents, with a slightly unusual sample selection procedure. The study began with selection of 200 primary sampling units and then drew a sample frame representative of the entire adult population of the United States. Because not every adult U.S. resident is required to submit an IRS return, the survey administrators further selected the respondents who represent the taxpayers' sample. Interviewers determined this on the basis of all household members who filed a federal return, or where the spouse filed a joint return with the respondent. The method cannot identify respondents who should have filed under IRS regulations but did not.

2. We also used the second set of responses to these questions—which measured whether the respondent knew anything about the actual change in each dimension of tax policy—to develop a second domain-specific information measure, which we called the hard information scale. We replicated our models using the hard information scale in place of the soft scale, and there was little appreciable difference in the estimated results. These results are available from the authors.

3. There is good evidence that procedural fairness matters in attitudes about taxation and tax compliance (Scholz and Pinney 1995) and in support for criminal justice (Tyler 1990), so one may wish to reserve judgment about its potential effects upon attitudes regarding the agencies and bureaucrats who administer such programs.

Chapter 8
Mass Opinion and Representation

1. There is a large and growing body of work on the use of the redistricting process to enhance minority descriptive representation through the development of "majority-

minority" districts. See Canon (1999), Kousser (1999), Lublin (1997), and Swain (1993) for excellent introductions to this subject.

2. This extensive literature defies easy summary, but important works are Achen (1975), Arnold (1990), Bianco (1994), Clausen (1973), Fenno (1978), Fiorina (1974), and Miller and Stokes (1963).

3. There are many studies dealing with aggregated public opinion, including Beck (1991, 1992), Kernell (1978), Kiewiet and Rivers (1985), MacKuen (1983), Ostrom and Simon (1992), Ostrom and Smith (1992), Smith (1992), and Williams (1992).

4. The goodness-of-fit index improves to .95 when one drops the spending measures.

5. The only one of these value measures that is not constructed using virtually identical survey questions in the two NES studies is the racial resentment measure. So, it is possible that the differences we see in these distributions from 1992 and 1996 could be due to the different survey instruments we used in each NES study to construct the racial resentment measures. But the other two measures that had seemingly large-scale change in this period—economic individualism and egalitarianism—did not change drastically in their measurement.

6. We must also point out, however, that in 1992 and 1996 we do have different measures of racial resentment. So the difference in the estimated effect of racial resentment between 1992 and 1996 could be either completely or partially the result of differences in measurement strategies between these two NES studies.

7. All of the uncertainty effects are statistically significant in the empirical estimates. Interested readers should examine the estimation results presented in the appendix to this chapter available on our website at www.pupress.princeton.edu/alvarez.

8. In our estimation results, all the estimates of the effect of chronic information on error variance are negative and are statistically significant, with one exception: the company affirmative action policy choice model.

9. The estimated effect of uncertainty in the two aggregated racial policy choice models is negative and statistically significant in each of the estimation models.

10. We find that the estimated effect of chronic information is negative in both aggregate models, but is only statistically significant in the model for whether welfare benefits should continue for women who have more kids while on welfare.

11. Both estimates of chronic information in the aggregate models are positive, but both fail to reach statistical significance.

Chapter 9
Do Elites Experience Ambivalence Where Masses Do Not?

This chapter was written with Henk Goemans.

1. The two surveys were conducted by separate organizations with separate modes. The civilian survey was a telephone interview conducted by Princeton Survey Research Associates. The civilian sample also includes African Americans. The method of selection within household employed a hybrid of random flip (for household, with exactly two eligible individuals) and "next birthday" (for households with more than two eligible individuals).

The military elite sample was a mail-back survey conducted by Peter Feaver, with a listed sample drawn from the staff colleges (with military at the captain level [GS 03-04]), war colleges (GS 05-06), and general "knife and fork" schools. Feaver requested a survey of the entire class of all institutions, of both Army and Navy War Colleges, and the joint school at the National Defense University. Surveys were hand-delivered to respondents, and returned collectively. Feaver obtained a similar listed sample of reservists by the rosters on correspondence courses at the same schools.

2. "[T]here is the conflict between military obedience and military competence when that competence is threatened by a political superior. What does the military officer do when he is ordered by a statesman to take a measure which is militarily absurd when judged by professional standards and which is strictly within the military realm without any political implications? This situation . . . represents a clear invasion of the professional realm by extraneous considerations. The presumption of superior professional competence which existed in the case of a military superior giving a questionable order does not exist when the statesman enters military affairs. Here the existence of professional standards justifies military disobedience. The statesman has no business deciding, as Hitler did in the later phases of World War II, whether battalions in combat should advance or retreat" (Huntington 1957, 74).

3. We note here that six outliers from each analysis were deleted: those who would tolerate casualties in excess of one million. One individual put acceptable casualties as five million, a number approximately equal to the entire U.S. peacetime military. These respondents were so far off the charts as to make us question their fundamental grasp of numbers.

4. The link function for negative binomial models is an exponential, hence, an interpretation of the coefficients for the choice model and is straightforward: multiply each coefficient by the natural logarithm of 10 (2.3), and the result represents the order of magnitude change in the dependent variable from a unit change in the corresponding independent variable.

5. Please note that the light lines and dark lines for mass noncoincident and mass coincident, respectively, overlap in the Taiwan panel of figure 9.5.

6. We present the choice component estimates of the heteroskedastic ordered probit model for the five questions on civilian control in an appendix to this chapter on our website at www.pupress.princeton.edu/alvarez.

References

Aberbach, Joel D., and Jack L. Walker. 1970. "Political Trust and Racial Ideology." *American Political Science Review* 64:1199–220.

Achen, Christopher H. 1975. "Mass Political Attitudes and the Survey Response." *American Political Science Review* 69:1218–23.

———. 1992. "Breaking the Iron Triangle: Social Psychology, Demographic Variables, and Linear Regression in Voting Research." *Political Behavior* 14:195–211.

Adams, Greg D. 1997. "Abortion: Evidence of an Issue Evolution." *American Journal of Political Science* 41:718–37.

Adorno, T. W., Else Frenkel-Brunswik, Daniel J. Levinson, and R. Nevitt Sanford. 1950. *The Authoritarian Personality*, Part 1, New York: Wiley.

Almond, Gabriel. 1950. *The American People and Foreign Policy*, New York: Praeger.

Alvarez, R. Michael. 1997. *Information and Elections*. Ann Arbor: University of Michigan Press.

Alvarez, R. Michael, and John Brehm. 1995. "American Ambivalence Toward Abortion Policy: A Heteroskedastic Probit Method for Assessing Conflicting Values." *American Journal of Political Science* 39:1055–82.

———. 1997. "Are Americans Ambivalent Toward Racial Policies?" *American Journal of Political Science* 41:345–74.

———. 1998. "Speaking in Two Voices: American Equivocation about the Internal Revenue Service." *American Journal of Political Science* 42 (2): 418–52.

Alvarez, R. Michael, and Charles H. Franklin. 1994. "Uncertainty and Political Perceptions." *Journal of Politics* 56:671–88.

———. 1997. "Attitudes, Uncertainty and Survey Responses." Unpublished manuscript.

Alvarez, R. Michael, and Jonathan Nagler. 1995. "Economics, Issues, and the Perot Candidacy: Voter Choice in the 1992 Presidential Election." *American Journal of Political Science* 39:714–44.

———. 1998. "Economics, Entitlements, and Social Issues: Voter Choice in the 1996 Presidential Election." *American Journal of Political Science* 42:1349–63.

Arnold, R. Douglas. 1990. *The Logic of Congressional Action*. New Haven: Yale University Press.

Bartels, Larry M. 1986. "Issue Voting Under Uncertainty: An Empirical Test." *American Journal of Political Science* 30:709–23.

———. 1993. "Messages Received: The Political Impact of Media Exposure." *American Political Science Review* 87:267–85.

Baumgartner, Frank, and Bryan Jones. 1993. *Agendas and Instability in American Politics*. Chicago: University of Chicago Press.

Beck, Nathaniel. 1991. "Comparing Dynamic Specifications: The Case of Presidential Approval." *Political Analysis* 3:51–88.

Berelson, Bernard, Paul Lazarsfeld, and William McPhee. 1954. *Voting*. Chicago: University of Chicago Press.

Berger, Mark, and John Brehm. April 1997. "Watergate and the Erosion of Social Capital." Paper presented at the annual meeting of the Midwest Political Science Association, Chicago.

Berlin, Isaiah. 1992. *The Crooked Timber of Humanity*. New York: Vintage Books.

Bianco, William T. 1994. *Trust: Representatives and Constituents*. Ann Arbor: University of Michigan Press.

Bobo, Lawrence. 1983. "Whites' Opposition to Busing: Symbolic Racism or Realistic Group Conflict?" *Journal of Personality and Social Psychology* 45:1196–210.

Box-Steffensmeier, Janet M., Kathleen Knight, and Lee Sigelman. 1998. "The Interplay of Macropartisanship and Macroideology: A Time Series Analysis." *Journal of Politics* 60:1031–49.

Box-Steffensmeier, Janet, M., and Renee Smith. 1998. "Investigating Political Dynamics Using Fractional Integration Methods." *American Journal of Political Science* 42:661–89.

Brady, Henry, and Paul Sniderman. 1985. "Attitude Attribution: A Group Basis for Political Reasoning." *American Political Science Review* 79:1061–78.

Brehm, John. 1993. *The Phantom Respondents*. Ann Arbor: University of Michigan Press.

Brehm, John, and Wendy Rahn. 1997. "Individual Level Evidence for the Causes and Consequences of Social Capital." *American Journal of Political Science* 41:999–1023.

Brewer, Paul. 1999. "Values, Public Debate, and Policy Opinions." Ph.D. diss., University of North Carolina.

Brody, Richard. 1991. *Assessing Presidential Character: The Media, Elite Opinion, and Public Support*. Stanford: Stanford University Press.

Cacioppo, John T., and Wendi L. Gardner. 1999. "Emotion." *Annual Review of Psychology* 30:191–214.

Calvert, Randall L., and Michael MacKuen. April 1985. "Bayesian Learning and the Dynamics of Public Opinion." Paper presented at the annual meeting of the Midwest Political Science Association, Chicago.

Campbell, Angus, Philip E. Converse, Warren E. Miller, and Donald E. Stokes. 1960. *The American Voter*. New York: Wiley.

Canon, David T. 1999. *Race, Redistricting, and Representation: The Unintended Consequences of Black Majority Districts*. Chicago: University of Chicago Press.

Carmines, Edward G., and James A. Stimson. 1980. "The Two Faces of Issue Voting." *American Political Science Review* 74:78–91.

———. 1989. *Issue Evolution*. Princeton: Princeton University Press.

Casady, R. J., and J. M. Lepkowski. 1991. "Optimal Allocation for Stratified Telephone Survey Designs." *Proceedings of the Section on Survey Research Methods, American Statistical Association*.

Chavez, Lydia. 1999. *The Color Bind: California's Battle to End Affirmative Action*. Berkeley: University of California Press.

Chong, Dennis. 1993. "How People Think, Reason, and Feel about Rights and Liberties." *American Journal of Political Science* 37:867–99.

Clausen, Aage. 1973. *How Congressmen Decide: A Policy Focus*. New York: St. Martin's Press.

Combs, Michael, and Susan Welch. 1982. "Blacks, Whites and Attitudes toward Abortion." *Public Opinion Quarterly* 46:510–20.

Condorcet, Marie-Jean Antoine-Nicholas de Caritat, Marquis de. 1955. *Esquisse d'un tableau historique des progrès de l'esprit humain*, translated by June Barraclough. New York: Noonday Press.

Conover, Pamela J., and Stanley Feldman. 1981. "The Origins and Meanings of Liberal/ Conservative Identifications." *American Journal of Political Science* 25:617–45.

Converse, Philip E. 1964. "The Nature of Belief Systems in Mass Publics." In *Ideology and Discontent*, edited by New York: Free Press.

Dahl, Robert A. 1956. *A Preface to Democratic Theory*. Chicago: University of Chicago Press.

Dawson. Michael C. 1994. *Behind the Mule: Race and Class in African-American Politics*. Princeton: Princeton University Press.

Delli Carpini, Michael X., and Scott Keeter. 1996. *What Americans Know about Politics and Why It Matters*. New Haven: Yale University Press.

Downs, Anthony. 1957. *An Economic Theory of Democracy*. New York: Harper & Row.

———. *Inside Bureaucracy*. New York: Harper & Row.

Durkheim, Emile. 1897. *Suicide: A Study in Sociology*. Reprint, New York: Free Press, 1951.

Enelow, James M. and Melvin J. Hinich. 1984. *The Spatial Theory of Voting*. New York: Cambridge University Press.

Erikson, Robert S., Gerald C. Wright, and John P. McIver. 1993. *Statehouse Democracy: Public Opinion and Policy in the American States*. New York: Cambridge University Press.

Feaver, Peter. 1999a. "Civil-Military Relations." *Annual Review of Political Science* 2:211–41.

———. 1999b. "Agency, Oversight, and Civil-Military Relations." Unpublished manuscript.

Feaver, Peter, and Christopher Gelpi. 1999a. "The Civil-Military Gap and Casualty Aversion." Paper prepared for the TISS Project on the Gap Between the Military and Civilian Society, Durham, NC.

———. 1999b. "Civilian Hawks and Military Doves: The Civil-Military Gap and the American Use of Force, 1816–1992." Paper prepared for the TISS Project on the Gap Between the Military and Civilian Society, Durham, NC.

Feldman, Stanley. 1988. "Structure and Consistency in Public Opinion: The Role of Core Beliefs and Values." *American Journal of Political Science* 32:416–40.

Feldman Stanley, and Marco Steenbergen. 2001. "The Humanitarian Foundation of Public Support for Social Welfare." American Journal of Political Science 45:658–77.

Feldman, Stanley, and John Zaller. 1992. "Political Culture of Ambivalence: Ideological Responses to the Welfare State." *American Journal of Political Science* 36:268–307.

Fenno, Richard J. 1978. *Home Style: House Members in Their Districts*. New York: Addison-Wesley.

Festinger, Leon. 1954. "A Theory of Social Comparison Processes." *Human Relations* 7:117–40.

Fiorina, Morris P. 1974. *Representatives, Roll Calls, and Constituencies*. Lexington, MA: Lexington Books.

Fox, J., and J. S. Long. 1990. *Modern Methods of Data Analysis*. Newbury Park, CA: Sage.

Franklin, Charles H. 1991. "Eschewing Obfuscation? Campaigns and the Perceptions of U.S. Senate Incumbents." *American Political Science Review* 85:1193–214.

Gaertner, S. L., and J. F. Dovidio. 1986. "Aversive Racism." In *Prejudice, Discrimination, and Racism,* edited by J. F. Dovidio and S. L. Gaertner. New York: Academic Press.

Gamson, William A., and Andre Modigliani, eds.. 1979. *Conceptions of Social Life : A Text-Reader for Social Psychology.* Washington, DC: University Press of America.

Gerber, Elizabeth R., and John E. Jackson. 1993. "Endogenous Preferences and the Study of Institutions." *American Political Science Review* 83:639–56.

Ginsburg, Faye D. 1989. *Contested Lives.* Berkeley: University of California Press.

Glasgow, Garrett. 1999. "Issue Publics in American Politics." Ph.D. diss., California Institute of Technology.

Goffman, E. 1959. *The Presentation of Self in Everyday Life.* Garden City, NY: Doubleday.

Goodsell, Charles T. 1985. *The Case for Bureaucracy: A Public Administration Polemic.* Chatham, NJ: Chatham House.

Green, Donald, Brad Palmquist, and Eric Schickler. 1998. "Macropartisanship: A Replication and Critique." *American Political Science Review* 92:883–99.

Hall, Elaine J., and Myra Marx Ferree. 1986. "Race Differences in Abortion Attitudes." *Public Opinion Quarterly* 50:193–207.

Hamilton, Alexander, James Madison, and John Jay. 1961. *The Federalist Papers.* New York: New American Library.

Harris, Louis, and Associates, Inc. 1988. *1987 Taxpayer Opinion Survey.* Report to U.S. Internal Revenue Service.

Harris-Lacewell, Melissa. 1999. "Barbershops, Bibles, and B.E.T.: Dialogue and the Development of Black Political Thought." Ph.D. diss., Duke University.

Hastie, Reid, and Bernadette Park. 1986. "The Relationship Between Memory and Judgement Depends Whether the Task Is Memory-based or On-line." *Psychological Review* 93:258–68.

Hawthorne, Michael R., and John E. Jackson. 1987. "The Individual Political Economy of Federal Tax Policy." *American Political Science Review* 81:757–74.

Heider, Fritz. 1946. "Attitudes and Cognitive Organization." *Journal of Psychology* 21:107–12.

———. 1948. *The Psychology of Interpersonal Relations.* New York: Wiley.

Hochschild, Jennifer L. 1981. *What's Fair? American Beliefs about Distributive Justice.* Cambridge: Harvard Univercity Press.

Holbrook, Allyson L., Jon A. Krosnick, Penny S. Visser, Wendi L. Gardner, and John T. Cacioppo. 2001. "Attitudes toward Presidential Candidates and Political Parties: Initial Optimism, Inertial First Impressions, and a Focus on Flaws." *American Journal of Political Science* 45: 930–50.

Holbrook, Thomas M. 1994. "Campaigns, National Conditions, and U.S. Presidential Elections." *American Journal of Political Science* 38:973–98.

Huntington, Samuel. 1957. *The Soldier and the State.* Cambridge: Harvard University Press, Belknap Press.

Hurwitz, Jon, and Mark Peffley. 1987. "How Are Foreign Policy Attitudes Structured? A Hierarchical Model." *American Political Science Review* 81:1099–120.

Jackman, Mary R. 1978. "General and Applied Tolerance: Does Education Increase Commitment to Racial Integration?" *American Journal of Political Science* 25:256–69.

Jacoby, William G. 1994. "Public Attitudes Toward Government Spending." *American Journal of Political Science* 39:314–35.

Jordan, Donald L., and Benjamin Page. 1992. "Shaping Foreign Policy Opinions: The Role of TV News." *Journal of Conflict Resolution.* 36:227–41.

Katz, Irwin J., and R. Glen Hass. 1988. "Racial Ambivalence and American Value Conflict: Correlational and Priming Studies of Dual Cognitive Structures." *Journal of Personality and Social Psychology,* 55:893–905.

Katz, Irwin, J. Wackenhut, and R. Glen Hass. 1986. "Racial Ambivalence, Value Duality, and Behavior." In *Prejudice, Discrimination, and Racism,* edited by J. F. Dovidio and S. L. Gaertner. Orlando, FL: Academic Press.

Kelley, Stanley, Jr., and Thad W. Mirer. "The Simple Act of Voting." *American Political Science Review,* 68:572–91.

Kernell, Samuel. 1978. "Explaining Presidential Popularity." *American Political Science Review* 72: 506–22.

———. 1986. *Going Public.* Washington, DC: Congressional Quarterly Books.

Key, V. O., Jr. 1966. *The Responsible Electorate.* New York: Vintage Books.

Kiewiet, D. Roderick, and Douglas Rivers. 1985. "The Economic Basis of Reagan's Approval." In *The New Direction in American Politics,* edited by John E. Chubb and Paul E. Peterson. Washington, DC: Brookings Institution.

Kinder, Donald R. 1983. "Diversity and Complexity in American Public Opinion." In *Political Science: The State of the Discipline,* edited by Ada Finifter. Washington, DC: American Political Science Association.

———. 1986. "The Continuing American Dilemma: White Resistance to Racial Change 40 Years After Myrdal." *Journal of Social Issues* 42:151–71.

Kinder, Donald R., and Laurie A. Rhodebeck. 1982. "Continuities in Support for Racial Equality, 1972 to 1976." *Public Opinion Quarterly* 46:195–215.

Kinder, Donald R., and Lynn M. Sanders. 1996. *Divided by Color: Racial Politics and Democratic Ideals.* Chicago: University of Chicago Press.

Kinder, Donald R., and David O. Sears. 1981. "Prejudice and Politics: Symbolic Racism Versus Racial Threats to the Good Life." *Journal of Personality and Social Psychology* 40:414–31.

———. 1985. "Public Opinion and Political Action." In *The Handbook of Social Psychology,* edited by Gardner Lindzey and Elliot Aronson. Reading, MA: Addison-Wesley.

King, Gary. 1989. *Unifying Political Methodology: The Likelihood Theory of Statistical Inference.* Cambridge: Cambridge University Press.

———. 1997. *A Solution to the Ecological Inference Problem.* Princeton: Princeton University Press.

Kousser, J. Morgan. 1999. *Colorblind Injustice: Minority Voting Rights and the Undoing of the Second Reconstruction.* Chapel Hill: University of North Carolina Press.

Lacy, Dean. 1993. "Nonseparable Preferences and Public Policy Agendas." Unpublished manuscript.

Lacy, Dean, and Emerson M. S. Niou. 1998. "Elections in Double-Member Districts with Nonseparable Preferences." *Journal of Theoretical Politics* 10:89–110.

Latane, B. 1966. "Studies in Social Comparison." *Journal of Experimental and Social Psychology.* Supplement 1.

Lazarsfeld, Paul, Bernard Berelson, and Hazel Gaudet. 1944. *The People's Choice.* New York: Columbia University Press.

Lester, David. 1998. "Preventing Suicide by Restricting Access to Methods for Suicide." *Archives of Suicide Research* 4:7–24.

LeVine, Robert A., and Donald T. Campbell. 1972. *Ethnocentrism: Theories of Conflict, Ethnic Attitudes, and Group Behavior.* New York: Wiley.

Lippmann, Walter. 1922. *Public Opinion.* New York: Macmillan.

———. 1927. *Phantom Public.* Reprint, New Brunswick, NJ: Transaction, 1993.

Lipset, Seymour Martin, and William Schneider. 1978. "The Bakke Case: How Would It Be Decided at the Bar of Public Opinion?" *Public Opinion* (March/April): 38–44.

Lodge, Milton, Kathleen McGraw, and Patrick Stroh. 1989. "An Impression-Driven Model of Candidate Evaluation." *American Political Science Review* 83:399–414.

Long, J. S. 1997. *Regression Models for Categorical and Limited Dependent Variables.* Thousand Oaks, CA: Sage.

Long, Susan B., and Judyth A. Swingen. 1991. "Taxpayer Compliance: Setting New Agendas for Research." *Law and Society Review* 25:637–83.

Lublin, David. 1997. *The Paradox of Representatiion: Racial Gerrymandering and Minority Interests in Congress.* Princeton: Princeton University Press.

Luker, Kristin. 1984. *Abortion and the Politics of Motherhood.* Berkeley: University of California Press.

Lukes, Stephen. 1973. *Individualism.* Oxford: Basil Blackwell.

Luskin, Robert C. 1987. "Measuring Political Sophistication." *American Journal of Political Science* 31:856–99.

MacKuen, Michael B. 1983. "Political Drama, Economic Conditions, and the Dynamics of Presidential Popularity." *American Journal of Political Science* 27:165–91.

MacKuen, Michael B., Robert S. Erikson, and James A. Stimson. 1989. "Macropartisanship." *American Political Science Review* 83:1125–42.

———. 1992. "Question Wording and Macropartisanship." *American Political Science Review* 86:597–611.

———. 1995. "Dynamic Representation." *American Political Science Review* 89:543–64.

Mansbridge, Jane J. 1986. *Why We Lost the ERA.* Chicago: University of Chicago Press.

McClosky, Herbert. 1964. "Consensus and Ideology in American Politics." *American Political Science Review* 58:361–82.

McClosky, Herbert, and John Zaller. 1984. *The American Ethos: Public Attitudes toward Capitalism and Democracy.* Cambridge: Harvard University Press.

McConahay, John B. 1986. "Modern Racism, Ambivalence, and the Modern Racism Scale." In *Prejudice, Discrimination, and Racism: Theory and Research*, edited by J. Dovidio. New York: Academic Press.

Miller, Warren E., and Donald E. Stokes. 1963. "Constituency Influence in Congress." *American Political Science Review* 57:45–56.

Myrdal, Gunnar. 1944. *An American Dilemma: The Negro Problem and Modern Democracy.* Reprint, New Brunswick, NJ: Transaction, 1997.

Nadeau, Richard, Richard G. Niemi, and Jeffrey Levine. 1993. "Innumeracy about Minority Populations." *Public Opinion Quarterly* 57: 332–47.

Neustadt, Richard E. 1980. *Presidential Power: The Politics of Leadership.* New York: Wiley.

Nie, Norman H., Sidney Verba, and John R. Petrocik. 1979. *The Changing American Voter.* Cambridge: Harvard University Press.

Niemi, Richard, G., and Larry M. Bartels. 1985. "New Measures of Issue Salience: An Evaluation." *Journal of Politics* 47:1212–20.

Niskanen, William A., Jr. 1971. *Bureaucracy and Representative Government*. Chicago: Aldine-Atherton.

Ostrom, Charles W., Jr., and Dennis M. Simon. 1985. "Promise and Performance: A Dynamic Model of Presidential Popularity." *American Political Science Review* 79:334–58.

Ostrom, Charles, W., Jr., and Renee M. Smith. 1992. "Error Correction, Attitude Persistence, and Executive Rewards and Punishments: A Behavioral Theory of Presidential Approval." *Political Analysis* 4:127–83.

Page, Benjamin I. 1978. *Choices and Echoes in Presidential Elections*. Chicago: University of Chicago Press.

Page, Benjamin I., and Robert Y. Shapiro. 1992. *The Rational Public*. Chicago: University of Chicago Press.

Perrow, Charles. 1987. *Complex Organizations: A Critical Essay. 3rd. ed.*, New York: Random House.

Petty, Richard E., and John T. Cacioppo. 1986. *Communication and Persuasion: Central and Peripheral Routes to Attitude Change*. New York: Springer-Verlag.

Pitkin, Hanna F. 1967. *The Concept of Representation*. Berkeley: University of California Press.

Popkin, Samuel L. 1991. *The Reasoning Voter*. Chicago: University of Chicago Press.

Prothro, James W., and Charles M. Grigg. 1960. "Fundamental Principles of Democracy: Bases of Agreement and Disagreement." *Journal of Politics* 22:276–94.

Rabinowitz, George, James W. Prothro, and William Jacoby. 1982. *Journal of Politics* 44:41–63.

Rahn, Wendy, John Brehm, and Neil Carlson. 1999. "National Elections as Institutions for Building Social Capital." In *Civic Engagement in American Democracy: Frontiers of Theory and Research*, edited by Theda Skocpol and Morris Fiorina. Washington, D.C.: Brookings Institution.

Rawls, John. 1993. *Political Liberalism*. New York: Columbia University Press.

RePass, David E. 1971. "Issue Salience and Party Choice." *American Political Science Review* 65:389–400.

Rivers, Douglas. 1988. "Heterogeneity in Models of Electoral Choice." *American Journal of Political Science* 32(3): 737–57.

Rivers, Douglas, and Nancy L. Rose. 1985. "Passing the President's Program: Public Opinion and Presidential Influence in Congress." *American Journal of Political Science* 29:183–96.

Rokeach, Milton. 1973. *The Nature of Human Values*. New York: Free Press.

Saunderson, T., R. Haynes, and I. H. Langford. 1998. "Urban-Rural Variations in Suicides and Undetermined Deaths in England and Wales." *Journal of Public Health Medicine* 20:261–67.

Schattschneider, E. E. 1960. *The Semi-Sovereign People*. New York: Holt, Rinehart & Winston.

Scholz, John T., and Neil Pinney. 1995. "Duty, Fear, and Tax Compliance." *American Journal of Political Science* 39:490–512.

Schuman, Howard, Charlotte Steeh, and Lawrence Bobo. 1985. *Racial Attitudes in America: Trends and Interpretations*. Cambridge: Harvard University Press.

Schuman, Howard, Charlotte Steeh, Lawrence Bobo, and Maria Krysan. 1997. *Racial Attitudes in America: Trends and Interpretation*. Cambridge: Harvard University Press.

Shepsle, Kenneth A. 1972. "The Strategy of Ambiguity." *American Political Science Review* 66:555–68.

Shipler, David K. 1997. *A Country of Strangers: Blacks and Whites in America*. New York: Knopf.

Simon, Dennis M. and Charles M. Ostrom. 1989. "The Impact of Speeches and Travel on Presidential Approval." *Public Opinion Quarterly* 53 (Spring): 58–82.

Smith, M. Brewster, Jerome S. Bruner, and Robert W. White. 1956. *Opinions & Personality*. New York: Wiley.

Smith, Renee M. 1992. "Error Correction, Attractors, and Cointegration: Substantive and Methodological Issues." *Political Analysis* 4:249–54.

Sniderman, Paul M., and Edward G. Carmines. 1997. *Reaching Beyond Race*. Cambridge: Harvard University Press.

Sniderman, Paul M., and M. Hagen. 1985. *Race and Inequality*. Chatham, NJ: Chatham House.

Sniderman, Paul M., and Thomas Piazza. 1993. *The Scar of Race*. Cambridge: Harvard University Press, Belknap Press.

Sniderman, Paul M., and Philip E. Tetlock. 1986. "Symbolic Racism: Problems of Motive Attribution in Political Analysis." *Journal of Social Issues* 42:129–50.

Stanley, Harold W., and Richard G. Niemi. 1995. *Vital Statistics on American Politics*. 5th ed. Washington, DC: CQ Press.

Stenner, Karen. 1995. "Threat, Authoritarianism, and Racial Violence in America 1960–89." Paper presented at the annual meeting of the Midwest Political Science Association, Chicago.

———. 1996. "Societal Threat and Authoritarianism: Racism, Intolerance, and Punitiveness in America, 1960–94." Ph.D. diss., State University of New York at Stony Brook.

Stimson, James A. 1991. *Public Opinion in America: Moods, Cycles, and Swings*. Boulder, Co.: Westview.

Sullivan, John L., James E. Piereson, George E. Marcus. 1978. "Ideological Constraint in the Mass Public: A Methodological Critique and Some New Findings." *American Journal of Political Science* 22:233–49.

———. 1979. *Political Tolerance and American Democracy*. Chicago: University of Chicago Press.

Sullivan, M. J. Ormel, G. I. J. M. Kempen, and T. Tymstra. 1998. "Beliefs Concerning Death, Dying, and Hastening Death among Older, Functionally Impaired Dutch Adults." *Journal of the American Geriatrics Society* 46:1251–57.

Swain, Carol M. 1993. *Black Faces, Black Interests: The Representation of African Americans in Congress*. Cambridge: Harvard University Press.

Swanwick, G. R. J. and A. W. Clare. 1998. "Suicide in Ireland 1945–1992: Social Correlates." *Irish Medical Journal* 90:106–8.

Tocqueville, Alexis de. 1969. *Democracy in America*. Edited by J. P. Mayer. Garden City, NY: Anchor Books.

Tourangeau, Roger, Lance J. Rips, and Kenneth Rasinski. 2000. *The Psychology of Survey Response*. Cambridge: Cambridge University Press.

Tyler, Tom R. 1990. *Why People Obey the Law*. New Haven: Yale University Press.

Walt, Stephen. 1987. *The Origins of Alliances*. Ithaca: Cornell University Press.

Williams, John T. 1992. "What Goes Around Comes Around: Unit Root Tests and Cointegration." *Political Analysis* 4:229–36.

Wilson, James Q. 1967. "The Bureaucracy Problem." *The Public Interest* 6:3–9.

———. 1989. *Bureaucracy: What Government Agencies Do and Why They Do It.* New York: Basic Books.

Wilson, J. Matthew. 1999. "Group Identification and Political Behavior in the United States." Ph.D. diss., Duke University.

Yamagishi, Toshio, and Midori Yamagishi. 1994. "Trust and Commitment in the United States and Japan." *Motivation and Emotion* 18:129–66.

Zaller, John. 1992. *The Nature and Origins of Mass Opinion.* Cambridge: Cambridge University Press.

Zaller, John, and Stanley Feldman. 1992. "A Simple Model of the Survey Response." *American Journal of Political Science* 36:579–616.

Zechman, Michael J. 1978. "Dynamic Models of Voting Behavior and Spatial Models of Party Competition." Chapel Hill, NC: Institute for Research in Social Science.

Index